PATRIOTS, LOYALISTS, AND REVOLUTION IN NEW YORK CITY, 1775–1776

REACTING TO THE PAST is an award-winning series of immersive role-playing games that actively engage students in their own learning. Students assume the roles of historical characters and practice critical thinking, primary source analysis, and argument, both written and spoken. Reacting games are flexible enough to be used across the curriculum, from first-year general education classes and discussion sections of lecture classes to capstone experiences, intersession courses, and honors programs.

Reacting to the Past was originally developed under the auspices of Barnard College and is sustained by the Reacting Consortium of colleges and universities. The Consortium hosts a regular series of conferences and events to support faculty and administrators.

Note to instructors: Before beginning the game you must download the Gamemaster's Materials, including an instructor's guide containing a detailed schedule of class sessions, role sheets for students, and handouts.

To download this essential resource, visit https://reactingconsortium.org/games, click on the page for this title, then click "Instructors Guide."

PATRIOTS, LOYALISTS, AND REVOLUTION IN NEW YORK CITY, 1775–1776

SECOND EDITION

Bill Offutt

BARNARD

The University of North Carolina Press

Chapel Hill

Cover illustration: Johannes Adam Simon Oertel, *Pulling Down the Statue of King George III, N.Y.C.*, ca. 1852. Wikimedia Commons.

ISBN 978-1-4696-7067-6 (pbk.: alk. paper)
ISBN 978-1-4696-7235-9 (e-book)

ABOUT THE AUTHOR

BILL OFFUTT is Professor of History and Faculty Advisor for the Pforzheimer Honors College at Pace University. He received his AB from Stanford University and his J.D. from Stanford Law School. Abandoning the law, he then went to graduate school and earned a Ph.D. in Early American History at Johns Hopkins University under Professor Jack P. Greene. His first book, *Of Good Laws and Good Men: Law and Society in the Delaware Valley 1680–1710*, was published by Illinois University Press. His academic interests focus on the relationship between law and society, particularly the methods by which legal systems obtain and keep their legitimacy. He has taught classes on colonial America, revolutionary America, the Civil War, Constitutional history, and American women's history. In addition to his own Reacting game, he has taught eight other Reacting games to students at Pace, and he has participated in numerous Reacting conferences as gamemaster and/or player.

CONTENTS

PATRIOTS, LOYALISTS, AND REVOLUTION IN NEW YORK CITY, 1775–1776

1

PART 1: INTRODUCTION

BRIEF OVERVIEW OF THE GAME

It is April 1, 1775. The residents of the British colony of New York are involved in a political and social struggle of enormous intensity, in which the future of millions of people on a continental scale seems contingent on the actions and reactions of every member of that society. For ten years, the actions of the British government (levying taxes, instituting regulations, sending in military troops) have led to many colonial responses of defiance, which have produced repeated political crises and escalating confrontations involving violence and intimidation. The legitimacy of the existing political and economic system of the British empire is now under attack, following Boston's infamous tea party of 1773, the stunning punishments the British government leveled on Massachusetts in response, and the subsequent intercolonial economic retaliation against the British proposed by the first ever Continental Congress in 1774. The British North American colonies now teeter on the brink of political chaos, economic catastrophe, social upheaval, and possibly war—incomprehensible possibilities just a few years before.

The vast majority of New Yorkers, formerly lacking much political enthusiasm or principles beyond self-interest, now face a choice of two factions within a political elite that happily prospered from and cooperated with British rule. The Patriots are now passionately opposed to the existing British government, believing that the British have spent the previous decade plotting to destroy colonial rights and liberties. The Loyalists are just as passionately committed to the British government's defense, claiming it ensures the rule of law and provides prosperity, protection, and justice amid chaos and disorder. Many if not most New Yorkers are waiting for the next crisis before picking a side. Those New Yorkers—moderate undecided elite and disfranchised men, women, and slaves—will be swayed to the Patriot or Loyalist side by a combination of principle, self-interest, and opportunistic desire to join the side whose success is most assured.

When the game begins, you have just been called—either by election or by personal interest—to attend a Provincial Congress for the entire New York colony held in New York City Hall. New York's regular colonial assembly has been dissolved by the royal governor, who then fled the scene in fear for his safety. The Provincial Congress thus is not a regular governing body but an extraordinary new institution, erected to meet the needs of an ongoing crisis of political power and authority. This Congress must deal with the collapse of the existing order and government under the pressure of events in Massachusetts and the divisions between Patriots and Loyalists in the elite. Without the power to command any regular institutions of government—power enjoyed by tax collectors, bureaucrats, or an army—the Provincial Congress will have to enforce its own decisions about New York's role in the British Empire, about the necessity of revolution, and about who should make these decisions for society in the first place.

Some of the players in this episode of Reacting to the Past have the power to vote in this Congress, having been elected by their neighbors; some are from the city, others are from nearby counties, and still others are from regions more than one hundred miles away. Other players, including laborers, slaves, and women, sit in the gallery of the Congress without votes, but they are hardly spectators—they make comments and ask questions from the balcony or at the podium, add petitions to the agenda, and engage in street actions to influence the course of events. All will draw on their knowledge of history, on the writings of great philosophers and lowly pamphleteers, and on their own personal views on culture, economy, and society to advance their own interests as well as the interests of New York.

Now, in early April 1775, no one knows there will be a war; no one knows that a Declaration of Independence will be produced; and no one knows who will be victorious. The game asks you to determine the fate of New York in 1775–76, and the outcome depends on your collective actions and choices during the sixteen months of historical time covered by the game. The choices made in the game may (and in fact often do) deviate from what "really" happened, but all choices available in the game were real possibilities at the time. The game requires you to understand and internalize the choices and contingencies of that time; it allows you to feel the anxieties and triumphs of those alive in that moment, and thus make the history of Patriots, Loyalists, and all colonial Americans your own. You probably know something about the results of the American Revolution, including that the Revolutionary War led to the founding of the United States of America. What the game asks you to do is to forget that outcome, as best you can, and to immerse yourself in the chaotic world of colonial America in 1775. You will not "reenact" the history of that time—you will make it.

PROLOGUE

New York City, February 9, 1775: An Evening in a Tavern[1]

*I*t is a matter of liberty, sir." That word, "liberty," caught your attention. You looked up from your tankard of stonewall, a hard cider fortified with rum. The words were spoken by a young man, perhaps not yet twenty, seated alone, staring down at the table. He was dressed in the fashion of the radicals: brown coat made of homespun broadcloth—fabric not manufactured in England—and no collar or lapel. His hair, unpowdered, was cut so short that it required no braids in the back.

"Liberty, is it?" answered an older man, seated at an adjacent table with a British officer in a resplendent red uniform. The older man looked at the radical, awaiting a response with a forced smile on his face. He was heavyset, and wore a long, deep green waistcoat of corded silk with red and yellow embroidery over a shirt with lace cuffs and collar. His wig, powdered and clean, was white.

"You call it liberty when a man can't dock his ship?" the older man continued, speaking to the younger. "What about my liberty?"

The keeper of the tavern looked up, spoon in hand. She had been frothing eggs to add to the flip, a concoction of beer, sugar, cream, and rum. "Then you must be Watson, captain of the *James* out of Glasgow?" she asked.

"That I am."

"Tried to dock at Murray's last week?" she asked.

"I did indeed," Watson said. "And again today, this time with the help of Captain Montagu." He lifted his tankard in salute to the officer.

The men at a table near the fireplace fell silent and glanced at each other.

"Last week we had just sailed past the narrows," Watson continued. "I set the *James* on a course for Murray's, dodging ice from the Hudson all the way. Then a sloop tacks our way, its deck swarming with armed men. 'They're pirates,' one of my crew yells. 'Can't be pirates,' I say. 'They're too fat.' Then one of the brigands on the sloop shouts at me. 'Turn back,' he says, 'or we'll seize your boat and crew.' I responded with all due courtesy."

The officer guffawed.

"So the sloop follows us into Murray's. When we approach the dock, Murray's men, seeing the ruckus on the sloop, refuse to take my ropes. So I sail over to the Jersey shore and anchor near the oyster beds."

The tavern keeper, carrying a tankard, walked toward Watson and set it down. Watson raised it to his lips, sniffed the egg-white foam, and took a deep drink.

"'Tis good indeed," he declared. "Everyone said that I'd find the best flip in all of New York at the tavern of the widow de la Montagne and they were right. To you, madam, and to the king"—he raised the mug toward the picture of King George III on the far wall.

The men by the fireplace rose from their table and slipped out the door.

"The sloop captain—that was either Sears or McDougall," the widow explained. "In charge of the Liberty Men. You're fortunate they didn't board the ship and seize your cargo."

"Lucky they didn't try," the captain said. "I'd have stuck them with my sword."

"And you, sir, would have been arrested," the young man again spoke up. "They were doing their duty."

"Their duty, you say?" Watson asked, setting down his tankard. "You," he said, and repeated the word with emphasis. "*You* speak to me of duty? I am captain of a six-hundred-ton ship. What of my duty to the owners of that ship? My duty to the owners of the cargo? My duty to the crew? What do you know of duty?" He ended by muttering something to the British officer; they both laughed.

"I know, sir, that you should not have sailed for New York," the young man replied.

"Is that so?" Watson's smile was gone.

"Last September," the young man continued, "the Continental Congress in Philadelphia voted to put an end to all shipping to or from England. This was in retaliation for Parliament and King George closing the Boston port."

"They closed the port," Watson growled, "because pirates like your Sears had dumped a shipload of East India tea into the Boston harbor. That was in December of 1773, over a year ago."

"And so"—the young man continued, ignoring Watson's words—"the Continental Congress instructed every town throughout the colonies to elect a committee"—here he pulled a broadsheet out of his pocket, unfolded it, and read aloud—"'whose business it shall be attentively to observe the conduct of all persons touching this association; and when it shall be made to appear, to the satisfaction of a majority of any committee, that any person within the limits of their appointment has violated this association, that such majority do forthwith cause the truth of the case to be published in the gazette; to the end that all such foes to the rights of British-American may be publicly known, and universally condemned as the enemies of American liberty; and thenceforth we respectively will break off all dealings with him or her.'"

"The vote selecting the New York committee was held at the intersection just outside the tavern," the widow added. "Hundreds of men shouting out their votes—and calling for drinks. The way I heard it, 'rum and cider' won the election by a landslide."

The tavern erupted in laughter. One man with a frizzy white beard piped up, "Rum or cider, Delanceys or Livingstons, what's the difference?"

"After you've had your fill of any of 'em," the widow added, "your head will ache in the morning."

More laughter.

"You're wrong," the young man declared. "Well, maybe not in the past. New York elections used to be a tug-of-war between the Delanceys and Livingstons but no more. The Liberty Men won, and they'll win the election for the new Provincial Congress next month. Things will change now."

"The Liberty Men won because Sears was working for Livingston," the bearded man said. "Next time he'll be on Delancey's payroll."

"That's a lie," the young man said.

"I didn't vote for Sears or for the Liberty Men or Livingston," another man said, coat covered by a mechanics apron. He stood up and walked toward Watson's table, hat in hand. "Excuse me, sir," he said. "I'm not afraid to unload your cargo, and there are plenty more carters like me down by the wharves."

"I thank you," Watson replied. "But your Liberty Men—your *dutiful* Liberty Men—have deprived you and me both of the liberty of earning a living. Earlier today I again failed to bring the *James* into Murray's. Captain Montagu here of His Majesty's warship *Kingfisher* escorted me in; he even put armed soldiers aboard the *James*. But someone must have tipped off Sears, because when the *James* approached Murray's, a mob scrambled onto the dock."

"Some of them were yelling like Indians," Montagu added. "Homage, I suppose, to the ruffians who dumped the Boston tea. I called off the landing because the mob would have destroyed the cargo and sunk the *James*."

"Why didn't you get help from Fort George?" the cartman asked. "They must have seen what was going on. One volley of musket fire and the mob would have run to Westchester."

"That's what the merchants who owned my cargo told the governor a few hours ago," Watson said. "But the Governor said that his authority was being 'superseded,' as he put it. He said that the Liberty Men, if provoked, might run amok and burn down the town. Isn't that right, Montagu?"

"The governor's concern was not unfounded," Montagu replied. "I'm sure you noticed that the cannons at the Fort are not aimed toward the harbor, but at the city itself. Nowadays we worry more about armed ruffians in New York than the Indians or the French. Some in the Crown government propose that, for safety, we move out of Fort George and onto the *Asia*, anchored in the Hudson."

"I, for one, am leaving for Barbados," Watson declared. "On the tide tomorrow morning."

"But maybe around sunset"—the words came from a man who was sitting alone by the kitchen—"you'll change your mind. Perhaps you'll turn around, sail up the East River, and unload your cargo at midnight in one of the hidden coves opposite Montressor's island. Right, captain?"

"Try and they'll catch you," the young man warned. "Sears and the Committee on Inspection are on the lookout for smugglers."

"They needn't trouble themselves about the *James*," Watson sniffed. "I've had my fill of New York. A wondrous colony indeed. A breeding place for pirates and smugglers."

"Where the pirates make illegal laws and smugglers obey legitimate ones," Montagu added. "Yes, 'tis wondrous."

"A breeding ground, too, for spies," the widow whispered, glancing toward the door through which another man had just departed. "I suggest you lower your voice."

"I've had enough of this *liberty*." Watson spat out the word, and turned toward the young man. "You speak of liberty," Watson called out, "but perhaps you should read the words of John Locke. Ever heard of him? About a century ago, he wrote wise things. He said that if a man's property is not secure, he has no liberty. He is slave to his belly, or to anyone who has power."

"But we have no liberty now," the young man replied. "You should read McDougall's 'Statement of Grievances'—"

"More wonders," Watson interrupted, learning toward Montagu. "In New York the pirates write learned treatises!"

"—the king and Parliament impose unconstitutional taxes," the young man continued, "they suspend our legislatures, they ignore our courts—"

"And so you promote liberty through thievery and assault," Watson retorted.

"Look at the counties along the Hudson!" the cartman exclaimed. "Mobs are burning manor houses and farms and seizing land. That's not liberty, that's chaos."

"It's not easy to break the chains of our bondage, but if we fail to do so, we'll remain slaves," the young man countered.

"What about Black Dan there?" another man asked, gesturing to the black man who was carrying a keg of rum from the cellar. "You give him liberty and he'll slit the widow's throat."

Black Dan set down the keg, picked up a long knife, and fingered the blade, testing its sharpness. He opened his eyes wide and smiled innocently.

The tavern roared with laughter.

Then the door burst open and a dozen men rushed inside. "I am Alexander McDougall of the Committee on Inspection and I arrest Captain Watson of the *James* for violating the orders of the Continental Association as set forth by the Continental Congress."

"Damn your eyes, you bloody sot!" Watson said, standing and raising the tankard as if to strike McDougall. The Liberty Men rushed at Watson and knocked him onto the floor. One man kicked him furiously. Montagu tried to intervene but quickly was overwhelmed as more Liberty Men poured into the tavern.

"Parade 'em through the streets!" one of them shouted.

Watson and Montagu were dragged from the tavern. Outside, a crowd cheered. Within a few minutes, as the procession made its way south, the tavern fell silent. You found yourself alone in the tavern with only the widow and Black Dan.

"Here's a shoe with a silver buckle," the widow said. "And a wig, trampled into the dirt floor."

"They broke the picture of King George," Black Dan said.

"Just sweep up the glass and throw the picture away," the widow said. "It riles people."

While collecting glasses and plates, she asked, "What do you make of this talk of liberty?"

Black Dan paused. "I like the words of the Liberty Men. But I ask myself: Why do they talk of liberty when they own so many slaves? Not like you, but the big planters from Virginia with whole fields of slaves. I like the Livingstons—and the Delanceys—because I always like rich people. I like King George and Parliament because they own Fort George and a mighty fleet. Slaves like those who can help them."

"But I help you," the widow said.

"Yes, Madam, that you do," Black Dan replied, "and I appreciate it. Give me a few more shillings each week and I'd appreciate it more."

"But you'd just buy your freedom and leave."

"That I would," he said, smiling broadly. "As that boy said, 'It's all a matter of liberty.'"

Now she laughed. "Who do you hope wins the elections for the Provincial Congress?"

The slave paused. "Don't think it much matters. It all depends on who controls New York at the end of the day. The rest of it's just words, ain't it?"

March 31, 1775: A Walk Through the City

Nearly two months later, on an early spring morning, you reflect that the arguments heard that night have only intensified. You emerge from a quieter Montagne's tavern, on Broadway near Warren Street (see the map on p. 11). Broadway's paving stones are heaving up after a hard winter of frost and thaw, leaving holes in one of New York's few "paved" streets. Across Broadway is the Commons, roughly ten acres at the northern edge of town, the largest open space left on the southern tip of Manhattan. The mud is rampant, as young grass is trampled and munched upon by various horses, cattle, and pigs. The animals have left their dung everywhere. Combined with a warm sea breeze, those fragrances remind you of the daily agricultural rhythms in this most urban of colonial places. As you reflect on recent events and debates, you can't help wondering who will control New York in the end. Everywhere you look you see a possible answer to this question—but none are fully convincing.

Just to your left at the north end of the grassy field are the barracks built to house British soldiers, now empty after the British officers decided their men would be safer elsewhere. Those soldiers are now staying at Fort George at the foot of the island and on board His Majesty's ship, *Asia*, docked on the East River. Next to the barracks is the city's new poorhouse, overflowing with young men suffering the consequences of a decade of economic upheaval that left them with few opportunities. Beyond the poorhouse is the new jail, named Bridewell to mimic London's prison, with a public gallows conveniently located in front. You wonder how much business the hangman will soon have, due not to the usual crimes but to the political turmoil engulfing this town. You have heard the word "treason" bandied about, and you know the traditional punishment for traitors: their intestines are cut out and shown to them as they hang on the gibbet. This practice is referred to as "drawing," customarily followed by decapitation. The arms and legs are then attached to four horses, "quartering" the traitor before a raucous crowd.

But just who are the traitors? Treason is disloyalty, giving aid and comfort to your country's enemies, but right now it is difficult to know where your loyalty should lie. With king and country (the British Empire), along with the Loyalists, or with liberty and colony, with the Patriots? Each casts the other as the true enemy of the people of New York, and right there on the Commons is the focal point of much bloodshed so far: a "Liberty Pole." Planted deep in the softening soil is the fifth such pine tree shorn of its branches, rising forty feet and festooned with banners and posters, defended by a half-dozen scruffy Patriots day and night. The first pole was erected as part of the Stamp Act resistance nearly ten years ago, and melees have broken out repeatedly around the various poles, British soldiers and Loyalists rushing to chop it down and Patriots rushing to defend it—as if the fate of this piece of wood determined the fate of the world. The pole is a symbol of political chaos and disorder, a cynical reminder that this year's traitor is next year's hero. The winners define the traitors, but the ones who will control this city will be determined by you and your fellow New Yorkers.

You walk down Broadway, toward the tip of the island; it is only about a mile, twenty minutes of walking. To the right is St. Paul's Chapel, an outpost of the Church of England, the dominant religious authority and favored by Loyalists. Beyond the spire you spot the field beyond the church, known as the "holy ground"—the largest meeting space for prostitutes in the city. It is a dangerous place, patrolled by British officers to control fights between the prostitutes and their numerous customers; one colonel demeaned the women his enlisted men regularly patronized as "bitchfoxy jades, jills, haggs, strums."[2] You don't see much activity from the denizens of the holy ground this morning—most of their business is transacted at night—but you do see dozens of men and women on Broadway, going about their daily routines. None can be self-sufficient living in town, so women are acquiring food and fuel (firewood), often trading eggs and

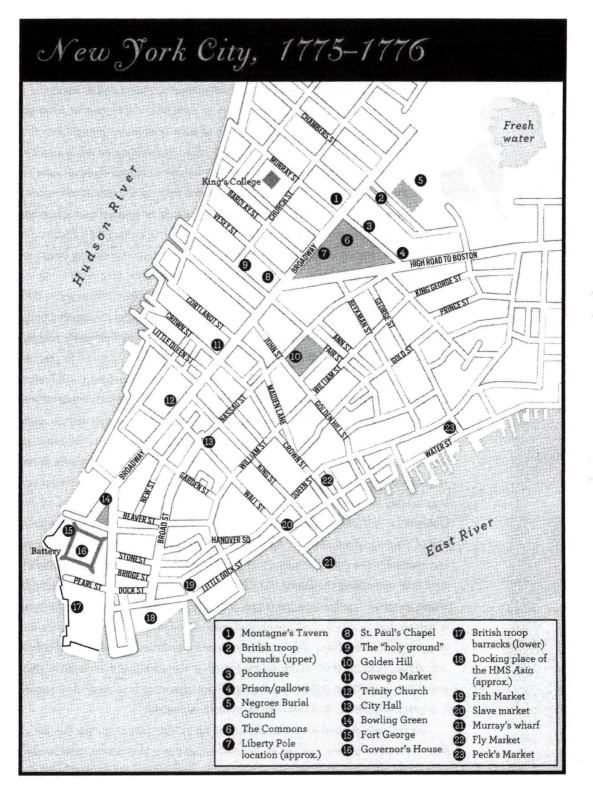

New York City, 1775–1776

Fresh water

King's College

Hudson River

CHAMBERS ST

MURRAY ST

BARCLAY ST

CHURCH ST

VESEY ST

1 Montagne's Tavern
2 British troop barracks (upper)
3 Poorhouse
4 Prison/gallows
5 Negroes Burial Ground
6 The Commons
7 Liberty Pole location (approx.)

HIGH ROAD TO BOSTON

KING GEORGE ST

PRINCE ST

BEEKMAN ST

GEORGE ST

ANN ST

FAIR ST

GOLD ST

JOHN ST

WILLIAM ST

MAIDEN LANE

GOLDEN HILL ST

NASSAU ST

CORTLANDT ST

CROWN ST

LITTLE QUEEN ST

BROADWAY

WILLIAM ST

KING ST

CROWN ST

QUEEN ST

WATER ST

WALL ST

NEW ST

BROAD ST

GARDEN ST

HANOVER SQ

BEAVER ST

STONE ST

BRIDGE ST

DOCK ST

LITTLE DOCK ST

PEARL ST

Battery

East River

8 St. Paul's Chapel
9 The "holy ground"
10 Golden Hill
11 Oswego Market
12 Trinity Church
13 City Hall
14 Bowling Green
15 Fort George
16 Governor's House

17 British troop barracks (lower)
18 Docking place of the HMS *Asia* (approx.)
19 Fish Market
20 Slave market
21 Murray's wharf
22 Fly Market
23 Peck's Market

milk that they produce at home. Young men are out and about, hungrily looking for a day's worth of pay on the docks, in the warehouses, or in the many small shops. Artisans run most of these shops, where one can get handmade-to-order goods such as shoes, clothing, hats, and furniture—these are small manufacturing sites as well as stores.

Other men are opening their front doors or their stalls in the open-air Oswego Market—shopkeepers and merchants showing all sorts of products brought into the city from distant lands including Queens, Staten Island, and Albany, as well as London, Jamaica, and the Orient. If the Patriots have their way, those store shelves will soon be empty—they want to stop importation through what they call a Continental Association. This is their way of helping the beleaguered residents of Massachusetts, who are groaning under the Intolerable Acts. Groaning too, and much closer than Boston, are the slaves you see on the street, black men working construction or driving fancy carriages for wealthy merchants.

As you walk further, you see a small field to your left, Golden Hill, where in 1770 British soldiers bloodied Patriots in a melee following the felling of the fourth Liberty Pole. But what you notice most are the many churches, seemingly from every country. By the time you reach Trinity Church, the headquarters of the Church of England in America, you have seen houses of worship for Dutch, Moravian, German, and French congregations. Along with the dominant Anglicans, there are Baptists, Presbyterians, Lutherans, Quakers, Methodists, and even a few Jews here, and you wonder: how could so many faiths ever unite to do anything? From Trinity, you look down Wall Street all the way to the East River and see ships unloading their cargoes, including slaves, at the first marketplace established on Wall Street. Continuing down Broadway, the houses are more tightly packed together as you come to the Bowling Green, set up by the Dutch in the 1600s as a market, now a park with flowers and lawn bowling. At the north end of Bowling Green sits a tall statue of King George III on a horse, commissioned and erected by the grateful citizens of New York in 1770 to celebrate the king's beneficent role in repealing the Stamp Act. But beyond this symbol is the harsh reality of British authority: Fort George, the home of the Royal Governor Tryon, with cannons to defend the city's harbor and a garrison of men trained in modern military tactics and weapons—the British Army. The cannons, you note, are still directed at the city. Political and military force recently destroyed the French in the world war that ended in 1763; what hope would New York's divided people have against such an array of weaponry and manpower, should the British choose to flex their muscles?

As you walk along the water's edge at the tip of Manhattan, you see the sails of ships in the water of New York harbor. Some are headed over to Brooklyn, some headed up the river, some headed out to sea, some are inbound with goods from the Caribbean and England, and some are just sitting and rotting in dry dock, waiting for better trade conditions. Flying the flag of empire, the Union Jack, and sitting in a berth on the East River, is the *Asia*, a proud warship armed with 64 cannons capable of sinking any enemy ship likely to enter the harbor—and also capable of firing a broadside sufficient to level multiple buildings at once. What flag will fly over the harbor this time next year? Will this seemingly never-ending turmoil result in war, and if so, who will win? You know that in times like these, many people could be destroyed, but many others are capable of using their wits and their muscles to take advantage of the situation. You compare the movement in the water with what you've seen on land, and you resolve not to get stuck like those ships still in port.

To do that, you will need to understand New York's political dynamics, both in recent history and in the new Provincial Congress. You continue to think as you walk north on Broad Street toward City Hall at the corner of Broad and Wall, the meeting place for the ninety-three representatives from all over the colony who will gather tomorrow to begin charting the future for your colony, your city. You will need many candles tonight, to read and understand the philosophical and historical foundations of the various political positions and factions. You will need to understand the people, their personal histories and motives. You will need information about what is going on in Boston, in Philadelphia, in Williamsburg, in London, and in the backrooms of Manhattan taverns where talk flows freely and plans (or plots?) are hatched. You need to read deeply, you need to study, you need to think strategically, you need to anticipate and adjust, and you need ultimately to persuade others to follow your opinion as to what is to be done at every turn.

You are now at the steps leading up to City Hall, with its doors open to the future. There is not much time and you must get to work, for you know that your life will soon be transformed by the events about to occur. There is no doubt that the coming experience will make you a different person, a prospect that both thrills and terrifies you. You must be engaged mentally, physically, and emotionally; you must go beyond the limits of what you already know (or think you know) about everything to achieve your mission: to prevail in the struggle for New York.

HOW TO REACT

Reacting to the Past is a series of historical role-playing games. After a few preparatory lectures, the game begins and the students are in charge. Set in moments of heightened historical tension, the games place students in the roles of historical figures. By reading the game book and their individual role sheets, students discover their objectives, potential allies, and the forces that stand between them and victory. They must then attempt to achieve victory through formal speeches, informal debate, negotiations, and (sometimes) conspiracy. Outcomes sometimes part from actual history; a postmortem session sets the record straight.

The following is an outline of what you will encounter in Reacting and what you will be expected to do.

Game Setup

Your instructor will spend some time before the beginning of the game helping you to understand the historical context for the game. During the setup period, you will use several different kinds of material:

- You have received the game book (from which you are reading now), which includes historical information, rules and elements of the game, and essential documents.

- Your instructor will provide you with a role sheet, which provides a short biography of the historical figure you will model in the game as well as that person's ideology, objectives, responsibilities, and resources. Your role may be an actual historical figure or a composite.

In addition to the game book, you may also be required to read historical documents or books written by historians. These provide additional information and arguments for use during the game.

Read all of this contextual material and all of these documents and sources before the game begins. And just as important, go back and reread these materials throughout the game. A second and third reading while *in role* will deepen your understanding and alter your perspective, for ideas take on a different aspect when seen through the eyes of a partisan actor.

Students who have carefully read the materials and who know the rules of the game will invariably do better than those who rely on general impressions and uncertain memories.

Game Play

Once the game begins, class sessions are presided over by students. In most cases, a single student serves as a kind of presiding officer. The instructor then becomes the Gamemaster (GM) and takes a seat in the back of the room. Though they do not lead the class sessions, GMs may do any of the following:

- Pass notes

- Announce important events (e.g. Sparta is invading!). Some of these events are the result of student actions; others are instigated by the GM

- Redirect proceedings that have gone off track

The presiding officer is expected to observe basic standards of fairness, but as a fail-safe device, most Reacting to the Past games employ the "Podium Rule," which allows a student who has not been recognized to approach the podium and wait for a chance to speak. Once at the podium, the student has the floor and must be heard.

Role sheets contain private, secret information which students are expected to guard. You are advised, therefore, to exercise caution when discussing your role with others. Your role sheet probably identifies likely allies, but even they may not always be trustworthy. However, keeping your own counsel, or saying nothing to anyone, is not an option. In order to achieve your objectives, you *must* speak with others. You will never muster the voting strength to prevail without allies. Collaboration and coalition building are at the heart of every game.

These discussions must lead to action, which often means proposing, debating, and passing legislation. Someone therefore must be responsible for introducing the measure and explaining its particulars. And always remember that a Reacting game is only a game—resistance, attack, and betrayal are not to be taken personally, since game opponents are merely acting as their roles direct.

Some games feature strong alliances called *factions*: these are tight-knit groups with fixed objectives. Games with factions all include roles called Indeterminates, who operate outside of the established factions. Not all Indeterminates are entirely neutral; some are biased on certain issues. If you are in a faction, cultivating Indeterminates is in your interest, since they can be convinced to support your position. If you are lucky enough to have drawn the role of an Indeterminate you should be pleased; you will likely play a pivotal role in the outcome of the game.

Game Requirements

Students in Reacting practice persuasive writing, public speaking, critical thinking, teamwork, negotiation, problem solving, collaboration, adapting to changing circumstances, and working under pressure to meet deadlines. Your instructor will explain the specific requirements for your class. In general, though, a Reacting game asks you to perform three distinct activities:

Reading and Writing. This standard academic work is carried on more purposefully in a Reacting course, since what you read is put to immediate use, and what you write is meant to persuade others to act the way you want them to. The reading load may have slight variations from role to role; the writing requirement depends on your particular course. Papers are often policy statements, but they can also be autobiographies, battle plans, spy reports, newspapers, poems, or after-game reflections. Papers provide the foundation for the speeches delivered in class.

Public Speaking and Debate. In the course of a game, almost everyone is expected to deliver at least one formal speech from the podium (the length of the game and the size of the class will determine the number of speeches). Debate follows. It can be impromptu, raucous, and fast-paced, and results in decisions voted on by the body. Gamemasters may stipulate that students must deliver their papers from memory when at the podium, or may insist that students wean themselves from dependency on written notes as the game progresses.

Wherever the game imaginatively puts you, it will surely not put you in the classroom of a twenty-first-century American college. Accordingly, the colloquialisms and familiarities of today's college life are out of place. Never open your speech with a salutation like "Hi guys" when something like "Fellow citizens!" would be more appropriate.

Never be friendless when standing at the podium. Do your best to have at least one supporter second your proposal, come to your defense, or admonish inattentive members of the body. Note-passing and side conversations, while common occurrences, will likely spoil the effect of your speech; so you and your supporters should insist upon order before such behavior becomes too disruptive. Ask the presiding officer to assist you, if necessary, and the Gamemaster as a last resort.

Strategizing. Communication among students is an essential feature of Reacting games. You will find yourself writing emails, texting, attending out-of-class meetings, or gathering for meals on a fairly regular basis. The purpose of frequent communication is to lay out a strategy for advancing your agenda and thwarting the agenda of your opponents, and to hatch plots to ensnare individuals troubling to your cause. When communicating with a fellow student in or out of class, always assume that he or she is speaking to you in role. If you want to talk about the "real world," make that clear.

Counterfactuals

To facilitate the smooth operation of this game and to open debate of some key ideas that might otherwise be submerged, the author has manipulated some elements of the history of the American Revolution and of New York in this period.

First, the political situation is simplified. For instance, the game assumes that the royal governor is not present at all; in fact, Governor Tryon was in and out of Manhattan during this period, including some time he spent in the harbor on a British ship. In the game, the Provincial Congress, comprising a single body of elected representatives, meets continuously; in reality, from April 1775 to August 1776 there were three separate Provincial Congresses, each with changing membership. The courts of New York City are considered closed for the duration of the game unless the Provincial Congress chooses to reopen them; actually, New York City's courts were only intermittently closed but, when open, held disorganized and chaotic sessions, while county courts outside the city continued their regular sessions.

Second, the timing of various revolutionary events is condensed and somewhat altered. While each event in the game actually occurred in history, some incidents during the revolution occurred later than this sixteen-month period, and some events may occur in the game out of chronological order. These slight chronological alterations improve game flow, and aid discussion of critical revolutionary issues, especially pertaining to matters of women, slaves, and laborers.

Finally, many characters reflect real individuals based on historical research, but some characters are fictional composites, designed for the purposes of the game. All characters' role sheets contain reasonable interpretations (historically plausible, but still educated guesses) about motivations and interests. Members of the Crowd (laborers, slaves, women) each have particular names and identities, but each should be seen as a single representative of dozens of people in New York similarly situated and motivated. Thus, for example, freeing a slave character by purchasing him from his master means that, for game purposes, one is purchasing and freeing fifty slaves, not just one. Similarly, if an individual in the Crowd decides to join the military, the game assumes that he represents hundreds of similar men volunteering.

These counterfactuals condense rather than change history, allowing you to consider, evaluate, and debate, in mere weeks, issues that emerged and were decided over the course of years. They also create both urgency and contingency around what may be decided in any class. With counterfactuals, creativity, and chaos, possibility and disaster can coexist, allowing students in all roles the chance to experience "the thrill of victory, the agony of defeat."

PART 2: **HISTORICAL BACKGROUND**

CHRONOLOGY

1754–63   French and Indian War (Seven Years' War)
- British launch a military buildup in colonies (1756–59) to defeat French in Canada and Indians on frontier.
- Britain ask colonies to contribute men and money to war effort; contributions made but not at level desired by the British government; some smuggling with French occurs.
- New York is center of British military buildup; local economy prospers.
- 1759: Defeat of French in Quebec; most British forces withdrawn to fight in Caribbean starting in 1760.

1763   Treaty of Paris ends French and Indian War; Proclamation Line of 1763
- Border drawn along spine of Appalachian Mountains, forbidding colonists from settling on the western side of the line in order to separate whites from Indians, who had launched Pontiac's Rebellion (1763).
- Colonial land speculators from Virginia and Pennsylvania outraged; opportunity for future settlement restricted.
- British retain significant army contingent in New York City following end of war.

1764   British Parliament passes **Sugar Act** and **Currency Act**
- Sugar Act lowers duties (tax rates) on sugar and molasses but increases enforcement. Currency Act forbids colonial issuance of paper money.
- Colonial merchants (especially those who smuggled sugar) protest.

1765   Parliament passes **Quartering Act**
- Act requires colonies to provide (and pay for) housing and provisions for British soldiers stationed locally. New York's Provincial Assembly refuses to comply.

1765   Parliament passes **Stamp Act**
- Act places tax on all printed matter, especially legal documents, using an impression or stamp on the paper to indicate that tax has been paid; appoints tax collectors in each colony, scheduled to take effect November 1 to allow set up of stamps and paper supplies.
- Massive political protest by colonial legislatures results; mobs rampage in various towns; non-importation of British goods adopted as protest; all Stamp Tax collectors resign before November 1, rendering tax collection impossible.

- New York anti–Stamp Act mob confronts British soldiers near Fort George at the southern tip of Manhattan; massacre narrowly avoided.

1766 Parliament repeals Stamp Act, passes **Declaratory Act**
- Declaratory Act asserts Parliament's right to pass legislation binding the colonies "in all cases whatsoever" ("all cases" including the right to impose taxes).
- Colonial political leaders greet Declaratory Act with alarm; most colonists celebrate restoration of the pre-1765 status quo.
- New York celebrates with erection of liberty pole on the Commons, across from British barracks. Pole chopped down by British soldiers. Sons of Liberty re-erect liberty poles with increasing defenses three more times. New York commissions statue of King George III to commemorate the repeal, to be erected in Bowling Green in 1770.

1767 Parliament passes **Townshend Acts**
- Under the Townshend Acts, British customs officials collect taxes in the ports on imported products from Britain (e.g. glass, iron, paper, tea). British government uses the funds to pay officials of the empire stationed in the colonies. The Acts also establish American Board of Customs Commissioners and special Vice-Admiralty Courts to ensure that mobs cannot pressure officials into resigning (as occurred following passage of the Stamp Act).
- Colonial legislatures resume political protests, led by Massachusetts (whose legislature is dissolved by the British in response); non-importation adopted in most places in 1768–69, enthusiastically by artisans but reluctantly by merchants.
- Royal governor suspends New York Assembly until it complies with Quartering Act requirements; new election brings Delancey Party to power. Delancey-controlled Assembly passes appropriation to comply with Quartering Act. New York merchants adopt non-importation in late 1768.

1770 Parliament repeals all Townshend Acts taxes except tea tax (as one remaining symbol of its authority)
- March 5: Boston Massacre. Angry mob hurls verbal abuse and projectiles at British soldiers in Boston; soldiers respond by firing into the crowd, killing five colonists and wounding six.
- April: news of Townshend Acts' repeal reaches colonies—celebration follows along with ending of non-importation. Most colonists ignore the issue of the remaining and wholly symbolic tea tax.
- Destruction of fourth liberty pole in January leads to Battle of Golden Hill, a bloody melee between soldiers and the mob. Alexander McDougall jailed for

eighty days for writing pamphlet that accuses Assembly of betraying New York by acceding to the Quartering Act. Fifth liberty pole erected, stands until 1776.

1773   Parliament passes **Tea Act** on May 10

- Tea Act reduces tea tax while giving British East India Company agents a monopoly on tea sold in the colonies.
- Colonial governments or mobs in every colony halt importation of tea, except in Boston where a ship loaded with tea docks. Boston Tea Party (December 16) destroys 342 chests of tea worth ten thousand pounds.
- New York committees force all local tea agents to resign their positions and to refuse to take custody of any shipped tea. No tea ships land in Manhattan until 1774, when New York stages its own miniature tea party.

1774   Parliament passes **Coercive** or "**Intolerable**" **Acts** as well as **Quebec Act**

- As response to Tea Party, the Coercive Acts impose the following changes:
  1. **Boston Port Act** effectively closes seaborne trade of Boston until destroyed tea is paid for, thereby crippling Boston's economy.
  2. **Massachusetts Government Act** gives royal governor power to appoint upper house of the legislature (the Council); essentially abolishes town meeting government.
  3. **Quartering Act** requires Massachusetts to pay expenses of British Army stationed there.
  4. **Administration of Justice Act** moves trials of any British official accused of crimes outside of Massachusetts.
  5. **Quebec Act**, not part of response to Tea Party but passed at the same time, places the area west of the Appalachians and north of the Ohio River under administration of Quebec's government, and grants Quebec Catholics more rights.
- Massachusetts' Committees of Correspondence call for immediate intercolonial boycott of all British goods; other colonies hesitate.
- Leaders in every colony call for a Continental Congress in September to consider coordinated response to Coercive Acts; delegates from twelve colonies attend. Declaration of Rights and Grievances approved, enumerating colonial rights and Parliament's violation of them. Continental Association formed to implement trade boycott in stages, with local committees to inspect for compliance.
- New York's Assembly, under Delancey's control, rejects resolutions of Continental Congress including establishment of Association, in late 1774. Ignoring this, radicals form Committee of Sixty to enforce Association without sanction of law.

CRISIS IN THE COLONIES, 1763–1775

In 1766 Benjamin Franklin, agent for the British colony of Pennsylvania, was interviewed in Parliament. He was asked to describe "the temper of America toward Great Britain before the year 1763." Franklin replied, "The best in the world. They submitted willingly to the government of the Crown, and paid, in their courts, obedience to acts of Parliament. . . . They had not only a respect but an affection for Great Britain; for its laws, its customs, and manners, and even a fondness for its fashions, that greatly increased the commerce."[1] Less than a dozen years later, this amicable relationship between the colonies and Britain was gone, replaced by antagonism, suspicion, mob violence, and threats of worse to come.

The causes of this rapid deterioration lay in a series of social developments and political controversies, some consciously provoked by political leaders, others occasioned by long-term processes of which the subjects were but dimly aware. Historians divide these causes somewhat arbitrarily among categories—social, economic, political—and the discussion that follows will keep to that framework in tracing the development of various problems as they mutated into the crises of 1763–1775. But for the people of New York, the lived reality of these crises was more vivid than such historical abstractions. Crisis became the background of their daily lives; they had to try to make sense of a dizzying whirl of events and make choices that would best secure a future for themselves and their families in the face of great unknowns.

SOCIAL DISCONTENT, THE FERTILE SOIL OF THE REVOLUTIONARY CRISIS

Overview

In considering the society of the American colonists in general and New York in particular in 1775, two key points should be kept in mind. First, *people who are happy with their present circumstances and comfortable with their future prospects don't revolt.* Revolutionary crises cannot occur without a significant fraction (if not a majority) of society feeling aggrieved, and needing to dramatically express their discontent over their present social situation and future prospects. Such discontent forms the "fertile soil" in which ideas of rebellion or revolution may be planted. There will remain many who are happy enough with the way things are, even during such upheavals, and will resist the revolt; the critical question will be how to balance the needs of the unhappy (taking into account the intensity of their distress) versus those of the satisfied.

Second, *American colonial society does not take personal autonomy for granted: many people are unfree, and many others are quite limited by society and law.* Modern Americans operate under the assumption that freedom is the normal condition, that all competent adults are entitled to personal independence of action, to choose for themselves (within the law) their own occupations, significant others, diversions, geographic locations, and so forth. Colonial Americans would have thought that assumption bizarre in the extreme, because the vast majority of the adult population were dependents (e.g., married women, slaves, indentured servants). Even an adult white male who worked for a wage, rented land, or was in debt was considered a dependent. To gain and keep **personal independence**—to own one's land or business, to be free of debt, to control one's own destiny, and to be able to provide independence in the form of property to one's children—was an essential part of the colonial "pursuit of happiness." For many, it was a fruitless pursuit.

Yet such personal autonomy, usually measured in terms of owning enough land or other property, free and clear of debt, was seen as essential to political participation and marked one as a person of status in society. It was understood that anyone without economic independence could not speak or vote freely; his vote and voice would be controlled by his landlord, employer, or creditor, and would thus be invalid. Yet all in colonial society—whether voters or not—who held grievances could express those grievances both legitimately and illegitimately. These protests would contribute to either intensifying or resolving the crisis facing New York.

Growth in the Colonies, 1700–1770

As of roughly 1770, the North American British colonies contained slightly over 2 million people. That population had grown from roughly 250,000 in 1700, meaning that the overall population was doubling every twenty to twenty-five years, a extraordinarily fast growth rate of approximately 3 percent per year. Yet despite the strains associated with rapid population growth, the American colonies had seen relative prosperity and real economic growth (especially measured by household consumption and per capita production) in the previous seventy years. In contrast, England was estimated to have 6.4 million people in 1770, with a population growth rate of less than 1 percent annually. Many observers on both sides of the Atlantic, including Benjamin Franklin, noted that within a few generations, the colonial population would exceed that of the mother country. This projection was viewed with optimism and pride in the New World, and with some foreboding in London.[2]

The British colonial population surge was due roughly equally to a high birth rate and to immigration (half of those immigrants had

Personal independence was the supporting idea behind the right to vote and hold office. Ownership of sufficient property (land or personal wealth) was proof of personal independence, which was considered essential to exercising political judgment free of improper motivations or pressures.

entered the country involuntarily, as slaves). These British colonists lived on a strip of land roughly two hundred miles wide, from the Appalachian Mountains to the Atlantic Coast. The population was overwhelmingly rural and primarily engaged in agricultural occupations, with 95 percent of the population living on farms or in towns smaller than 2,500 people. Towns such as Philadelphia (40,000), New York City (25,000), and Boston (16,000) had a political and economic significance beyond their mere numbers. Virginia, at 447,000, was the largest colony in terms of population, followed by Pennsylvania, Massachusetts, Maryland, and then New York at 162,000. Overall, approximately 21 percent of the colonial population was enslaved, and black slaves (as well as a few free blacks) were found in every colony (roughly 12 percent of the population in the New York colony; 15 to 20 percent in New York City).[3] Furthermore, a large number of white people lived in various states of dependency, including indentured servants (a contract in which a servant promised four to seven years' work in exchange for boat passage to the colonies), apprentices, wage laborers, renting farmers, wives, and children. Even among those white males considered independent, such as those who owned land or their own businesses, hierarchy dominated social interactions.

The Elite: Merchants and Large Landlords

That hierarchy was deeply rooted in social thought. According to historian Gordon Wood, before the 1760s, social thought in the colonies started with the principles of monarchy (all were subjects of the king), hierarchy (fathers ruled families, with mothers as their deputies; wealthy elite ruled communities), and traditional personal ties.[4] Society was considered as a single organism, and each part had its own special rank and role in the body. The wealthy elite wished to be known as **gentlemen**. They were the heads of society, and felt entitled by their birth, wealth, and status to rule and to receive deference from common people.

Gentlemen saw themselves as substantively better than average men: they had more refined manners, tastes, thoughts, ways of walking and talking, dancing and gambling. A gentleman was a man of leisure and not required to labor; he guarded his reputation and his honor jealously while indulging in high levels of luxury consumption. Gentlemen ruled by means of informal networks, family connections, and patronage (providing jobs and government benefits to lesser men who would then be loyal and subservient). Politics was rarely about principles: it was based on personal ties and relationships among the elite, often motivated by self-serving greed and status. When a man of lesser rank wanted something from the government, he was supposed to take a humble approach: to bow, doff his hat, and petition meekly as if he were a child asking for a favor from his father. Years later, men who had distinguished themselves during the Revolution would remember with both shame and wonder how they had quaked in the presence of such elite, beginning and ending every sentence with "sir" or "your honor."

Gentleman officially denoted the lowest rung in the British landed aristocracy. Colloquially, to be a gentleman meant to come from a good family and to be independently wealthy, making money from property and not from work. By English standards, the colonies had no gentlemen; elite colonists begged to differ.

In the founding years of the colonies, this English model of gentlemen rulers was inapt; social and economic conditions were too new and too chaotic to produce or sustain such a stable aristocratic class. Over time, however, colonial elites acquired more wealth and stability, enabling them to aspire to the status of gentlemen (even if they technically couldn't be considered gentlemen due to having engaged in work or merchant activity). The wealthiest began to copy English manners and buy the latest English consumer goods; they built houses that mimicked English mansions; they sent their sons on grand tours of Europe and to study in England; they set up exclusive social clubs; and they wanted to rule their communities as English aristocrats did. They knew more of what was going on in England than they knew of neighboring colonies,

TIP

If your role is not one of the elite, you must decide how much subservience to give those in the game who believe themselves gentlemen. Giving too much deference will make you seem like a toady; giving too little may hurt your character's personal relationships with the elite.

and they admired the English government. These gentlemen got along well with the English-appointed royal governors in each colony, generally complied with the Navigation Acts (see "Origins of the Colonial Economic System" on page 37), supported the British Empire, and viewed their colonial legislatures, which they dominated, as little Parliaments. The top 5 percent of society in the north, comprising mainly merchants, and the top 5 percent in the south, comprising plantation owners with enormous amounts of land and slaves, consciously imitated English ways as the distribution of wealth began to resemble England's—skewed heavily to the top. The rich were getting richer, the poor were getting poorer, and the middle was losing ground in terms of current property and future opportunities.

In New York, many of these elites were merchants, traders who pursued a variety of strategies to achieve wealth. First, there was money to be made in transportation: owning and operating merchant vessels that transported other people's goods for a price. Second, there was the buying and selling of merchandise on one's own account. These northern merchants became adroit at creating complex patterns of exchanges around the Atlantic, with a profit on each leg. For example, northern merchants would buy from nearby colonial farmers wheat, corn, and other food crops, and sell that cargo at a profit in the West Indies, where plantation owners preferred importing food and using their own scarce land for growing sugar. This archetypal merchant would then buy sugar and carry it to England, where again he would be offered more for the sugar than he had paid. From England, he would buy consumer products and bring them back to New York, for sale in Manhattan or distribution to storekeepers and consumers throughout the region.

Merchants would also make profits by extending credit to consumers and shopkeepers, thus collecting interest as well as making a profit on the sale of goods. Finally, merchants also became landowners (and vice versa—large landowners in the Hudson Valley diversified into merchant activity). Land produced profits either from renting, whether it was a town lot or a fifty-acre farm, or from speculation, with merchants buying up large plots to subdivide and resell at a profit. To protect those interests, merchants and large landowners naturally became the dominant forces in the colony's political system, from which they could benefit as well. The gentlemen—from families like the Livingstons, Delanceys, and Philipses—combined trade and land ownership to sit at the top of the colonial hierarchy.

Farmers

While some white men, as merchants, ran the economy and politics of the northern colonies, most white men were farmers. Personal independence in rural areas meant owning your own land free and clear of debt or rent, which made one a "yeoman" farmer. Tenant farmers and farm laborers aspired to the status of yeoman, while many yeomen hoped to acquire yet more land to attain the status of "planter." Between 50 and 70 percent of white adult males in rural areas qualified as yeomen by owning their own land, and thus could vote. The standard for voting eligibility in most colonies was fifty acres of land (or paying sufficient taxes on personal property if one lived in town), and that amount was about as small as a farm could get and still be economically viable. Owning fifty acres was seen as a proxy for the personal independence one needed to participate in politics. Most of the remaining adult white males were either younger sons working for their fathers, land-renting farmers, or laborers (sometimes indentured servants or slaves). All hoped to end their demeaning economic dependence through landownership, and thus attain the status of yeoman and voter.

Yeomen farmers operated on the basis of a household economy, which required productive work from everyone—husbands (in the fields, harvesting crops for both consumption and profit), wives (in vegetable gardens and orchards, supervising penned-in animals, producing cloth, and preserving foods), children, indentured servants, and occasionally slaves. Few if any farmers could achieve complete self-sufficiency, and farm families engaged in market transactions throughout the year for necessities they could not produce by themselves. Women would trade household products with other women of the neighborhood (e.g., eggs for fruit); men would sell crop surpluses in local markets, in exchange for critical supplies or new consumer products imported from Britain. But few farmers would produce primarily for the marketplace—these were not profit-maximizing plantations. Rather, farmers aimed at a competency, for themselves and for their male children to have the opportunity to gain economic independence as farmers as well. Yeomen's farms could grow in size, or land in outlying areas or new towns could be purchased, in order to provide "new" land for multiple sons as they came of age. The goal was to preserve the independence of the family's males for the long term.

For at least three generations, northern colonial farmers prospered with these strategies because land was plentiful. Farm sizes averaged one hundred and fifty acres in the early 1700s; patriarchal fathers could provide their sons (of whom there were often many—the average number of children surviving to adulthood was seven in some areas) with land by dividing their existing farm or helping to set up new towns for their sons to settle new land. However, by the 1760s the land supply east of the Appalachian Mountains had been divided up, and the average size of family farms had dropped to fifty acres. Land was becoming more expensive, making it harder to provide for children. A man needed at least fifty acres to have a good chance of making his farm profitable—a yeoman who sold land to pay debts or taxes or to set up a son on his own farm would impoverish himself if his own holding dropped below fifty acres. In order to maintain a family's standard of living on fifty acres, the land had to be worked more intensively, with less time lying fallow to restore fertility and less ground for farm animals to graze. The result was declining crop yields as land began to wear out. Meanwhile, thanks to the growing availability of a wide range of consumer products imported from Britain—cloth and carpets, mirrors and glass, china and cutlery, books—and to easy credit provided by English merchants (see Origins of the Colonial Economic System, pages 37–38), farm families had more things to buy, and more desire to buy them. Thus, the average northern family farmer in the 1760s and 1770s was confronting a diminishing future: less income from market sales of his produce, little if any land to give to the next generation, and increasing risk of debt as he bought more consumer goods than his crops could pay for.

Beginning in the 1760s, farmers began to fear tenancy and the dependence it implied—descending from the independence of a yeoman to the feudal position of a serf under a lord. Tenancy meant a farmer rented his land from a landlord instead of owning the land outright, which resulted in the farmer becoming **disenfranchised** if he did not own enough other goods that were taxed.

There was evidence all around them of this possibility—younger sons were forced to rent land (at ever higher prices) in order to start farms and families. More men wandered the back roads between small towns looking to find employment as farm or wage laborers, and towns were "warning out" such vagabonds so they wouldn't end up on poor relief. Many yeomen could see that their own accounts with local merchants never quite cleared: as each year passed they were always a bit further in debt as the crops they sold failed to cover the year's purchases. Anything that might increase debt increased the risk of losing land, and increased taxes were a prime threat.

Yet farmers' worries about impoverishment or inability to provide for their sons' futures were not sufficient to produce a rebellion; only when political changes posed another threat—this time to their personal independence—would these rural property owners become radicalized.

Artisans and Workingmen

Unlike rural areas, where land determined one's wealth and social status, the major towns of Philadelphia, Boston, and New York had more complicated social hierarchies. The 10 percent of urban dwellers who were

Those adult males who did not own sufficient property or pay minimum tax levels (such as wage laborers or tenant farmers) were **disenfranchised**, meaning they could not vote. These men could become franchised if they obtained enough property. Certain people (married women, slaves) were always dependents who could never own property and thus were always ineligible to vote.

Artisans were skilled craftsmen who owned their own tools and, at the top of their profession as masters, ran their own shops and employed journeymen, apprentices, servants, and slaves in their trade. The artisan group included blacksmiths, carpenters, tailors, and shoemakers. Practically all manufactured goods made in New York came from artisans.

merchants, shopkeepers, and landowners included many wealthy elite, but also many who might be called middle-class or bourgeois. More than 50 percent of the free urban male population, with a range of wealth and status, made their living through a skilled trade of some sort. Beneath them were another 20 percent considered common laborers: seamen, cartmen, or longshoremen. Below these laborers were indentured servants and slaves.

Among the tradesmen, who called themselves **artisans** or mechanics, there were definite hierarchies. At the bottom was the apprentice, who worked for his room and board while learning the trade. The next level was journeyman, who worked for wages in someone else's shop. At the top was the master, who was his own employer as a small-scale producer. That meant he was a property owner (of his tools and shop), and might employ journeymen, apprentices, servants, and slaves. In this hierarchical world, status within the tradesmen could be determined with precision, yet tradesmen had more contact with the elite (as customers and suppliers) and those below them (their employees and bound labor) than they did with members of their own trade.

Much like farmers, however, this group shared the goal of gaining personal independence: of becoming a man who worked for himself, free of rent or debt. Webs of dependency made this goal difficult to achieve, even for master craftsmen. Starting an artisanal business required capital, which meant going into debt, and raw materials, which meant relying on a merchant supplier. Customers in many trades ordered "bespoke" goods; these were expensive custom-made products, which tradesmen relied on the elite to purchase with regularity. Towns also required licenses, another cost of doing business. These barriers to entry had been growing during the eighteenth century, making it increasingly difficult for journeymen to move up to master, and more difficult for masters to sustain and expand their own shops.

Certain moral values, such as hard work and thrift, were considered necessary to achieving personal independence. Artisans believed in a labor theory of value, which specified that they were entitled to the fruits of their own labor and that honest work produced not only income but also respectability. (Sections 25–31 of the John Locke reading on pages 104–106 provides the philosophical grounding for this view of the right to property.) Those with aspirations to status and wealth adopted individualistic virtues that frowned on debt, corruption, extravagance, and drink in favor of economy, industry, and prudence. Their slogan became "Liberty and Property," a nod toward Lockean notions of the foundations for a just government, and an indication of their design for social mobility. But journeymen, whose hopes of upward mobility were dwindling due to rising costs of entry and periodic depressions, often spent more of their time and money in taverns, drinking alongside the laborers. There was a growing fear among journeymen of downward mobility, descent into the working class, and never acquiring a competency—all of which would mean never achieving personal independence.

The boom and bust cycle of the colonial economy reached its zenith in the years prior to the revolution. New York's economy expanded dramatically in the 1750s, thanks in part to British military buildup that used New York as its central port during the French and Indian War (1754–63). Such growth included a building boom—New York City added perhaps a thousand buildings in those ten years, which meant more work for both skilled and unskilled workers in the construction trades. At the ports, the traditional basis of the economy, there continued to be growth in the grain trade, particularly to the West Indies and southern Europe. This merchant activity meant plentiful opportunities for work in ship construction and maintenance, in loading and unloading, and as sailors on merchant vessels. And, of course, population growth produced more opportunities to provide services, such as chimney sweeping, wood cutting, and hauling. Thus a growing working class—unskilled laborers who were dependent on wages to survive—formed and occupied a rung of the economic hierarchy beneath the tradesmen and even underemployed journeymen.

When the war ended and the massive military spending suddenly dwindled to a trickle, the colonial economic boom quickly became a bust. Even without the war, one recurring problem for the workingmen of New York City had been the unreliability of work. This was a pre-industrial economy, geared to the rhythms of the seasons, to the arrival and departure of ships, and to the seemingly unfathomable actions of politicians, merchants, and economic forces located in England and around the Atlantic. Now, credit crises in London (in both the post-war early 1760s and again in the early 1770s) profoundly depressed the colonial port economies. Increases in British taxes would reduce purchasing power still further. Thus, both unemployment and abject poverty became constant threats to workingmen throughout the 1760s and 1770s. The city spent large amounts of money erecting and maintaining almshouses, where the desperate unemployed lived and worked in appalling human warehouse conditions.

Another factor cutting into the job prospects and wages of local workingmen in the 1760s was the arrival of immigrants, including British soldiers, who were allowed to seek part-time employment in the local economy and were willing to work for roughly half of what locals demanded. Most European professional soldiers came from the lower, uneducated classes to take this poorly paying but secure job; colonists saw them as rough, crude, barbaric sorts who often abused local women as a way to ease their boredom. Americans despised these "standing armies," preferring the local militia, part-time soldiers called up in an emergency, who they viewed as virtuous for sacrificing for their country in its time of need. Unemployed men, already vulnerable, might literally lose their independence if the British navy needed more men and **impressed** them into service off the street.

Finally, the population rise reflected immigration from England, Scotland, and Ireland. Many came through the city on their way to finding

Impressment refers to the British navy's practice of forcing (by means of "press gangs" in port cities) men of military age and seafaring experience to crew naval warships. Although similar in many ways to a draft, it differed in that it occurred without warning and at gunpoint in the streets and homes of those men impressed.

a farm on which to work, but others stayed to compete with the locals. These arrivals brought their own vivid memories of British elite oppression and the rights of average people to take to the streets against the government, for many had done so back home during the social and political conflicts in the 1760s.[5]

One final challenge in this period was the reduction in the use of indentured servants by New York employers and the decline in the importation of slaves. Employers were discovering one great advantage of wage labor—the ability to hire just the right number of men for a particular job and then let them go when the job was done. Given the seasonality of the shipping and construction industries, which anchored New York's economy, it was starting to make less sense for employers to pay the carrying costs in room and board (not the mention those of catching runaways or putting down a slave rebellion) that a servant or slave required year round.

Laborers' standard of living fell after 1763, following the end of the spending for the French and Indian War. Although prices for most goods remained stable, food prices rose in the late 1760s and early 1770s. Wages fell dramatically from wartime levels, down to two to three pounds per month—when work could be had at all. It is difficult to give that wage in modern figures given the change in value of money and the switch from pounds to dollars, but an educated guess would place it at less than ten to fifteen thousand dollars per year in purchasing power today. Thus, at best, workingmen were living close to the economic edge. New York City's growing funds for poor relief supported not only the city's indigent widows, elderly, sick, and orphans, but also its adult men who had fallen on hard times. Those who had to seek such public relief resented it deeply, and blamed their plight on the affluent of the city. The affluent, of course, blamed the poor themselves, citing their laziness, drunkenness, and lack of thrift. Class divides widened as the wealthy purchased luxury goods such as carriages and mansions while the poor struggled to eat on a daily basis.

Workers actively sought to remedy their economic plight. Some proto-union organizing efforts occurred among sailors and carpenters, who tried to bargain collectively for better wages. Many more sought out evangelical churches, which had been founded during the Great Awakening, a religious revival of the 1740s, and which offered an egalitarian understanding of both life and the soul. These churches, Baptist and Methodist, with their enthusiastic services and high levels of congregational participation, appealed to the lower classes, as well as servants and slaves. Unlike the established Anglican or Dutch Reformed churches controlled by elite, these new churches proclaimed that all were equal before God and that an individual's holiness counted more than his place in the social hierarchy. The lower classes did not believe in a free market or nascent ideas of the law of supply and demand; they believed in a moral economy based on fair wages and just prices, as had existed since the Middle Ages. Their lives depended on the interlocking supports of family, religion, and community, for which they would fight.[6] Given a spark, a cause, the workingmen would be in the streets, and not just for someone else's purposes but in support of their own ambitions.

Artisans and workingmen found themselves on the same side in the streets, despite their different places in the hierarchy. Some members of the elite believed that they could control the actions of these lesser men, to use the crowd for their own purposes, but as the crisis wore on, artisans, mechanics, and workingmen began to awaken to their role as political actors rather than as dependents. Gouvernour Morris, a wealthy landowner, expressed the contempt the elite felt for the lower classes and the elite's fear of such discontent getting out of hand:

> The mob begins to think and to reason. Poor reptiles! It is with them a vernal morning; they are struggling to cast off their winter's slough, they bask in the sunshine, and ere noon they will bite, depend on it. The gentry begin to fear this.[7]

Slaves

What became the British colonial city of New York had begun as New Amsterdam in 1625 by Dutch colonists. The Dutch owned slaves nearly from the beginning of the city's history. Although the percentage of slaves in New York's population declined between 1664 and the early 1700s after the city transitioned to British rule, the slave population expanded relentlessly through the middle of the eighteenth century. As of 1771, there were more than 3,100 slaves in New York City, nearly 15 percent of the population. Many had been imported directly from Africa in the previous two decades. Although not a slave society in the manner of the southern colonies, where slave labor was the bedrock of plantation labor, New York was not just a society with a few enslaved men—it was, along with other northern colonies, a "society with slaves." Slavery was an important element in the economic, social, and political life of the city, and slaveowning an appropriate and morally acceptable way to gain wealth, power, and status.

Northern slavery was initially concentrated in the cities; it was expected of an elite household to use some slaves as domestic servants (e.g. gardeners, butlers, and coachmen for men; cooks and maids for women). However, mid-eighteenth-century urban slavery expanded into the shops of artisans, where slaves worked in a wide variety of manufacturing roles, especially those connected with the sea (shipbuilding, ropemaking, etc.). Similarly, the operations of merchants in the port relied in part on slaves, often as sailors or dockworkers. Slavery also moved into the fields as farmers in New Jersey, Long Island, and up the Hudson River turned to slaves instead of increasingly scarce white indentured servants. Northern agricultural slaves were not organized into gangs as on southern plantations; rather they served many different roles at different times of the year, working alongside the farmer's family, hired day laborers, and servants. Thus, slaves in the city and in the countryside were an integral part of the labor force in various geographic and economic sectors of the north.

The growth in the number of slaves in New York was fueled primarily by the slave trade from the Caribbean and Africa, rather than occurring through natural population growth. Through the 1730s, most imported slaves came from other New World colonies such as Jamaica or Barbados, but later waves contained higher and higher percentages of Africans (by one estimate, up to 70 percent of slave imports to New York after 1741 were Africans). This African wave unbalanced the sex ratio, making it much more heavily male, and increased death rates due to diseases brought off the ships. Most slaves were owned in small groups, with one, two, or three to a household, whether for an artisan in the city or a farmer in Queens. The result was a population that did not sustain itself, as marrying became more difficult (white masters often discouraged marriage between slaves of different masters) and maternal fertility declined due to the skewed sex ratio and the higher mortality rate. At the same time, as whites imported more slaves, they freed fewer blacks and the free black community, already small, began to shrink as well. It is estimated there were only one hundred free blacks (compared to over 3,100 slaves) in New York City by 1771.

Given the difficulties of establishing a family life, what could slaves in New York City do to improve their lives? One chance that many in the past had taken—earning enough on the side to buy their freedom from their master—had drawn hostile attention from the authorities. The slaves' shadow economy, where handicrafts, garden crops, oysters, and after-hours labor could be sold to whites, shriveled as New York barred slaves from trading independently and made it a crime for free persons to buy from slaves by the mid-eighteenth century. Another potential outlet lay in religion. Many Africans tried to retain their cultural habits, including their names and modes of worship, but more acculturated slaves began to seek out the evangelical faiths that had sprung from the Great Awakening. Many Methodist and Baptist churches embraced blacks as equals, and offered solace in Biblical stories of freedom after captivity. Another option was running away, a practice that was on the rise as evidenced by the increasing number of newspaper ads placed by masters seeking the return of runaways. But most slaves probably engaged in regular small acts of resistance—stealing, drinking, violating curfew, slacking on the job—which made life bearable. They enjoyed moments in taverns, with fiddles at home, or at celebrations like Pinkster Day, a spring festival derived from Dutch customs that gave slaves time off to gather with family and friends.

However, all New Yorkers of the mid-eighteenth century, free or slave, knew that slave revolts were a real possibility. Any society with slaves had to fear violence by individual slaves against their masters. In 1775, for example, two New York City slaves were hanged for conspiring to murder their masters; the executed were described as "two Tory Negroes" who were "engaging to murder their masters who were supporters of Liberty."[8] But masters' worst fears concerned larger plots, greater conspiracies designed to channel violence into a bloody all-out rebellion for freedom, revenge, or both. In April 1712, slaves plotted to set fire to a series of houses and kill the white inhabitants as they fled. For this conspiracy, in which eight whites were killed, eighteen blacks were executed with a variety of torture tactics, including burning alive, breaking on the rack, and hanging in chains. Furthermore, the whites left the heads and body parts of the executed out in public as an example to others.

In 1741, authorities came to believe that an even larger conspiracy, hatched at a white-owned tavern on the Hudson River during winter, was afoot. After several suspicious fires (including the burning down of Fort George at the tip of Manhattan), one hundred and fifty-two blacks and twenty whites were arrested as conspirators, and eighty-one blacks confessed to the plot. Thirty blacks—most of whom were slowly burnt to death—joined four hanged whites for a total of thirty-four people executed, a number vastly exceeding the twenty executions at the Salem Witch Trials during which none were burnt. Yet the conspiracy's existence was debated immediately after the executions, and is still an open question discussed by historians today.[9] It is safe to say that rumors of slave revolts outpaced their actual occurrence throughout colonial America, and the actions taken by whites based on those rumors were gruesome, horrific, inhuman, and reliant on terror tactics in order to deter future attempts at revolt. Nonetheless, hideous tortures of real or imagined conspirators could not remove the specter of slave revolt that hung over New York City throughout this period. Many of those who witnessed the 1741 trials, including the justice who conducted the investigation and wrote up his own account defending the convictions, were still alive in 1775.

New hope for slaves appeared, in the 1770s, from an unexpected source. The continued legal existence of slavery was questioned by the 1772 *Somerset* decision in England. The result of that case, wherein slavery was held incompatible with the laws of England (and only England—the practice of slavery in its colonies was unaffected by the decision), heartened opponents of slavery in the colonies and led many slaves to think that if they only could get to England, they would be free.

In the 1770s, the Quakers began discussing prohibiting slave ownership among their members and, along with other religiously motivated slaveowners, began to free their slaves. Slaves themselves now saw new options—to appeal to their masters' consciences, to petition colonial legislatures to follow the *Somerset* precedent, and to run away with the knowledge that there might be some out there who would hide them or get them to England, where freedom ruled. Starting in January 1773 and continuing through 1774, petitions signed by slaves began arriving at the Massachusetts legislature (some directly addressed to the legislature, some in the form of widely distributed pamphlets) calling for freedom and making proposals to settle the newly freed slaves on unimproved land (often meaning land still claimed and occupied by Indians). Though these petitions went nowhere, the fact that slaves were employing one of the most ancient English political rights—the petition for redress of grievances—meant that legislatures and the people as a whole now had to debate such issues. A revolution, many slaves began to think, might bring them the personal independence they desired above all else.

Women

Women's official place in late colonial life was constrained by rules of coverture. Coverture attached to all women when they married in all English colonial jurisdictions. A married woman became civilly dead, with her legal existence merged into that of her husband, who had control of all assets and authority over all decisions. This doctrine existed for centuries prior to the 1770s, and only began to be eroded in the mid-nineteenth century by the Married Women's Property Acts. Until marriage, women were controlled by their fathers; after marriage, a woman became a *feme covert*, a "covered woman." Roughly 90 percent of all adult women were married in the colonies. To quote the great English legal scholar Blackstone in 1765, "by marriage the husband and wife are one person in law; that is, the very being or legal existence of the woman is suspended. . . ."[10] Adult married women could not make contracts or work for wages without their husband's permission. Nor could they sell or manage any property without their husband's permission, even property owned prior to and brought into the marriage. Adult married women could not be legal guardians, could not serve as executors or administrators of estates, and could not sue in court without permission. Without ownership or control of property, married women were dependents, and neither the law nor society allowed them to exercise independent judgment. As such, women could not vote, hold public office, or serve on juries; married women were treated like children—legally incompetent and barred from public life.

Coverture did not apply to the small minority of women who were single adults or who were widowed. Such women could own property, enter contracts, bequeath possessions by will, serve as legal guardians, and administer estates. In the early years of many British colonies, the high death rate meant widowhood was common, creating many *feme soles*. These women would accumulate property and manage farms and businesses if they were "lucky enough" to have their husbands die. Given the surplus of men in the early years of most colonies, such widows generally did not remain single very long; however, many widows made prenuptial agreements that allowed them to continue controlling property after remarriage. If a widow did not remarry, she could carry on her husband's farm, business, or artisanal trade, and towns often granted widows licenses to manage inns and taverns. Such businesswomen had to learn to deal with suppliers and obtain credit, as well as keep accounts and extend credit to customers in a cash-poor economy. Some widows became prominent in their hometowns for their business acumen as well as inheritances, even writing letters to the editors of New York newspapers asking to be given the same opportunities in court as men.

The social reality of women's lives bore very little resemblance to that painted by patriarchal laws, as married, widowed, and single women engaged in the public sphere far more than the law would suggest was possible. Women could not be condescended to as mere dependents because their labor and their dealings were essential to family economic survival. In the colonial economy, in which 90 percent of the people worked in agriculture, women's work was absolutely essential. On farms, the division of labor was such that men usually engaged in commodity production in the fields, the surplus of which might be sold at market for cash, while women were responsible for farm production "inside the fence." That meant that wives raised chickens, grew vegetables, tended to dairy production, gathered and dried fruits, made cider, and preserved food. Only the largest, wealthiest farms could be self-sufficient; women on most farms engaged in a wide network of neighborhood trading, exchanging with a nearby woman surplus of one product for something her household lacked. Women also produced cloth, a tedious and time-consuming process that involved spinning yarn, weaving it into material, and stitching it into usable clothing, blankets, and rugs.

Furthermore, women had to manage the household, which meant coordinating the work of children and servants. Children had to be educated and directed into productive household work at the earliest possible age, and that was the wife's job. The result was that women were managers of property, deputy husbands, inside and outside of the house, and they could take over the whole enterprise if the husband was absent. In the real colonial world, the fact that

> An average woman would marry in her early to mid-twenties and start having children, on average one child every other year, for the next fifteen to twenty years.

their work was essential to success on the farm meant that women gained independence, respect, and confidence in an array of public roles. The law, which technically considered women dependent, rarely interfered, as women occupied essential positions in both the family and political economy.

A particularly striking example of women's socioeconomic significance was their critical contribution to the success of men's strategy of resistance to British taxes through **boycotts** in the early 1760s and 1770s. In order for the boycotts to be effective, women by the thousands had to be enlisted in the political process. Simple actions—eating, drinking, and clothing choices—became imbued with deep political meaning. Women stopped buying British goods, stopped consuming taxed products, and started manufacturing replacements at home, especially cloth. To protest the Stamp Act, the 1765 British law designed to raise revenue for the empire from the colonies by taxing paper products and particularly official documents, a group of engaged brides-to-be in New York refused to be married if their groom obtained a stamped marriage license.[11] As economic conditions worsened and political tensions threatened to break out into armed struggle, calls went out—both to and from women—for a return to a simpler life of sacrifice, frugality, and economy, denouncing the luxury, extravagance, and dissipation that came from excessive wealth. Women's letters and diaries from this period reflected an increasingly political tone, as the issues at stake and the proper responses to them became subjects for debate. One prominent example of women's

> **Boycott** means to refrain from buying, selling, or interacting with a person or company to make a political point. The term itself began in reference to an individual Irish land agent—Charles Boycott—who in the 1880s was subject to such pressure. Colonists referred to such actions as non-importation, non-exportation, or non-intercourse; the term "boycott" is an anachronism and would not have been used then, but is used here for convenience.

collective action occurred in Edenton, North Carolina, where fifty-one women signed onto the Association in 1774 to protest the Coercive Acts (see below) and faced ridicule for their action from the British press. But American Patriots rallied to support them; as one male commentator had said about a similar action, American men knew they had "to persuade our wives to give us their assistance, without which 'tis impossible to succeed."[12]

Significantly, women were also essential participants in street actions and public ceremonies. In the late 1760s, women calling themselves the Daughters of Liberty gathered in groups of twenty to forty to hold ritualized ceremonies supporting resistance to the British. Subsequently, such women participated in mobs and marched in funeral processions for fallen Patriot victims of the Boston Massacre. When Alexander McDougall of New York was imprisoned for his writings, "45 virgins of this city went in procession to pay their respects" at the jail to show their support.[13] Some women were cited by British authorities for participating in mobs, even to the extent of tarring and feathering their political opponents. As the struggle for power intensified, Patriot women harassed Loyalists, clamored outside of merchants' warehouses for supplies they believed were being hoarded, and reported on their neighbors for trading with the British or engaging in conspicuous consumption. By 1776, Abigail Adams, in her now famous letter to her husband John, was suggesting that women would "foment a Rebelion" because of the "unlimited power" in the hands of husbands, who, like all men, "would be tyrants if they could." Women, she wrote, "will not hold ourselves bound by any Laws in which we have no voice, or Representation."[14]

THE ECONOMIC CRISIS FACING THE COLONIES

The American Revolutionary crisis is unusual in the history of revolutions in that a large number of the elite became revolutionaries. Revolutions are not typically led by a society's social, economic, and political leaders; instead, revolutionaries come from below and tend to want to replace those elites. Why and how some members of the colonial elite—in New York and elsewhere—engaged with and encouraged the revolutionary forces is a critical question.

It is in the deteriorating circumstances of the economic elite of the colonies—merchants in the north, plantation owners growing tobacco and rice in the south—within the British Empire's economic system that one finds the cause for unhappiness among the colonial privileged. For many years, their control over their own fortunes and over the fortunes of their colonies had been growing larger and stronger, but now this economic autonomy (as well as its profits) was eroding. Eliminating competition both from within and without their home base to regain and expand their economic independence would be an essential driving force in their resistance to Britain during the revolutionary crisis.

Origins of the Colonial Economic System

The economic model of the British Empire in the seventeenth and eighteenth centuries has been called **mercantilism**, defined (in terms of the colonies) as a government's attempt to orchestrate the economies of the colonies to maximize the wealth of the mother country. Mercantilist government policies organized the national economy toward that goal and did not favor free markets in trade goods. Most European economic thinking in the 1600s through the mid-1700s was rooted in mercantilism; Adam Smith's classic treatise favoring free trade and free markets, *The Wealth of Nations*, would not be published until 1776. European governments sought to avoid buying products from other nations or other nations' colonies (such as sugar and tobacco from Spanish, Portuguese, and Dutch colonies, and timber and naval supplies from Scandinavia), striving instead to maximize the processing, refining, and re-exporting of colonial commodities. Under mercantilism, British trade to and from the colonies in its empire became the dynamic element in its trading economy, growing two to three times faster than trade with other countries. Underpinning mercantilism in Great Britain was a set of laws collectively known as the Navigation Acts (first passed in 1651), which controlled and channeled trade to and from the American colonies.

Mercantilism assigned an empire's colonies the primary economic role of suppliers of raw materials, with manufacturing (and its enormous profits) generally restricted to the home country. The key elements were these:

TIP

Any discussion of economic policy during the game must take into consideration the Navigation Acts, which were enforced by the dominant British navy as well as customs officials and courts. In particular, players must always be aware of what economic activity was legal or illegal.

1. Only British Empire vessels (English, American colonial, Scottish) were allowed to take goods into or out of the colonies to other ports within the empire. This gave a legal monopoly in the shipping trade to the British, to the exclusion of French, Dutch, Portuguese, and Spanish merchants.

2. Certain colonial-made goods, known as enumerated goods because they were on a numbered list, had to be exported to Great Britain first. Only if the British had exhausted their demand for them could the commodities then be re-exported to other countries in Europe for sale. The reverse was also true. In particular, British merchants and consumers could tap other nations only if the colonial sources had not supplied sufficient quantities. The products on the list by 1760 included tobacco, sugar, molasses, indigo, naval

Mercantilism is an economic philosophy based on the idea that national wealth is built through a positive balance of trade—more exports than imports—with the rest of the world.

supplies, hemp, and rice. The British had secured the market from non-British competition for both buyers and sellers.

3. Colonies were restricted from producing certain manufactured products in order to limit competition against the English manufacturers. Colonists could harvest beavers and other furs, for example, but could not produce fur products—they had to ship the pelts to Great Britain to be manufactured into hats and coats, which would then be sold back to the colonists at a high profit. Similar restrictions applied to wool (home manufacturing was allowed, but textile production for market was restricted) and to iron ore.

Despite these limitations and restrictions (or perhaps because of them) the Navigation Acts had been a tremendous success for the colonies in general and New York in particular as of the mid-eighteenth century. Trade to and from the North American colonies expanded faster than the population, indicating real economic growth. Colonists experienced a consumer revolution, as average American farm families purchased more and more imported products and paid for them with farm produce sold both locally and throughout the Atlantic world. Thanks to the protection offered by the British navy and the assured markets, colonial merchants in the North and tobacco plantation owners in the South had established central and extremely lucrative positions in the colonial economy. In the North, merchants invested in more ships, more warehouses in towns, and more networks for both distributing imported goods to the countryside and gathering products to fill their ships' cargo holds. In the South, large planters did not do the shipping themselves, but operated as middlemen, selling not only their own tobacco but bundling their neighbors' crops in the load as well (for a percentage of the profits, of course). In both the North and the South, these men could offer credit for these transactions, allowing small farmers to borrow money for imported goods they purchased and pay it off later when the farmers sold their crops (usually with interest if the debt was carried longer than six months).

WARNING ! *Remember that a free market was not the engine of this prosperity. Guaranteed markets through mercantilism reduced risks and assured profits for preferred vendors and customers. Arguing for a free market and free trade regime was a risky economic innovation in this period.*

British Challenges

English merchants observed this growing colonial trade and decided to engage heavily in the colonial markets, threatening both the power and the profits of the locals. They did so in two ways. First, they invested money in the form of easy credit terms for purchasers. These English merchants were able to give twelve months of credit with zero percent interest (versus six months by the colonials), encouraging both colonial merchants and consumers to buy more products. Of course, if the debt was not paid off within a year, interest would start to accrue, much like a credit card after the grace period has expired. Most of this debt was kept in a "book"; periodic payments never quite met the full principal, but the debtor was never forced to pay in full. Second, lacking in warehouses and distribution systems, the English merchants would auction off goods directly to small-town merchants and consumers themselves. These sales were called "vendues" (from the French *vendre*, to sell) and were advertised by boys walking through the port and neighboring towns, beating drums (this is the origin of the phrase "to drum up business"). Purchasers would come down to the wharf and buy what they wanted off the ship, selling their own farm products to the ship for its outbound voyage. Unlike the system in place for trading with American merchants, there were no warehousing costs and no distribution network with its middlemen to pay. The cheaper credit and cheaper products worked to the benefit of the English merchants between 1748 and 1752, as exports from Britain to the northern colonies boomed and American merchants suffered from the competition. American merchants faced mounting debts, warehouses full of unsold goods, and potential loss of control over their economy.

As luck would have it (at least for the economy), war broke out. The French and Indian War led to an enormous military buildup in the colonies as the British navy and army demanded ships, supplies, lodging, and provisions to fight the French in Canada and the Indians on the frontier. A spending spree of real money (gold and silver from the British treasury, as opposed to soft or paper money) ensued, and the wartime economic boom cleared out excess inventories and brought profits to both American and English merchants. But by 1760, British victories in North America led the military to move its forces to other war theaters. With the rapid decline in British military spending, economic conditions rapidly returned to their pre-war circumstances. Money, particularly gold and silver, now left the colonies as the balance of trade shifted: the demand for American farm produce dropped while the American colonial desire for imported consumer goods remained as strong as ever. Once wartime profits were spent, English merchants extended easy credit (again) and made easy sales (again), while American merchants saw their warehouses filling up with unsold merchandise (again).

By 1763, in a period of peace, English merchants faced rising interest rates and a credit crisis back in Great Britain. Feeling overextended in terms of what they had lent to American merchants and consumers, they began to fear that they would never be repaid. They therefore began to demand immediate payment on debts from their American customers, both merchant and consumer. To pay what they owed to the English, the Americans would turn to their books and call in their debtors to pay up. If a debtor couldn't pay, the creditor would go to the courthouse, obtain a judgment for the debt, and seize whatever of value (crops, farm implements, animals, and ultimately land) could be sold to pay off the debt. At the same time as this financial crisis, the British Parliament passed, in 1764, the Currency Act forbidding colonial governments from issuing paper money, thus further deflating the money supply available for paying off debts. The result by 1764–65 was a depression, as shipping ground to a halt, unsold inventories continued to grow, unemployment in shipping towns skyrocketed, and court judgments dispossessed large numbers of colonial farmers of their property. John Dickinson described the process on the American side this way: "Thus, the consumers break [force bankruptcy on] the shopkeepers, the shopkeepers break the merchants, and the shock must be felt as far as London."[15]

In the north, the merchant elite saw control over their colonies' economies taken over by English merchants and politicians. Northern merchants' overarching goal became **economic sovereignty**, to reassert their control over their home markets and their own economic destiny in the colonies. They immediately began to seek ways to reduce their dependency, to diversify in order to avoid the catastrophe of indebtedness, to regain their autonomy. Many started to look at manufacturing, but of course under the Navigation Acts many of the most lucrative products were off-limits for colonials to produce. They considered gaining control through the money supply, but this strategy would require lobbying in Parliament to reverse the Currency Act and allow paper issuances and inflation, a doubtful prospect considering the influence of English merchants who desired payment in the sound money of gold and silver. American merchants had tried to undermine their English competition directly by regulating vendue sales in the 1750s, but the British government vetoed such prohibitions, allowing the English merchants to continue operating as before. At every turn, the lack of political autonomy prevented the colonists from achieving economic independence.

Since British laws blocked their goal, the economic elite turned to extralegal (neither sanctioned nor prohibited by law) methods to eliminate their English competition. What the colonial economic elite needed was a way to sell their overstocked inventories and to regain control of the outgoing produce (and the overall balance of trade) so that their businesses would profit from their colonies' economic activities. Thus was born the idea of *non-importation* (now called boycott). If colonial consumers stopped buying new imports from the English, their demand for those goods would not vanish. Instead they would have to buy the goods now stacked up in the colonial merchants' warehouses (the English merchants, having used vendue sales, had few such facilities). Non-importation did not imply nonconsumption—rather than buying newly imported tea, you could drink the tea that was already here. It did not imply non-exportation either: you could still sell outbound American produce, but since English ships weren't likely to dock if they couldn't unload their cargo, the export trade would have to go to American colonial ships now sitting idle in the ports. As long as American ships could return from their voyages and sell new imported cargo in a year or so, and as long as non-importation didn't go on too long, American merchants would profit from selling their unsold goods at home and their American commodities overseas, and would thus break the English merchant hold on the market.

But consumers and producers could not be expected to adopt non-importation simply out of loyalty to their local friends; there had to be a good reason to make them change their purchasing patterns so drastically. The merchants found such reasons in 1765 with the Stamp Act and again in 1768 with the Townshend Acts.

Both the Stamp Act and the Townshend Acts imposed unprecedented British taxes upon the colonists, taxes that were unconstitutional for some, a dangerous threat to liberty for others. Opposition to these taxes was popular. It was a fortuitous coincidence: merchants could oppose the taxes and adopt one-year non-importation agreements based on political principles while serving their own financial interests. Merchants made alliances with local artisans (encouraging local manufacturing to replace the non-imported goods) and with town laborers (who could police the streets for smugglers). Wealthy merchants, by forgoing luxury imports and emphasizing their frugality and support of home industry, appeared to be virtuous and self-sacrificing even as they profited by selling goods from their warehouses.

It was all very convenient, and assisted the merchant elite in the pursuit of economic sovereignty in the 1760s. Yet these successful campaigns to roll back the British taxes had an unintended effect: they unleashed popular forces that would prove hard to control and give rise to unruly mobs that might ultimately turn their grievances against the local elite as easily as against the British. A fateful choice would have to be made sooner than anyone expected. The desire for local autonomy and control over their interconnected economic and political futures would convince many of the wealthy elite to participate in rebellious activities. Yet many feared the unknown consequences of such upheavals to their own positions; after all, the tangible and long-standing economic benefits deriving from their connections to the British Empire were not something to be tossed aside casually over a few pounds in taxes.

POLITICAL IDEOLOGIES IN THE REVOLUTIONARY CRISIS

Overview

Most functioning societies contain a dominant ideology that prescribes the proper way to govern that society, along with many ideas that disagree with the mainstream. In most cases, those holding such dissenting ideologies try to work within the existing system and dominant ideology to obtain control of the government or to reform the existing processes with which they disagree, turning to violent rebellion or revolution only as a last resort. Individuals draw upon a wide range of dissenting ideas from a variety of value systems and ideologies, including those that are religious, social, economic, and political in nature. In crisis, the ideas that prevail are determined by how well those ideas seem to explain past circumstances and present conditions, plus predict (or compel) future actions. Revolutionary ideologies usually gain popular support only when deteriorating social, economic, and political circumstances suggest that no other alternative ideology seems plausible. Masses of people are then convinced that the present is intolerable, the current system is incapable of positive change, and thus the future will be worse unless they act now.

An **ideology** is a set of conscious and unconscious expectations, goals, and actions that explains to its believers a society's past and present condition and provides guideposts to what ought to happen in the future.

In the context of the crisis in the American colonies between 1763 and 1775, remember that citizens' varied perspectives on life and politics combined (often in inconsistent ways) different personal goals, attitudes, and feelings. In addition to the usual variations in belief that can be linked to things like social standing, economic situation, and religion, location mattered as well to the formation of political identities. The British and the Americans shared a common tongue as well as a history, but they analyzed the same circumstances and used the same words in quite different ways. A critical question for all New Yorkers at this time was which **ideological** lens provided the best view on their situation, for there were many to choose from.

British Perspectives on Politics and the Empire

For nearly two hundred years, the British had been creating overseas colonies to form an empire stretching from North America to the Caribbean and South America, from Africa to India. The North American colonies, first entered in the 1580s, constituted the oldest and largest (in territory and population) element of the British Empire. Nonetheless, in ways that mimicked existing views of society as a fixed hierarchy, the British viewed themselves as the mother country to their dependents, the child-like colonies. Even as late as the 1760s, this metaphor dominated British rhetoric regarding the place of the American colonies within the greater British Empire. Charles Townshend, who would later propose the Townshend Acts, spoke in 1765 of "these Americans, children planted by our care, nourished up by our indulgence until they are grown to a degree of strength and opulence, and protected by our arms."[16] Colonial life was considered backward, unsophisticated, immature, and on the frontier, even degenerate. Culture, civilization, economic development, and even freedom came from the center of the empire; North America was peripheral, at best a pale reflection of England. The colonies only thought of their own self-interest, while the British could see the good of the whole. Colonies often squabbled with each other over petty disputes, such as borders (the Mason-Dixon Line, for example, narrowly averted a war between Pennsylvania and Maryland). Therefore, colonists were like dependents, like children, incompetent and incapable of managing their own affairs.

Most important to British logic, colonies behaved in ways that were not only counterproductive but also defiant of the empire. During the French and Indian War, Parliament and the various ministries had tried to get the colonies to contribute men and money for the war effort, much of which was fought in North America against the French in Canada and the Indians along the Appalachian frontier. British officials were disappointed when colonial governments did not produce the quantity of men and money that the British believed necessary for success and well within colonial means. Furthermore, regular British army officers had only contempt for the military abilities of the colonial units that were sent to fight against the French regulars in Canada. Finally, the British were appalled that, even while British men were fighting and dying on the battlefield, various American merchants were continuing to make money by trading with the French, either through smuggling to and from the French West Indian sugar colonies or by trading overland into French Canada. From the British perspective, not only were the capabilities of the colonists in serious question, but also their loyalty.

As the war drew to a close, British officials began to scrutinize the administration of the North American colonies, and what they saw confirmed their worst fears. Despite various attempts dating back to the mid-1600s to regularize colonial administration and bring some coherence to governance of the empire, the colonies seemed completely out of control. Governors appointed from London could not govern effectively because local colonial legislatures held their governor's pay hostage until he caved to all of what the locals wanted. Customs officials, the frontline enforcers of the Navigation Acts, often collected their salaries while living in England, not even bothering to show up to the colonies they were supposedly regulating. When customs officials did go to the colonies, many were bribed by colonial smugglers to ignore certain "irregularities." Even if smugglers were caught and brought to trial, local colonial courts often found them innocent, for the jurors were often friends of (if not paid off by) these local merchant elites. The British looked on their previous policies as permissive and neglectful, and thus concluded that their children were out of control.

While some have argued that the British acts and taxes imposed after 1763 were designed to help pay the debts accumulated while fighting the French and Indian war, those debts were neither the cause nor the intended effect of British efforts. The real goal of these measures was to regain authority, to bind the colonies closer to Great Britain before it became too late and the colonies were lost forever. This fear drew from many undeniable pieces of evidence. The British feared a colonial population that was growing two to three times faster than that of the home country. They wondered what would happen in a generation or two when the colonies would hold more people than Britain. British trade had become increasingly tied to the colonies, not only as a supplier of raw materials and agricultural products but also as the prime market for British manufacturing exports. The consumer revolution in the colonies had led to a merchant and manufacturing boom in England to meet that demand. The British economy would be damaged irreparably if the colonial markets, now exclusively within the empire thanks to the Navigation Acts, were lost. The British also looked at the feeble military and financial performance of the colonies during the recent war, along with colonial trading with the enemy, and doubted the loyalty of the colonists. In short, the British feared that the colonies would want independence, and that Britain might soon be unable to prevent them from gaining it. The colonies needed to be brought into line—and quickly.

Tactics to control the wayward colonies lay in the hands of Parliament, the legislature of Great Britain. To understand the exalted position in the political system of Parliament, we need to digress slightly into constitutional thought in the 1760s. The British constitution was not written in a single document (and still isn't), but rather consisted of a series of laws, customs, history, and precedents that established the basic functioning of British government. This constitution was the result of hundreds of years of negotiations, arguments, and civil wars, and was said to produce a balanced government among the three great social groups and their political forms: the king (*monarchy*), the nobility (*aristocracy*), and the people (*democracy*). In terms of popular elections to give voice to the people, only 10 percent of adult males owned enough property to vote for representatives; this was seen as a positive feature that limited politics to the economically independent. The "King-in-Parliament" (a political concept referring to the House of Lords and the House of Commons, representing the nobles and the people, respectively) was said to comprise the whole state, but in reality, Parliament was **sovereign**.

Parliamentary sovereignty was hard fought and hard won in the 1600s against the King. The British were proud of their constitution, their laws, and their liberties, protected by Parliamentary sovereignty. The British people compared their freedom favorably to those poor wretches ruled in Europe by absolute monarchs.

What Parliamentary sovereignty meant in practice was that any law passed by Parliament was supreme and automatically constitutional, and had to be obeyed. For the colonies, Parliament had passed many laws, but almost all involved trade (e.g., the Navigation Acts) or other economic regulations. Most colonial administration had been carried out through agencies of the king such as the Board of Trade and the King's Council. Parliament had never directly regulated the internal workings of the colonies, preferring to leave this task to royally appointed governors and locally elected colonial legislatures, but still had the power to do it. Parliamentary sovereignty was such a well-accepted principle in the British Isles that if Parliament passed a law, it was expected that the colonies would obey, if not willingly then at least grudgingly.

However, if the colonies were so defiant that resistance broke out, the British now had an alternative method of law enforcement. Before the 1750s, the British navy regularly visited colonial ports, but there was no army in place, no way to police the land by force. Now, in 1763, an army needed to be stationed in a central location in the colonies to monitor the conquered French populace and the restive Indians. Military effort that had once been devoted to external defense could now be used for internal compliance. If the children's disobedient streak extended to defying Parliament outright, the British Army would be present to back up the law. Given what the British saw as the colonists' weak military performance, they had no doubt that any colonial resistance would be futile.

The outlines of the agenda were clear, consistent, logical, and reasonable given these British views: First, Parliament would pass laws to reinforce the existing Navigation Act regulations, install new controls on the internal colonial economy, and exert authority over the colonies through taxes. Second, the British authorities in the colonies would use tax revenue collected there to pay the royal governors and the customs officials directly, making them independent of colonial legislatures and able to resist bribes. Next, the authorities would set up new courts to remove the bias of local juries from the enforcement process. Fourth and finally, they would use the new tax revenue to defray the cost of the British military stationed in the colonies—after all, those free-rider colonists should pay for their own defense. Enacting this program was expected to produce grumbling (after all, who likes to have their taxes raised?) but ultimately obedience—obedience compelled if necessary by the force now available. It was constitutional because it was done by Parliament, and it was for the good of the whole empire.

WARNING ! *An army stationed in peacetime was regarded by most political theorists among the Patriots as a mortal danger to the people of a republic!*

The first efforts to rein in the colonists began on the colonial frontier following the French and Indian War, which ended in 1763 with the Peace of Paris. Under that treaty the British Empire acquired Native American lands to the west of the colonies, past the Appalachian Mountains. But later that year the king issued a proclamation (now called the Proclamation Line of 1763) which prohibited British colonial settlers from pushing west into those newly acquired lands. To the British, it made sense to separate two parties whose interchanges had been frequently bellicose. The line affected certain members of the economic elite, especially in Virginia where there had been much land speculation in the Ohio Valley that disregarded the rights of the natives to that land. But no one in the colonies at this point doubted the British Empire's authority to draw lines on a map.

A complementary development was the continuing presence of British troops in the colonies, allegedly to deal with military threats from Indians (after what is now known as Pontiac's Rebellion, during which a loose confederation of Great Lakes, Ohio, and Illinois Indians rebelled against British control, in 1763). Yet these troops were sent to New York City, where the British commanders insisted that New York's port and central location allowed them the greatest freedom to move military force toward the location of any trouble. In 1763, neither the Proclamation Line nor the stationing of the army in New York caused any real colonial disturbances.

In 1764, Parliament attempted to reinforce the Navigation Acts' greatest weakness, its lack of enforcement, by passing the Sugar Act. By cutting taxes on imported sugar and increasing enforcement (by installing more customs officials and using the British Navy for interdiction), Parliament tried to both increase the incentive to comply (lower taxes) while making enforcement more efficient. The result would be to raise the costs of smuggling: captured smugglers would be tried not by sympathetic local juries but by special vice-admiralty courts, before judges only. Here was an economic threat to the colonial sugar traders, many of whom had been involved in smuggling. Similar Parliamentary legislation to gain increased leverage over colonial life included the Quartering Act (which then affected New York in 1765, requiring the colony to pay for the British troops' housing and provisions while they were stationed there) and the Currency Act (which eliminated colonial-issued paper money, a source of inflation from the British perspective). Colonial legislatures sent protests against such unwelcome and distressing interference, which London officials ignored. Parliament also began discussing in 1764 the remaining element in its plan for administrative efficiency—a tax on the colonists to pay for the cost of the army and imperial administration in North America. Colonial lobbyists in London and colonial politicians in America protested as Parliament gathered data on how to implement their innovation and how much revenue would be generated.

Thus, in 1765, over the clear objections of colonial interests that such taxes levied without their consent were unconstitutional, Parliament passed its first-ever tax to be directly paid by colonists, the Stamp Act. The British people had been paying stamp taxes on many items for years; in fact, Americans pay stamp taxes today (they can sometimes be seen on the tops of cigarette packs and liquor bottles). The 1765 law required tax stamps to be placed onto most printed materials, including all legal documents (wills, contracts, deeds, licenses), newspapers, and playing cards. The British also required that the tax be paid in sterling (gold or silver only, none of that colonial paper money), and that violators would be tried in vice-admiralty courts, without juries. The Stamp Act would make virtually everyone in the colonies pay taxes, because the cost of using stamped paper passed, through an increased price, to every consumer. Implementing the tax required a period of time to appoint new tax collectors in the colonies and to get all the stamps and stamped paper into position. Thus, the law would not go into effect until November 1, 1765, six months after its passage.

The British may have expected some colonial grumbling, some protests, and some evasion of the Stamp Act, but they were in no way prepared for what occurred in 1765. What occurred would today be called a political firestorm, and it set in motion the crisis that begat the American Revolution. To understand why that happened, you need to understand how the Americans saw themselves and their politics. Using the same terms and the same sources as the British, the colonists arrived at opposite conclusions.

American Perspectives on Politics and the Empire

When Americans of the 1760s employed the mother-child metaphor to describe their relationship to the British Empire, it was to claim that the children had now grown to adulthood. Colonists believed they were due respect from a parent who, truth be told, had often neglected them, if not abused them. Americans looked at the same statistics—the growth in population, the increase in trade—with pride, not fear. The colonies now had real towns, with institutions such as newspapers and colleges, and professionals such as lawyers and doctors. Americans also looked at their contributions to the French and Indian War quite differently from the British. Many Americans were proud that they had taxed themselves to contribute money to the war as the British had asked, and they gloried in the military accomplishments of the colonial militias who had fought side by side with the British regular army. Each American colony could point to its own local political elite, who were elected to and controlled the lower houses of each colony's legislature (often called Assemblies, Houses of Burgesses, or Houses of Representatives). These elites were elected by a wider electorate than in England (roughly 50 to 70 percent of adult white men could vote, versus 10 percent or less in England), thus making the political system more responsive to the public. The child was now fully grown and no longer dependent, and deserved to be treated respectfully as an adult.

While this political arrangement was not formally established in British law, the American political leaders believed that a second, unwritten constitution with a different set of constitutional principles governed the empire. For the colonist, the "British Empire" was a political unit comprising Great Britain and its colonies, while the "United Kingdom" governed the British Isles with acknowledged Parliamentary supremacy. The constitution of the British Isles was separate and distinct from this second constitution, which, just like the one for Great Britain, grew from the history, customs, and laws that had evolved over 150 years of colonial life. Therefore, Parliamentary sovereignty applied only to the British Isles, not to the empire.

By custom and history, Parliament did not interfere with the local governance of the colonies; rather, it confined itself to regulation of trade that was outside the borders of a colony (e.g, the Navigation Acts that enforced mercantilism and regulated colonial trade). It would be an unconstitutional violation of the rights of colonial self-government to undermine local colonial political institutions, to interfere with the colonial legislatures' control over internal governance. Equally important, the empire's constitution was said to allow colonists to pursue their own economic and social opportunities without restraint. It would therefore be unconstitutional to put up barriers to expansion into the West, or to take money out of colonists' pockets through taxes, unless the local colonial political institutions consented.

The colonists could point to history, custom, and law as the foundation of this constitution, and they had a case. After all, when there is no single constitutional document, there is no logical or historical reason why there couldn't be two constitutions in operation, one for the home islands and a different one for the empire. Until the 1760s the two theories of the constitution over the empire (in the British view, one of Parliamentary sovereignty; for the Americans, one of local autonomy and governance) had never had to be reconciled because they had never directly confronted each other.

Republicanism is the set of beliefs and behaviors needed to create and maintain a republic, which is minimally defined as government by the elected representatives of the body politic. As such, it includes a complex ideology about the common good, the virtues of its citizens, and the importance of property and liberty.

When the confrontation came, the colonial political elite shared a set of political beliefs, an ideology that did not have many adherents in England and could not have been clearly described by average colonists before the revolution. The usual name given to this belief system was **republicanism**, and it derived from many sources. Colonial political elites looked to the classics and the ancient Roman republic, to Enlightenment thinkers such as Locke, to the English common law, and to a set of thinkers known as Whigs in England, a minority who had opposed the governing elite as corrupt. Their political beliefs are summarized as follows:

- Ultimately, all legitimate political power is derived from the people.

- Each well-ordered, functioning society is like a single organism, possessing a single common good.

- Republican government operates through the consent of the people and can therefore achieve the common good.

- Republican government can easily be lost to corruption and power-hungry men, who will naturally seek to destroy the people's liberties for their own power.

- The key to survival for a republic is the virtue of its citizens. These citizens must be ever vigilant to threats to their liberties.

- Virtue is defined as setting aside one's own self-interest to pursue the common good. Self-sacrifice is required, up to and including fighting and dying for the common good.

- Only those who have achieved personal independence (as defined by property without debt) and who, with the time bought by this economic independence, have achieved sufficient education, possess the full virtuous qualities necessary for leading the people.

- The average citizen, imbued by virtue and recognizing the value of independence in achieving virtue, will elect the wealthy, well-educated elite who possess superior virtue and will thus direct society to its common good.

- Colonial society is an asylum for liberty, and colonial people are still simple and virtuous, not tainted by the vice, luxury, and avarice that has produced corruption and the decline of the people's liberties in England.

This ideology was held by many in the colonial political elite, which led them to view all politics in terms of evil versus good, a conflict of power versus liberty. POWER and the men who sought it for their own evil purposes were

the dominion of some men over others, the human control of human life: ultimately force, compulsion. . . . Most commonly the discussion of power centered on its essential characteristic of aggressiveness: its endlessly propulsive tendency to expand itself beyond legitimate boundaries. . . . The image most commonly used was that of the act of trespassing. Power, it was said over and over again, has "an encroaching nature; if at first it meets with no control [it] creeps by degrees and quick subdues the whole." Sometimes the image is of the human hand, "the hand of power," reaching out to clutch and to seize: power is "grasping" and "tenacious" in its nature; "what it seizes it will retain." Sometimes power "is like the ocean, not easily admitting limits to be fixed in it." Sometimes it is "like a cancer, it eats faster and faster every hour." Sometimes it is motion, desire, and appetite all at once, being "restless, aspiring, and insatiable." Sometimes it is like "jaws . . . always opened to devour." It is everywhere in public life, and everywhere it is threatening, pushing, and grasping; and too often in the end it destroys its benign—necessarily benign—victim . . . liberty, or law, or right.[17]

<aside>

NOTE

The word POWER is set in small caps to indicate that it is shorthand for a complex set of ideas that extends beyond the definition you might find in your dictionary.

</aside>

If POWER is what men really want, they will not reveal themselves honestly but rather conspire in secret and take incremental steps as part of a long-term plan. What republicans must do, what men of virtue must do, is remain vigilant for the signs that corrupt, power-hungry men are destroying a republic.

- First, they must look for whether there is a standing army among the people during peacetime. All countries need armed force when threatened or at war, but an army in peacetime is dangerous. Power in its crudest form comes from the barrel of a gun, and conspirators love to use men with guns for their own evil plots. Many republics throughout history have been lost to military officers who used their army in peacetime to overthrow the government and install themselves as dictators or emperors.

- Second, they must watch for new government offices to appear by political appointment or patronage. Such officials, known as "placemen," do not serve the people's interests; they are concerned merely with getting and keeping their "place," with its status and income. Such placemen are loyal to those who put them in office, not the public good; they are tools of their patrons.

- Finally, virtuous citizens must be alert to the loss of ancient rights. Among the most basic of English constitutional rights are the rights to self-government (including regular elections), to jury trial of the neighborhood, and to an independent judiciary loyal to the law.

If these signs appeared, republican ideology required that virtuous men mobilize to stop the plot before it was too late—before the republic died from these threats.

Because POWER was insidious, conspiratorial, and always looking for an opening, the virtuous must be constantly suspicious. Every act must be scrutinized carefully; one action consistent with these warning signs might be an error, but two or more acts implied a plot, a plan, a conspiracy. Once this interpretative framework—*they're conspiring against us!*—took hold, it was virtually impossible to disprove; even benign actions by the other side were seen as exceptionally clever parts of the plot (perhaps to lull you to sleep before they struck!). And of course the conspirators would deny what they were accused of doing—that was what conspirators did to cover their tracks—so every denial further confirmed the theory.

If you believed that such a POWER conspiracy is under way, what could be done to stop it? The virtuous people had one essential weapon to stop such a conspiracy—themselves. The community must rise up as a public body, as an extralegal force, to attack the enemy with numbers, risking their lives if necessary. In short, the answer to a power threat to liberty was mob violence, threatened or actual, to express the collective will of the people acting for the common good—according to Locke, the highest law (see section 158 on p. 122).

Mob Action in Service of the People's Will. Mobs were an essential and normal part of colonial political life, the primary way that the majority of adults who could not vote (property-less white males, women, and slaves) could make their voices heard. A mob consisted of large numbers of people, gathered in the streets, organized on short notice to confront threats to the common good or actions against the will of the people. The confrontation invariably involved raucous speeches and verbal abuse of the offender, along with intimidation and threats of violence (or actual violence) against the offenders and their property.

It may seem strange today that masses of people out in the street, out of the control of any lawful established authority, were accepted as extra-institutional aspects of politics. Nonetheless, in both England and its colonies, mob action was so common as to be routine and to have its own informal set of rules. Mobs were the way common people defended their interests; they could serve the "public good" throughout the colonies at a time when there was no professional police force. Mobs acted on a particular public problem that had not yet been resolved, took focused action against that grievance, and dispersed (at least in theory) once the grievance was redressed. The line between legal and illegal force was very thin.

In a few cases, mobs formed regularly, as in the yearly Guy Fawkes Day riots celebrating Protestant control over England; the offenders during these riots were Catholics and the demonstrations were mainly for public entertainment. Most mobs occurred more spontaneously, attacking perceived dangers to the health and morals of the community, such as brothels or smallpox victims. Mobs of farmers in New Jersey in 1740 released those arrested for cutting trees claimed by the crown for the Royal Navy; such attacks on jails to free neighbors represented popular justice over royal law. Other mobs attacked customs officials to free the seized ships of colonial merchants. Tenant riots involved thousands in the Hudson River valley in 1765–66, where the great landowners controlled the local government and courts.

In New York in the 1750s, there were mob riots when the merchants attempted to devalue the currency, and riots when the British Navy sent press gangs through town to impress (forcibly carry away) as many as four hundred residents for involuntary military service. Stamp Act riots, liberty pole battles, and mass meetings in the 1770s were thus not aberrations but a normal way for average people to express their political views. People who could not vote nonetheless made their presence felt on political questions, a presence that the elite had to take into account.

For the vast majority of American colonists in the 1760s, this ideology of republicanism (including the role of mobs) was not yet fully persuasive, as it contended with other equally compelling ideologies. Prior to the 1760s, the dominant political thinking was conservative (or Tory). In this view, the British Empire was the greatest in the world; the British and their colonists were the freest people in the world. Therefore, any problems could be handled through the existing political system. Conservatives accepted the notion of society as an organic whole with a common good, but they stressed the existing hierarchy as the tried-and-true method for finding and creating that good. Governments should be balanced like Britain's (with a king, an aristocracy, and a people); the colonial political system was troubled due to insufficient adherence to hierarchical principles—too much democracy. What conservatives feared was not a power conspiracy but lawless mobs in the street who threatened all property rights, from the wealthiest merchants and landowners to the humblest farmers and artisans. Loyalty to king and country was the virtue on which safety in property and peace in society rested. After all, these conservatives concluded, the opposite of loyalty was treason.

Other colonists, primarily merchants and artisans, were attracted to the idea of the free market as a political and social ideology. These men believed in equality of opportunity; promotion of talent; rewards for the individualistic, bourgeois values of industry, frugality, and sobriety; and attacking both the extravagance of the idle wealthy and the laziness of the idle poor. Adam Smith would publish his classic *The Wealth of Nations* extolling free trade in March 1776, but Lockean notions of property—of the freedom to enjoy the fruits of one's own labor—informed nascent free market ideology even before Smith's work appeared. Fighting and sacrificing to retain one's rights to property was as virtuous as fighting for a republic. Colonials were beginning to reject as fantasy the idea that politics in a republic could be based on disinterested virtue. Rather, they started to believe that republics could be built on self-interest, that expanding individual economic opportunity through removal of restraints on the market would produce the greatest public good, that is, the greatest enjoyment of property. After all, the market could be used as a political weapon; boycotts depended on the virtue of consumers foregoing purchases to make a political point. Republicanism and free market ideologies overlapped at times, but they also conflicted in defining the common good.

Finally, many people were imbued with religious beliefs that stressed communal needs over individual needs and stressed the equality of all (men and women, rich and poor, free and enslaved) before God. Several denominations, from the older Quakers to the younger Baptists, called for political rights and social justice for all. For the enslaved, equality meant physical freedom; for the free without property, equality meant a vote and a role in government. Evangelicals saw oppressors among the very rich, but also among the free market advocates; in times of scarcity, the community needed the enforcement of a **just price** (price controls) and a moral economy greater than self-interest. The message would obviously have its greatest appeal among the lower levels of society—those parts disparaged by the elite as rabble. The main political outlet for these lower class people was the mob, yet no one knew what actions this mob might take.

There were many other political threads and ideologies floating through the colonial North American ether at this time. It is safe to say that, in New York in 1775, none of these viewpoints commanded a majority (even if one were to poll only the adult white property-owning males). Many people combined variations of these ideologies in their own personal views, ignoring inconsistencies. It was when the political explanation offered by the patriot elite—republicanism, POWER versus liberty—of British actions and of the social and economic turmoil affecting people's lives started to make sense (i.e., when the seed of resistance found fertile soil in many people's social and economic anxieties) that the crisis took off. Once all three aspects of popular unrest—social, economic, and political—became integrated, resistance could become revolution.

Colonial Resistance

While previous British acts of 1763 and 1764, designed to bring the colonies into more regular obedience to the Empire, provoked little overt opposition, the Stamp Act of 1765 set off a firestorm of protest in the midst of a severe colonial depression. The Stamp Act's purpose was to help reestablish British control of its wayward colonies by taxing colonists to pay the cost of British administration, including the army. All potential elements of revolution came into play during those six months before it was to take effect. There was harm to the economic elite (who used many legal documents that required stamps), and average town dwellers and farmers would incur significant costs during an already difficult time (building on farmers' existing fear of debt and poverty). Amplifying those monetary inspirations for opposition were the multiple signs of a political POWER conspiracy found in the Stamp Act. Loss of ancient rights was present in the lack of self-government, ability to consent to taxes, and trial by jury; a new swarm of officials would be needed to collect the taxes (placemen); and a standing army needed to be financed. Elite Patriot leaders argued successfully that the time to call on the political virtue of a republican people was now. Their ideology provided both an explanation for the grievance of the taxes—a ministerial plot—and a clear solution—concerted popular action.

Using Locke's writings as a guide, colonial politicians wrote impassioned arguments and colonial legislatures sent petitions opposing the tax as a violation of constitutional principles and colonial rights (see Daniel Dulany's pamphlet in the Core Texts section, p. 131). Intercolonial meetings were held, such as the Stamp Act Congress, to protest the law based on its adverse economic impact; merchants passed non-importation (boycott) agreements that stopped all sales of newly imported British goods until the act was repealed. Most important was the popular uprising as the people came out into the streets to riot against the Stamp Act and to mob the tax collectors. These targeted riots induced (with threats of bodily harm and property destruction) every single one of the tax collectors to resign his post before November 1. When the law went into effect, it was impossible to obey for lack of anyone to sell the stamped paper, and courts closed for lack of the official paper required.

Back in London, the impact of non-importation, combined with the sheer impossibility of enforcing a tax when there were no tax collectors, compelled Parliament to act. A new prime minister organized the repeal of the Stamp Act in early 1766, not because the colonists had convinced the Parliament that it violated colonial rights and was unconstitutional, but because the law had been unwise (for a defense of the Stamp Act's constitutionality, see Soame Jenyns pamphlet in the Core Texts section, p. 134). In order to uphold their principles (and save face), Parliament passed the Declaratory Act, which claimed authority for Parliament to legislate and tax the colonies "in all cases whatsoever." When word of the repeal reached North America, the public celebrated their success, and the crisis passed. Only a few politicians paid any notice to the Declaratory Act, but those who did began to see the outline of a continuing POWER conspiracy.

In 1767, the British ministry, led by Charles Townshend, sought to implement the Declaratory Act, this time through taxes imposed at the port and not inside colonial borders. These duties acted as import tariffs and were set at a very low level on imported products such as paper, glass, lead, paint, and tea. The money raised by these Townshend Act duties would pay the salaries of British officials stationed in the colonies. Furthermore, a new set of officials, the American Board of Customs Commissioners, would collect the taxes. Members of the board would be British, thus avoiding the possibility of local mobs pressuring the new agents into resigning. Finally, violations of the Townshend Acts would be tried in the vice-admiralty courts without juries.

Some colonial politicians, excited by republican theory with its insistence on the need for constant vigilance in case of a POWER conspiracy against liberty, now had the proof they needed. One violation like the Stamp Act might be an innocent mistake, but this second instance of depriving Americans of their ancient rights (self-government regarding consent to taxes, jury trials) and bringing in placemen was proof of a plot. Rhetoric heated up again, but there were few mobs and little street action because the impact of the taxes on average people was negligible.

There were calls for non-importation, but merchants were in a somewhat better position economically and less than enthusiastic to cut off trade and hurt business. Artisans and workingmen supported non-importation because they could then manufacture substitute goods for sale, and they helped enforce the boycott against merchants who smuggled. Non-importation did cut down British revenues to next to nothing and symbolic protests were widespread, but there wasn't a sense of imminent revolution in the streets as there had been during the Stamp Act crisis. Only the political roots of rebellion were fully engaged, with only partial impacts on the social or economic level.

Massachusetts was the primary political center of resistance, and Massachusetts did have some mobs, particularly one that freed a ship owned by John Hancock from the grasp of the customs officials. In 1768, the British Army, which had primarily been stationed in New York, moved much of its force to Boston. Again, here was more proof of a plot: a standing army in peacetime. The resulting friction between the people and the army culminated in the Boston Massacre of March 1770. Ironically, the original reason for the upheaval had been repealed, only the colonists didn't know it yet. A new prime minister, Lord North, thought the costs of the Townshend duties not worth the revenue benefits. However, to preserve Parliamentary authority, a symbolic tax on tea was retained. When colonials heard the news, there was more rejoicing. Colonial politicians who were worried about the POWER conspiracy noted the tea tax and contended that non-importation should continue, but most ignored such fears and consumed all sorts of British goods (including tea) once again.

From 1770 to 1773, relative peace descended throughout North America. Most turbulence seemed confined to Massachusetts, where politicians continued to see plots against colonial liberty in how their governors were paid. Massachusetts leaders set up Committees of Correspondence to fulminate about the ongoing plot against colonial rights and to spread awareness of this evil, sending out letters that were read and answered in many towns and counties throughout the colonies as a political education project. Then, in 1773, the British East India Company faced bankruptcy, holding 17 million pounds of unsold tea in its English warehouses. Parliament, whose members included many East India Company investors, decided to bail out the company through its trade with the colonies. The existing tea tax would be lowered to make the tea less expensive and thus presumably increase consumption. Furthermore, all middlemen merchants were to be eliminated, as only official East India Company agents would be allowed to sell tea. This streamlining promised to reduce the tea price still further. The bottom line, from the British perspective, was that colonists would consume more tea, the Company would sell all the tea that colonists consumed, and it would thus become profitable again. There is no evidence that Parliament was thinking any further than bailing out the Company in making these plans.

Colonial politicians didn't see it that way. Instead they saw a plot, a crafty scheme, a devious ploy to induce them to buy tea. They saw it in terms of the POWER conspiracy, reasoning that if colonists accepted the tea tax (many had for three years, but the politicians ignored this), soon they would descend a slippery slope into slavery. Merchants did have real cause for concern, as the British were establishing a monopoly on this important item of trade and cutting most of them out. Such actions seriously threatened their economic opportunities, and that monopoly could easily spread to other products, putting them out of business entirely. But on the social level, why should the average colonial resident be upset, let alone become revolutionary over this Tea Act? The price that tea-drinkers paid would be cheaper.

Yet the public came out in numbers and with such vehemence as hadn't been seen since the Stamp Act eight years before. On the surface, it seemed irrational: Why would large numbers of average people show up for mass meetings, mob local agents of the East India Company to resign (just as they had forced the Stamp Act officials to quit), and threaten the lives of East India Company ship captains so convincingly that many captains would not even try to land their cargo? The answer is that years of agitating about the POWER conspiracy had touched a chord in the average colonist. This republican ideology of public virtue facing off against conspiracies now resonated within a segment of the public as an explanation for their economic and social grievances. When a tea ship landed in Boston, the captain was told by the royal governor to pay the tea tax or else lose his vessel, while Boston leaders stationed guards around the boat to prevent tea from being off-loaded. At the climax, an estimated five thousand Bostonians (nearly one-third of the city's population) attended a mass meeting to try to convince the governor to let the ship sail out of the harbor without unloading tea and without paying tax. Unsuccessful in that effort toward compromise, elements in the crowd then executed what became known as the Boston Tea Party, dumping into the harbor 342 casks of tea worth ten thousand pounds sterling.

The British and their colonial allies were outraged at the wanton destruction of property and the breakdown of lawful government in Boston. They now saw the supremacy of the Crown and Parliament at stake and concluded that they must discipline their rebellious child or else lose the colonies forever. Ferocious feelings rose in Parliament against the colonies; Ben Franklin, agent for Pennsylvania, was hauled in front of a Parliamentary committee and publicly reviled. A consensus arose in Parliament that maximum force was required to put down the treasonous behavior in Boston. The resulting legislation, known collectively as the Coercive Acts in England and as the Intolerable Acts in America, certainly employed that force. Their provisions were:

> **TIP**
>
> The **Coercive Acts,** nicknamed **Intolerable Acts** by Patriots, are the trigger for the first issues in the game. They are on everyone's mind and tongue, and you must know all aspects and angles of them to argue well.

- The Boston Port Act (passed March 31, 1774) closed Boston's harbor, destroying Massachusetts' economy and impoverishing thousands, until the cost of the destroyed tea had been paid back.

- The Massachusetts Government Act (May 20, 1774) effectively abrogated the Massachusetts charter unilaterally. The royal governor would now appoint the upper house of the legislature (the Council); most local officials were no longer elected but appointed; jurors would not be randomly picked but rather selected by the sheriff. Moreover, town meetings were forbidden except with the consent of the royal governor. The goal was to quash the democratic portion of Massachusetts politics, giving power to the new, royally appointed governor, General Gage.

- The Administration of Justice Act (May 20, 1774) allowed any British official accused of a crime in Massachusetts to have his trial moved out of Massachusetts (where presumably he would be acquitted).

- The Quartering Act (June 2, 1774) required Massachusetts to pay for lodging and supplies for the army that was now in their midst.

- At almost the same time, a Quebec Act (June 22, 1774) passed, extending religious freedom to the resident French Catholics, reinstating French civil law, and most important, extending the boundaries of this ethnically and religiously alien land down to the Ohio River, seeming to cut off that land from future settlement by residents of Virginia, Pennsylvania, and New York.

To those American colonial politicians who believed in republicanism and virtue, the POWER conspiracy had been conclusively proven. At every level—deprival of ancient rights of self-government and jury trial, control by a standing army, infiltration by swarms of appointed placemen—Massachusetts' plight revealed the true culmination of a decade-long plot to destroy the colonies and render them slaves. And certainly, the British acts confronted Massachusetts with the imminent destruction of their economy, social order, and government. Massachusetts readied for war and desired the support of all colonies in a Solemn League and Covenant to end all trade (both imports and exports) with Britain. Massachusetts argued that if these Intolerable Acts succeeded, the British would have enslaved Massachusetts, and other colonies would be next to suffer the same fate. However, other colonies hesitated to act; the Massachusetts Patriots were too radical for many. Colonial conservatives did not want such radicals pulling the rest of the continent into war or revolution hastily. Massachusetts had indeed violated property rights with the Tea Party, and though Parliament had overreacted, a compromise could be arranged. Instead of immediately following Massachusetts' lead, multiple colonies called for a Continental Congress, with representatives from all colonies to meet in Philadelphia in September 1774. This hesitancy shows that there was no majority position in favor of rebellion yet; the case was still very much debatable.

From the Continental Congress emerged a compromise statement in October 1774, a Declaration and Resolves (also called the Declaration of Colonial

Rights), wherein the colonists drew on a variety of ideological sources, including the principles of natural rights, the British constitution, colonial charters, and mutual interest. These Resolves declared that colonists would consent to obey Parliamentary trade regulation but not any Parliamentary taxation. More important, to oppose the Intolerable Acts, the Congress created the Continental Association, which called for a phased boycott: non-importation of British goods starting December 1, 1774; non-consumption of British products starting March 1, 1775; and non-exportation of American products effective September 10, 1775, all contingent on British actions. The Association relied on popular assent and voluntary enforcement to work, as the Continental Congress had no police, no administrative officers, and no courts. To enforce the Association, local committees of observation and inspection were elected in every town, claiming the authority to search records and buildings, publish names of violators, identify opponents, and force public apologies. The fact that the Association succeeded in most colonies was a function of the public's approval of the Congressional proposals, but it was also the consequence of local activists organizing the members of previous mobs to enforce the Association through extralegal searches, seizures, loyalty tests, and humiliating punishments. The infrastructure of revolution was coming into view in many places, but competing ideas and interests (as well as inertia) still held sway over much of the populace, especially in New York. New York's Assembly had *not* adopted the Association in late 1774 and early 1775. Debating whether to adopt the Association in New York and confronting the increasing chaos in colonial government will be the first task you face in this game.

NEW YORK, SPRING 1775

The current situation in New York is explosively anxious, with no place to escape from the tension, and fresh memories of recent conflict and bloodshed. New York City is a face-to-face, personal society, a small town on a small island where everyone knows where you stand and what you have done. There are over 3,200 houses crowded together in less than one square mile on the lower tip of Manhattan, which means that rich and poor, black and white, Patriot and Loyalist, enemy and ally see one another daily. Prior to 1765, New York's political elite had been bitterly divided into factions based not on ideology so much as on personal animosities that stretched back for decades. On one side were the Livingstons and their allies. This faction included extremely wealthy landowners whose primary wealth came from leasing land to tenant farmers in the Hudson River valley, with secondary wealth coming from trade. In addition to land, this side also included lawyers trained in political argument. Their opponents were the Delanceys and their allies, whose wealth derived from merchant activity in the city of New York, but who also invested in land.

The issues the Livingston and Delancey factions had fought over for generations were many and varied, but there was little principle involved before the 1760s—both groups were primarily preoccupied with seizing control of the power and money that flowed from patronage and government jobs. Both sides wanted to emulate and recreate British society, which meant elite control of society, economy, and politics. However, many common folk owned enough property to vote, which complicated elite control to some extent. Because votes were cast in public by voice and not in secret, the elite often intimidated those voters who rented from or were in debt to them, or bribed them through offers of political jobs and cash. Before the Revolutionary crisis, the voting public tended either to defer to their local elite or to switch sides depending on which faction offered them the better deal. The loyalties of voters, like the loyalties of political leaders, were fluid and without principled content.

At the start of the Revolutionary Crisis in 1765, the two factions began to be challenged by a third group in New York City, who became known as the Sons of Liberty. The leaders of these men were upstart merchants, including privateers Alexander McDougall and Isaac Sears, as well as literate artisans such as carpenters, silversmiths, blacksmiths, and tailors, who owned and operated their own small businesses. The wealthier artisans, such as Abraham Brasher, employed servants and owned slaves. Their suppliers of raw materials were the merchants of the city; their customer base was the wealthy of both factions; their political attitudes drew from their tenuous middle-class independence as well as from discussions of pamphlets that occurred after work in the many taverns of the city.

Here in New York's bars, their tongues loosened by liquor, are the many laborers, sailors, servants, journeymen, young apprentices, and slaves who now make up the mass of the Sons of Liberty. Taverns, such as the widow Montagne's seen in the prologue, are ubiquitous in the city; it's been estimated that there is one licensed bar for every thirteen adult white men in town. These taverns are places for discussion and agitation around the long list of grievances and resentments of the common folk. These poor white and black men and women cannot vote, but they can form an effective mob. Artisans, merchants, and landowners all exploit members of this group; in terms of oppression, there isn't much difference between the Delanceys and the Livingstons. The Sons of Liberty leadership can find manpower outside the regular frame of government, but they have to be careful lest the mob get out of hand and turn on them.

There is one more element in Manhattan: the British Army. New York has the best port in the colonies and it is centrally located, with plentiful supplies as well as barracks to house the British troops. Allegedly needed to police a much enlarged North American empire that now includes increased numbers of hostile French and Indians, the British government stationed a sizeable force (at first only several hundred men, plus naval vessels, ultimately intended to comprise fifteen to sixteen regiments, roughly fifteen thousand men) in New York. The prime military sites in town are

TIP

Geography matters. Check the map on page 11 for these sites, as well as those referenced below.

Fort George (at the Battery on the southern tip of Manhattan) and the barracks that are located just north of the Commons, prison, and poorhouse.

These regular Army soldiers are underpaid and bored most of the time, leading them to seek part-time jobs in competition with the laborers who live here. These men also spend a lot of time in the taverns and the brothels that surround the Commons, activities that also produce conflict with New Yorkers. And under the Quartering Act, New Yorkers have to pay for these soldiers' quarters and provisions, a heavy tax in a time of economic depression. For nearly ten years, there have been regular violent confrontations in New York among these contesting groups. In 1765, public pressure forced the Stamp Tax agent for New York to resign (as those collectors did throughout the land), but the stamped paper was still on a boat in the harbor, and the people wished to prevent its landing. A mob of thousands formed on the Commons across from the barracks and marched down Broadway, gathering women, boys, laborers, sailors, artisans, and merchants, hanging effigies as they went. As the mob approached Fort George and its 130 defenders, the general ordered the cannon filled with shot and pointed at the approaching mob. But the mob did not try to breach the fort's walls; it instead turned to burn the lieutenant governor's carriages and then to destroy the house of a British major. For ten hours, the mob ran riot through New York City, attacking symbols of British power, and the colonial elite now wondered what had been unleashed.

When the Stamp Act was repealed in 1766, a mob celebrated by erecting a liberty pole on the Commons, a forty-foot pine tree shorn of its branches that sat directly across from the British Army barracks, adorned with ribbons, flags, and banners supporting liberty. British soldiers viewed that as an affront (it was) and cut it down on August 10, 1766; in anger over this action, a mob of two to three thousand people gathered on the Commons on August 11 and clashed with the soldiers, resulting in several wounded. A new pole was erected, but it lasted only a month before soldiers again chopped it down. Meanwhile, as poles went up and came down, new taxes in the Townshend Acts were approved in 1767 in Britain, resulting in new Patriot calls for non-importation. By January 1770 (before the Boston Massacre of the same year), the fourth liberty pole on the Commons was destroyed, leading to the Battle of Golden Hill (roughly the area along William Street between Fair—now Fulton—and John Streets; see the map on page 11) when soldiers swung their swords and drew bayonets in a bloody melee with the mob. This fracas (and a battle the next day on Nassau Street) produced the first bloodshed of the revolution, before the Boston Massacre; it also produced the fifth liberty pole, encased in iron bars and hoops, which would stand for six years.

The repeal of the Townshend Acts in 1770 led to three years of relative political calm in the colonies overall. However, within New York, lines had hardened as the elite divided in their sympathies. The Delancey faction moved toward reconciliation with the British and began to be called "Loyalists." The Delanceys achieved a bare majority in the Assembly, ended non-importation to bring about a brief economic recovery, and were able to convince some of the Sons of Liberty leaders to follow their more conciliatory approach, splitting the mob's leadership. The Livingston faction now moved, a little uneasily due to their fear of their mob allies, into clearly defined opposition to British rule, dubbing themselves "Patriots." Meanwhile, those Sons of Liberty who had allied with Livingston pursued a clear goal: to drive the British Army out of New York City so that the soldiers could no longer compete with laborers for jobs or fight with them in bars. In the New York Assembly, the Delancey and Livingston factions were often evenly balanced, leaving farmer representatives from rural counties such as Kings (Brooklyn), Queens, Richmond (Staten Island), and Westchester (which included the Bronx) with the swing votes that determined which faction gained the majority. The result was often political paralysis and deadlock in an Assembly meeting in the city, where most of the Assemblymen feared that the mob led by the Sons of Liberty would break loose again, perhaps against them if they took a wrong position.

In 1773, with the passage of the British Tea Act, the Sons of Liberty paid "visits" to the appointed tea agents for New York, convincing them to decline their posts and refuse to accept British imported tea. The Boston Tea Party of 1773 was followed by a much smaller Tea Party by New Yorkers who dumped eighteen chests of tea in the East River in April 1774. But the New York mob's violation of private property was overshadowed when word arrived of the British response to Boston—the Coercive or Intolerable Acts.

In New York, the Delancey faction was not interested in more confrontation. They successfully arranged that five Delanceyites would be the New York delegates to the Continental Congress of 1774 to put a brake on the crazed Bostonians and come up with an effective strategy to resolve the grievances peacefully. The Delanceyites and their allies in the mob and among the rural landowning elite were therefore disappointed when the Continental Congress proposed the Continental Association. Non-importation of new British goods would take effect almost immediately, to be followed by non-exportation of any American goods to Britain and non-consumption of anything made in Britain a year later if the British did not end their repressive measures against Boston. And how did the Congress, which lacked any legal authority, propose that the Association be enforced? Each colony was to set up local Committees of Inspection, whose job was to sniff out smugglers and violators. These committees might as well have been called "mobs," for if they found a merchant violating the Association, the committees were supposed to initiate a boycott of that merchant and have him publicized as an enemy of American liberty. Farmers like Samuel Seabury of Westchester worried that the Association would be the ruination of all farmers of New York, who would lose their foreign trade and thus be unable to pay their debts (see Samuel Seabury's pamphlet in the Core Texts section, p. 153).

At the beginning of 1775, Delancey and his allies still controlled the New York Assembly, which refused to ratify the Continental Association or appoint new delegates to the next Continental Congress, scheduled for May 1775. The Sons of

Liberty started to enforce—without any legal authority—the Continental Congress's directive that no goods be allowed in from Britain after February 1, 1775. The mob was showing signs of getting out of control, again, much to the fear and dismay of the existing elite on both sides. New York's political leaders called for a Provincial Congress—with delegates from every county—to meet in New York City, for the purpose of selecting delegates to the Second Continental Congress, despite the Assembly's refusal. In early April, just before the Congress was to convene, Isaac Sears was arrested for calling on each man to arm himself with twenty-four rounds. Delancey had him arrested, but a mob came down to the jail and freed him, without a single consequence. The rescue of Sears was another proof that the legitimacy of colonial political institutions was dissolving; when the colonial Assembly adjourned, its authority was gone, and it would never meet again.

After the Assembly dissolved, with Royal Governor Tryon having left in 1774, no one had clear authority to govern New York. The British army garrison from the upper barracks had been moved onto the warship *Asia* docked on the East River near Fort George, with its cannons positioned to hit any target in lower Manhattan. Although soldiers could no longer safely walk Manhattan's streets alone, and though most of the British Army and navy was now concentrated on Boston, there was still plenty of military punch available to support the British Empire in New York, should anyone wish to use it.

In colonial American government, the vast majority of administrative and legal functions occur in the county courts. For most colonists, the courts are the only government they deal with, the only authority that matters. For the purposes of this game, as of early 1775, the courts of New York County (Manhattan) have ceased to function, primarily because the officials necessary to run the courts (judges, sheriffs, clerks, constables, and jurors) have found it too risky to swear the oath of allegiance to the Crown at the start of court sessions. (Historical note: the actual situation in Manhattan courts was far more confused, intermittent, and ambiguous in terms of functioning). Without courts, all disputes in the city, both civil and criminal, are thrown into legal limbo—debtors can escape from their debts because there is no court process to hold them accountable, criminals who are apprehended cannot be legally tried, and the taxes necessary to run the city are going uncollected. Without functioning courts, no business is safe, no property is safe, and no person is safe. Most people are continuing to pay their debts and to refrain from stealing and committing violence, but it is not clear how long habitual compliance can continue in the absence of authority defined by law enforcement. Meanwhile, most courts in other counties remain open for business, operating under authority and taking oaths of office that swear loyalty to the king. It is in New York City where that equation has broken down and the fears of lawlessness are the greatest, where jails are broken into to release prisoners for political purposes, where mobs rule the streets, and where a new legislature without any official sanction will try to chart a course for the people of New York.

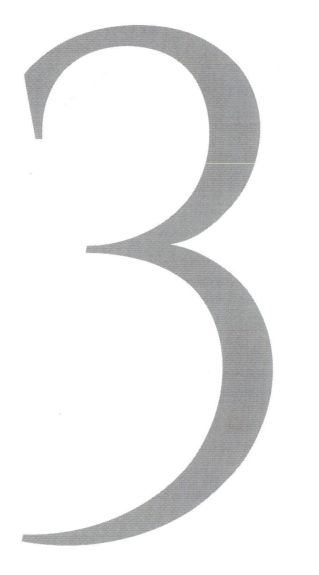

PART 3: **THE GAME**

MAJOR ISSUES FOR DEBATE

Principal Questions

There are five great interlocking questions for debate and action in this game:

1. What are the legitimate purposes of government and what makes a particular government legitimate?

2. How does the "rule of law" function in a legitimate government, and under what circumstances may the rule of law break down?

3. Under what circumstances does a government lose its legitimacy; what actions of government are illegitimate?

4. In what circumstances may people legitimately disobey, resist, or rebel against their current government?

5. When is it legitimate for people to use violence to obtain political objectives? When can they use organized, disciplined violence (a military) or sporadic, undisciplined violence (a mob)?

Political legitimacy most simply means popular acceptance of the governing political system. Philosophically, legitimacy also conveys the sense of moral approval of a governing system's institutions, offices, and actions—a belief that the system appropriately uses power. Legitimacy does not require popular acceptance of a particular politician or party in power, nor does it mean approval of every government act. Rather, recognizing that governments make mistakes and individuals in power change, political legitimacy rests (or not) on the whole system of law and political decision-making in a society.

These five somewhat abstract issues of political philosophy have been argued about for millennia. For colonial New York and for this game, the search for the answers begins with the political philosophy of John Locke (see the Core Texts section, pp. 100–31). But Locke's thought does not exist in a vacuum in 1775, because New Yorkers now have many pieces of evidence regarding the actions of the British government over the last twelve years. You must match recent events to the theory, as well as integrate new events into your worldview, to come to your own answers to these questions. Many of those answers will come from the New York Provincial Congress's decisions, which are at the center of this game.

Specific Issues Expected to Arise

Control and authority over New York, legitimate or otherwise, is up for grabs; the existing governmental system is wobbling under the stress. The Provincial Congress, which contains representatives selected from all over the colony (roughly half from the city, the other half from rural farm areas such as Brooklyn or Albany), has no official existence. Rather, it convenes in the absence of the royal governor and the regular legislative Assembly, which has been dissolved. There are no existing governmental institutions controlled by the Provincial Congress. It has no taxing power, no army, no police, no bureaucracy, and no courts under its authority; those institutions were all run by the existing government. In short, for it to accomplish anything it will have to rely on voluntary acceptance of its actions by individuals and by the people as a whole, sometimes in the form of a mob. Among the existing institutions, especially courts and military, the Provincial Congress will either have to use those that currently exist, modify them (perhaps radically), or create new versions while under the pressure of events in a crisis.

Recognizing its extralegal status, the Provincial Congress tried to widen participation, both of voters and of politically interested men, in order to increase its chances of popular approval. Thus, this Congress is larger in number than the old Assembly (ninety-three attend the first session of the Congress, compared to the thirty-one representatives composing the old Assembly). There are large numbers of men new to the colonial political process who are unattached to the Delanceys and Livingstons. These representatives, motivated by the events of the past few years to get involved politically, will not merely defer to their local elites or preexisting parties. These men now have the chance to change the future of New York. And watching every move of the new Congress is the crowd, the people of New York, including the laborers, women, and slaves who aim to take advantage of this chaos for their own benefit.

At a minimum, the Provincial Congress will have to decide these particular issues over the course of the game:

> **TIP**
>
> By the time the game begins, the Stamp Act is nearly ten years in the past, the Townshend Acts eight years old, and both have been repealed. Although they still linger as grievances, they are not the issues that focus colonial attention. The Coercive Acts are the immediate controversy.

1. Whether the Association will be approved for New York as a response to the Coercive/Intolerable Acts, and if so, how it will be enforced;

2. Whether courts in New York City should be reopened, and if so, under what personnel, laws, and oaths;

3. Whether troops will be raised for the defense of New York, the colonies, or both, and if so, which characters will be mobilized for this service; and

4. Whether New York should be committed to a plan of reconciliation with the British or to independence.

The debate on these issues will combine both principles and pragmatism, as New Yorkers deal with and argue over the problems confronting them in 1775–76. Additional issues will arise throughout the game, promoted by various characters' proposals and petitions brought before the Provincial Congress as well as by events that intervene.

RULES AND PROCEDURES

PROCEEDINGS OF THE PROVINCIAL CONGRESS

Layout of Congress

The classroom should be rearranged (if physically possible) to resemble a legislature. In the front area, the elected representatives' desks or tables should be arranged in a semicircle around a podium, which is to be considered "the floor" of the Congress. Patriots should sit on one side of the semicircle, Loyalists on the other side, with the Moderates in between. The Speaker should sit at a desk at the front, facing the Congress and next to the podium, so that she or he may call on Congressmen and the crowd for questions and comments for the speaker. The rear area of the classroom is to be considered the balcony, or gallery, where members of the public who are not voting members of Congress may sit (or stand or walk around as they choose). The public may cheer, boo, call out questions, and otherwise participate in debates from the gallery, but they are also permitted to come down from the balcony to the podium to present petitions and give speeches to the Congress.

The Speaker

The Provincial Congress is presided over by a Speaker. The election of the Speaker is the first order of business when the legislature convenes. The Speaker is elected by a majority vote of the Provincial Congress and can be removed as the result of a majority "no confidence" vote at any time. If the Speaker is absent when the legislature convenes for a new session, the legislature must elect a temporary replacement.

The Speaker has the following responsibilities:

1. Make sure that all topics receive full and complete debate; post new topics on the board as they emerge and post topics still under consideration on the board at the start of the session.

2. Choose the order in which topics are to be voted on. Debate is open and may continue on many different topics at once; only the Speaker may choose which topics are fully debated and ready for a vote.

3. Recognize and introduce speakers, including members from the gallery, at the podium,

4. Run debate, including calling on members of Congress and the gallery at their seats for questions to pose to each speaker.

5. Call for a show of hands for or against a motion or petition, and count the votes. There is no proxy voting. Those absent when a vote is conducted may not vote (although professors may allow virtual presence for voting at their discretion).

Respect the Podium

When someone is speaking from the podium, that person has the right to speak. Audience members (including spectators in the gallery) are welcome to hiss, boo, cheer, or shout "here, here" as the speech proceeds, but they must allow the speech to continue (unless a mob forms—see below). In a similar spirit, there can be no filibustering from the podium. After the speech concludes, anyone may ask questions. The Speaker manages this debate, until he decides to call for the next speaker or for a vote.

TIP

If debate becomes particularly chaotic, form a queue behind the podium. If you wait for a turn in the queue, the Speaker must recognize you in order, after the current speaker has finished.

Procedures

Although all inhabitants of New York may ask questions, make comments, present petitions, and speak to all questions (i.e., all characters, including women, slaves, and the landless, may come to the podium), only the elected representatives may vote in Congress. All decisions of the Provincial Congress are made by majority vote. In the event of a tie vote, the proposal or petition before Congress loses.

In terms of procedure in Congress, rudimentary Parliamentary procedures will apply. All proposals and petitions must be written; in the event of a proposal or petition occurring on the "spur of the moment" or being amended from the floor, the author is responsible for writing up the text which must be read aloud before the final vote on that item.

Proposals. Proposals are made by members of Congress and may have amendments offered to them from the floor; the author of the proposal may accept the amendment as "friendly," in which case it is written into the original proposal without a vote. If the author does not accept the amendment, then Congress should debate the amendment and vote upon it first, before the original proposal is voted upon.

Petitions. Petitions originate from members of the crowd, who do not have votes in Congress. The petition for redress of grievances was considered an essential part of British political practice, giving those without direct say in government (through voting in elections) the inalienable right to be heard. Some petitions concerned private or individual grievances, such as a request for the government to repair a road or compensate someone for damage done by official acts. The petitions in this game, however, concern public grievances, affecting a large portion of the community, in an attempt to redress the problems in a comprehensive manner. They must be written (they can be included in an essay paper if the author so desires) and submitted to the Speaker as well. The Congress must allow authors of the petitions the chance to speak on behalf of their causes, as well as allow regular debate by Congressmen and members of the crowd on the petition. A petition may be granted or denied, but Congress must vote on it in a timely fashion.

TIP

Petitions may not be amended; they are voted on as presented.

In general, Congress should operate with "open" debate, allowing students to make proposals and petitions in any order they wish without necessarily resolving one issue at a time. The Speaker or Gamemaster (GM) should list on the board, at the start of each session, those proposals and petitions still outstanding for Congress's consideration. The Speaker may determine the order of voting on the various issues; that is, it is not necessary that the proposals and petitions be voted upon in the order in which they were first offered. However, the Congress may, by majority vote, choose to override the Speaker and vote on a different measure first. The length of debate on particular topics is similarly flexible; in general the Speaker (in consultation with the Gamemaster) may determine when a topic has been sufficiently debated and is "ripe" for voting; however, any member of the Congress may "call the question" at any time, and if it is approved by a majority vote, then a final vote on the proposal or petition may be taken. All votes must be done in public by a show of hands—there will be no secret balloting in Congress.

If some players would like to take time to consider an issue in private, the Speaker (at his discretion) may call a halt to the current proceedings to allow time for meetings among players. This suspension is called a "faction break," the time allowed should be announced (usually five minutes is sufficient), and the Speaker is responsible for calling the Congress back into session as soon as the time has elapsed. No mob actions are allowed during faction breaks, but players may search for tea and the smuggler.

The Crowd: Mob Actions

Although the people in the crowd (laborers, women, and slaves) can neither vote in Congress nor vote in elections for Congress, they are expected to do more than just participate in discussions. The most effective way for these people to influence the outcome is to form a mob, which is done by:

- Gathering at least the minimum number of people required to form a mob;

- Agreeing upon one victim/target for the mob action;

- Making a political demand of that victim/target; and

- Threatening the victim/target with retribution should he or she not comply.

Mob actions are as important as legislative proposals and petitions to success in the game, and therefore they must be used strategically. Effective mobs are often planned before a game session, with target, demand, threat, and participants ready to move on an agreed-upon trigger.

Mob Procedures

Only one mob may form in any given Game Session (with the exception of the final session, where special mob rules may apply). It is not required that every Game Session have a mob, especially if the number needed to constitute a mob cannot be raised during a given session. In the event of a mob, all other business ceases until the mob action is resolved.

Forming a Mob: Number, Physical Presence, Demand, Threat

The minimum number of players needed to constitute a mob is set according to the number of laborers plus women plus slaves in the game (this will vary according to the size of the class). For example, in a class of twenty-four players, the minimum number of players required to form a mob would be nine; for a class of sixteen, the minimum mob size is six. A mob may be larger than the minimum, thus making its success more likely by avoiding the chance of a counter-mob (see below).

Note: Gamemasters may vary the number of mobs allowed during the whole game sequence, may set limited times when mobs may rise, and may alter the amount of physical presence needed in the execution of a mob. Your Gamemaster will announce any modifications to these rules during the time before Public Sessions begin.

With at least the minimum number of players deciding to mob, the mob must assemble and surround one other individual in the game for the purpose of persuading that character to alter his or her behavior. This rising of the mob is a physical event, and can occur in any space in the classroom, even in Congress, even if the victim is at the podium. When a mob rises, all other business ceases, and all other players must get out of the way.

> **TIP**
>
> A mob need not contain all the laborers, women, and slaves in order to rise; it merely requires that number of people. See the chart on page 95 for the minimum mob number for your class size. Members of Congress may join mobs if they believe it in their interest to do so; members of the crowd may choose not to join. The critical first question will be how many members of the mob are required, not who those members are.

The mob, while surrounding the intended victim on all sides, must clearly articulate:

1. The demand: what the victim must do in order to get the mob to disperse. The demand must be a concrete action, something within the victim's ability to carry out. A demand like "stop being a jerk" is not allowed, while demanding a particular vote on a proposal or petition is acceptable. The Gamemaster will rule on whether the mob demand is "doable."

and

2. The threat: what will happen to the victim if he does not agree. The mob must threaten the intended victim with one of the levels of danger listed below.

The mob should agree ahead of time (before surrounding the intended victim) as to how much force they wish to allude to in their threats to the intended victim. There are three levels of mob force that may be threatened; they are listed here from the most serious threat level to the least:

1. *Threatening serious bodily harm or death.* Students may verbally threaten death and accompany the threat with visible symbols (such as burning an effigy, parading around with a noose, drawings of the victim in casket) of what will happen if the intended doesn't change his or her behavior to satisfy the mob. Of course, such threats are representational, hypothetical reenactments of historical events; please, no real burning or hanging.

2. *Tar and feathering, followed by a parade* of the victim through the city streets (on a cart's tail). In real colonial practice, this punishment was not fatal but did produce disfiguring scars as well as deep humiliation. In terms of the class, this will require the victim to be publicly paraded through the hallway, cafeteria, and/or library with a demeaning sign around his or her neck. A victim who chooses tar and feathering may not participate or vote during the next 45 minutes of game sessions.

3. *Surrounding and shouting with curses* at the victim to convince him or her to confess his or her wrongdoing and promise to never offend the mob again. This promise should be presented to the victim as a written oath to be read, and the victim must write his or her next paper on why the mob was correct.

Members of the mob run the risk of serious bodily injury and even death should the victim choose to fight rather than submit (see victim's options below).

What are the causes for a mob to rise, and for the demands to be made? Here are some examples of targets and goals for mob action:

1. A merchant or landlord who has tried to aggressively collect debts from the people during the current crisis. Some characters may try to extort political allegiance from players by threatening to throw the debtor in

prison unless that player votes for their side. Any character threatened with debt collection may want to try to raise a mob in order to stop the collection—to demand that his or her creditor drop any efforts to collect the money owed.

2. Someone who has switched sides, or, even worse, someone who has promised to vote one way then votes another. Of course, those who pretend to be on one side and then work for the other are called *spies* or *traitors* and are clear targets for mob action.

3. Most importantly, and most frequently, anyone who has a vote in Congress may be a target of the mob, which will pressure them to vote a certain way on an issue (for example, to vote for the Association).

Once the victim has been surrounded by a mob of sufficient size and presented with the mob's demand and threat level, the victim will have five minutes to decide what to do in the face of this angry mob. The Gamemaster should keep an eye on the clock to be sure that no more than five minutes elapse before the victim makes a choice.

Mob Victim's Options

1. *Get enough other characters to come to his side to defend him* against the mob (this has the effect of persuading the mob to back down and go home). This is known as a *counter-mob*; a successful counter-mob must be as large as the mob that has formed. Victims count as part of counter-mobs. Therefore, in a class of twenty-four players in which a mob of nine has formed, the counter-mob would be successful if at least eight players came to the victim's rescue.

2. *Flee to the British ship* Asia *in the harbor*. During this period, the British regularly docked warships on the East River, both for transport of men and supplies and for potential use in conflict; the *Asia* was a ship-of-the-line carrying sixty-four cannons, and was present in New York's harbor in 1775. This choice has the effect of saving the character's economic and personal life, but it removes that person from participating in the remainder of that public session, including votes. If the mob forms late in the session (within the last fifteen minutes), a character who flees will not be allowed to participate or vote in the first half of the next public session.

3. *Submit by promising to do as the mob has asked*. All mob victims have the option of submitting to the mob—doing what the mob requests—and this action will end the mob for that session. However, a mob victim may lie in order to save his or her skin. Of course, if the victim is caught in a lie or doesn't live up to his or her agreement, he or she may be mobbed in the

next session for reneging. (Submission was probably the tactic most often used in real life.)

4. *Submit to either humiliation or tar/feathering.* The victim may choose to endure the penalty. In humiliation, the mob will be entitled to yell any insults (in character!) it desires against the victim in class for one minute (the Gamemaster must time the minute). During tar and feathering, the mob should attach to the victim papers bearing slogans and drawings illustrating his perfidy, and will be allowed to march the victim through whatever spaces (in or out of the classroom) the Gamemaster approves in order to simulate the actual practice of bearing the victim through town on a rail while covered in tar and feathers.

> **TIP**
>
> A mob victim may only call on the British Army when faced with death, and not merely to avoid a tar and feathering.

5. *Use deadly force.*

   a. When threatened with tar and feathering, the victim may employ self-defense by choosing to shoot into the crowd. Obviously choosing to shoot into a mob runs a risk—the action may backfire and the victim himself may be the one killed or wounded. Deadly force may not be used if the mob is yelling curses without any other physical threat.

   b. When threatened with death, however, the victim may choose either self-defense, by firing a gun into the crowd, or he may call upon the British Army to march a line of soldiers out from their barracks to defend him. Using self-defense is less likely to produce death or injury to either the victim or a member of the crowd than is relying on the British Army, which is more likely to kill or wound a member of the crowd.

> **WARNING !** *Depending on the threat level chosen by the mob and the response of the victim, mobs may result in death or serious bodily injury for either the victim or a member of the mob. Death is bad for your character and his or her victory objectives.*

Mob Action Outcomes

In the event that the victim chooses deadly force to defend herself, there will be a dice roll to determine the outcome. Some outcomes favor the victim, some the mob, and the Gamemaster won't tell you the odds ahead of time.

Mob victory is declared when the victim submits to the demands, refuses to submit but accepts tar and feathering, flees, is removed from the game temporarily (i.e., is in hiding), or is wounded or killed after choosing to fight. The mob loses and the victim achieves victory when a successful counter-mob forms, if there is a fight where no one is injured or killed but the mob disperses, or if there is fight during which a member of the mob is injured or killed. The table below summarizes the most common results.

RESPONSE BY VICTIM	INTIMIDATION	TAR AND FEATHERING	DEADLY FORCE/ THREAT OF DEATH OR SERIOUS HARM
Submission, either by agreeing to demand or accepting threat	Mob wins	Mob wins	Not an option (victim dies)
Flee	Mob wins	Mob wins	Mob wins
Counter-mob	Victim wins	Victim wins	Victim wins
Self-defense (victim fires at mob)	(not available)	Dice roll	Dice roll
Defense by British Army	(not available)	(not available)	Dice roll

Remember, joining a mob is a vital form of political participation for non-voting city residents (women, slaves, laborers). Without regular mob action, these characters cannot achieve their objectives. But joining a mob has risks of death or serious incapacitating injury (death is bad in the game—a character who dies will not get any game points; see Victory Objectives section on page 74), plus risks of retaliation (by husbands, masters, and employers, respectively) on the day after the mob has formed. Members of Congress may participate in mobs, or even try to get ahead of the mob in helping it choose the target and goal, but should there be violence they run the same risks of death as other members of the mob.

Smuggler

The game includes a *Smuggler*, one character whose job is to smuggle tea (a small cardboard sheet with the word *tea* written on it). The Smuggler may be any character from any faction. It is up to the Gamemaster to decide who will be a Smuggler, and to give that character the official tea placard to hide.

The Smuggler may hide his tea placard anywhere in the classroom *except*:

- on anyone's body (no personal body searching allowed);
- in the Gamemaster or preceptor's belongings; or
- other areas the Gamemaster designates as off-limits.

The Smuggler may hide the tea in his own or in other people's personal effects as well as in classroom spaces. Searches may be carried out at any time by anyone (if there is no Association approved) or only by members of a duly authorized Committee of Inspection (if the Association is in force). If students wish their personal effects not to be searched, they can give them to the Gamemaster to be placed in a "safe, no-tea zone" for the duration of the session.

The Smuggler earns points for each session during which she/he successfully hides tea in the classroom for the entire session; individuals (if no Association exists) or members of the Committee of Inspection earn points for discovering the smuggled tea and even more points for identifying and mobbing the correct Smuggler (but lose points for mobbing an innocent).

Personal Deals

All characters have the ability to make political deals, to trade their vote for something of value to them. In the political realm, this is called logrolling—you vote for my proposal, I'll vote for yours; you help me, I'll help you. Sometimes deals are made based on personal biases: because you like someone personally, or because you dislike someone and want to aid his or her opposition. These voting arrangements are not defined as Personal Deals for game purposes.

A few game characters possess assets, readily available wealth denominated by an amount of British pounds, which they can use to advance their political cause through Personal Deals in private. Your individual role sheet will contain information as to whether your character has the assets (and how much) to make a Personal Deal; that part of the role sheet is designated "Special Power." If a player's role sheet does not mention possible Personal Deals or Special Power, that character does not possess the wealth or power to do so (and the Gamemaster will halt any such fraudulent offers). Any character may be approached to accept a Personal Deal in private, but only a few may offer one.

The general rule is this: characters with Personal Deal assets are allowed one and only one Personal Deal during the course of the game. As defined here, Personal Deals involve an offer of a job, money, forgiveness of debt, land, freedom (for slaves), or other tangible gains. Some characters may combine their Personal Deal powers together to achieve political goals; if they do so, they forego these private deals for the rest of the game. If there is any doubt as to whether a deal is personal or relates to general politics, the Gamemaster will rule. If a Personal Deal is offered to a laborer, woman, or slave character, the Deal will be considered to cover dozens of laborers, slaves, or women similarly situated—that is, the individual players in laborer, slave, and woman roles are for this purpose considered to embody many people. This provision avoids illogical results such as a character ending the slave problem by buying one slave character and freeing him, or providing one laborer with fifty acres of land. The Gamemaster will make such parameters known to anyone who wishes to make Personal Deals with members of the crowd.

To be effective and enforced in game terms, all such Personal Deals must be in writing, signed by both parties involved, and delivered to the Gamemaster. The Gamemaster will accept the deal after ensuring it makes sense in the context of the historical time and the particular characters' descriptions; the Gamemaster will also make sure that this is not the second deal a character has struck. If the Gamemaster certifies the written deal, the characters are bound to follow that deal for the remainder of the game.

Other deals may be struck that are oral, but in the immortal words of Samuel Goldwyn, "an oral contract isn't worth the paper it's printed on." In other words, unless it's in writing in the Gamemaster's hands, characters may backstab, double-deal, and renege on oral agreements. In normal times, a man's word was supposed to be his bond, but a revolution is not a normal time, and men become suspicious of each other's loyalties. Ideally, a man was supposed to be self-sacrificing, motivated by his understanding of the common good, and an embodiment of republican virtues, but some may not be independent actors and others may be corrupt. Therefore, characters may say and promise anything, but only deals in writing filed with and accepted by the Gamemaster will be binding.

VICTORY OBJECTIVES

The critical question, the one that will determine overall success or failure for all characters is this: *who is in control of New York City at the end of the game?* Decisions you make on individual proposals, petitions, and issues will influence the final outcome, but so will the actions of the British government—including the British military, the most formidable military power at the time. In short, your characters must consider not only what other characters want and will do, but also what the British are capable of doing and what they are likely to do in response. For example, if the British government through its army is in control of Manhattan at the end of the game, the Patriots will have lost and the Loyalists will have won—but the Loyalist victory will be lessened by the fact that they succeed not through political tactics but by piggybacking on the efforts of the British military.

Thus, all characters wish to be on the "winning side" that controls New York City at the end of the game, which is (in real historical time) late 1776. Additionally, there are intermediate political goals throughout the game (passing or defeating legislation, for instance) which allow players to earn points. Finally, many players have personal victory objectives

TIP

Do *not* rely on any predictions you may have about who will win the American Revolution, as that outcome was unknown in 1776. Your victory is determined by whether your side is in control of New York City at the end of game time, which is late 1776.

listed in their role sheets, for which they can gain or lose points. Obviously, not all of the possible ways to earn points are available to every character, and not all of these will be used in every game. Remember, if your character dies, you lose all points accrued up to that point.

Should there be a mob clash, military encampment (camp diseases were a prime cause of mortality), or war battle, there will probably be casualties among the characters. Characters that are killed lose the chance for victory (obviously), but death is not the only possible outcome of these events. Wounded characters may return unimpaired or continue in the game with lesser abilities to participate in future sessions. The outcome of mob fights and military actions, as well as which characters are killed or wounded, will be determined by a combination of chance and the relative power of the forces at play. As in real life, there are contingencies—fortunes of war—that cannot be perfectly predicted, but advance preparation and planning improve your odds. In other words, a dice throw may determine outcomes, although characters and factions may improve or diminish their chances through their choices. But there is one truth, for this game as well as in life, that should be remembered: death is bad. Players whose characters die early in the game (i.e., not in the final session) will be given replacement roles, and the chance to rebuild their point total.

Each Gamemaster will use his or her own judgment to determine the "winner(s)" of the game and how (if at all) game performance points will affect student grades in the course. What follows below is a list of the various game elements that may allow individuals to accrue points and suggested amounts of points to be offered (of course, the Gamemaster has final and incontestable authority to award full or partial points):

ELEMENT	POSSIBLE POINTS
Quiz—if given	All students. 3 points for best performance. Gamemaster may assign points based on individual performance on quiz or may allow factions to compete as a whole.
Mobbing—successful	1 point for participants in successful mob action; success determined by whether political goal accomplished.
Mobbing—unsuccessful	2 points for victim who thwarted mob; 1 point for each member of counter-mob if it was employed successfully.

(continued)

ELEMENT	POSSIBLE POINTS
Tea smuggling	1 point per session that Smuggler keeps tea hidden in classroom; 3 points for individual who discovers smuggled tea, with 1 point each to all other members of Committee of Inspection if tea discovered.
Association	If Association passes: 1 point to all in Congress who voted for it (includes moderate supporters); if Association loses, 1 point to all in Congress who voted against (includes moderate opponents).
Courts	1 point to Loyalists if courts reopen; 1 point to other players who support re-opening depending on the details (per Gamemaster discretion).
Armed Force	2 points to the Patriots in Congress if Continental Army approved before halfway point in game; 1 point to Patriots if Continental Army approved after halfway point; 1 point if a New York Army separate from Continental Army is approved; 1 point for each Game Session to each non-member of Congress who served either in Continental or New York Army service. If no military training beyond militia approved, 2 points to all Loyalists.
Independence	2 points to all who vote in Congress for the prevailing side, 1 point to Crowd supporters of the winning side (Gamemaster will poll the crowd to determine which side each supports).
Private goal—positive	Individuals should consult their role sheets for these elements.
Private goals—negative	Characters who violate their role sheets in various votes or actions will lose 1–2 points for each such deviation, at the discretion of the Gamemaster.
OVERALL CONTROL OF NEW YORK CITY	10 points maximum if your side is in charge of New York City at the end of 1776. NOTE: the Gamemaster may award partial points—it is not required that he/she award all 10 to the side in control of the city (that depends on how control has been achieved).

OUTLINE OF GAME SESSIONS

Listed below is a suggested outline for game scheduling and planning. Some instructors may opt to include additional readings or additional discussion of the readings in the game book. They may also vary the amount of time spent explaining the workings of the game. So the amount of class time devoted to each "session" will vary from game to game; that is, something listed as a "session" may take more or less than one class to complete. Instructors may also distribute role sheets at different times than outlined here.

CONTEXT SESSION 1

HISTORICAL AND PHILOSOPHICAL BACKGROUND OF REBELLION

Required Reading:

- Game book: Introduction and Historical Background, pp. 3–61.

- Game book: John Locke, *Second Treatise of Government*, pp. 100–31.

This day should familiarize players with the general background of the American Revolution, with in-depth discussion of the John Locke text. Beyond discussing Locke, instructors may provide additional historical context on the American Revolution, either through lecture or discussion). Students must be prepared to discuss the Locke readings as well as the colonial revolutionary situation in social, economic, and political terms, as described in the Historical Background section of the game book. Instructors inform students if there will be a quiz on these readings.

> **TIP**
>
> When reading Locke, look for key words in his writings on the people, the common good, and the role of consent that tie into the list on page 48.

THE SITUATION IN NEW YORK CITY, APRIL 1775

Required Reading:

- Game book: Parts 3 and 4: The Game; Roles and Factions, pp. 63–95.

- Required reading:

  - Daniel Dulany, "Considerations on the Propriety of Imposing Taxes in the British Colonies for the Purpose of Raising a Revenue," 1765, p. 131

  - Soame Jenyns, "The Objections to the Taxation of our American Colonies by the Legislature of Great Britain, briefly consider'd," 1765, p. 134

  - Samuel Johnson, "Taxation No Tyranny," 1775, p. 136

  - Samuel Seabury, "Free Thoughts on the Proceedings of the Continental Congress in a Letter to the Farmer," 1774, p. 153

Recommended Reading:

- Barnet Schecter, *The Battle for New York* (New York: Walker and Company, 2002), 11–45.

- Gordon Wood, *The Radicalism of the American Revolution* (New York: Alfred A. Knopf, 1992), 11–42.

Gamemaster continues the lecture or discussion on the general background of the American Revolution, and engages the class in discussion of the particular situation in New York City as of 1775. The Gamemaster will review and demonstrate the operation of the game rules. Following such activities, the Gamemaster will distribute the role sheets to all students. Each instructor determines ahead of time whether to assign roles randomly or to designate certain students for particular roles. The role packets will be distributed to the students, though they are not to be opened until the instructor is satisfied that the allocation of roles is appropriate (e.g., Gamemasters may decide to "mix up" factions if students have already played games this semester, placing students who held "lead" roles in a previous game in lesser roles this time).

PRE-GAME PREPARATION

Quiz (if given)

Gamemasters are provided with materials to quiz all players on the game book readings given so far. The quiz is discretionary, and may be done individually or collectively by factions, open or closed book, with or without collaboration among faction members. Gamemasters should inform players if and when the quiz will be given.

Faction Meetings

There are four factions: Patriots, Loyalists, Moderates, and Crowd (women, slaves, and laborers). Each faction will meet in a separate part of the classroom to introduce themselves to their fellow faction members and to plan their faction's strategy. The Gamemaster will meet with each group separately to discuss roles, strategies, and potential papers. At some point, the faction members will mingle among the other factions to exchange information and seek allies for their position. At the end of this session (or if time is short, at the beginning of the first Game Session), the Provincial Congress will meet for organizational purposes, rearranging the classroom space as described above so that all members of the Congress sit at desks or tables in a semicircle around a podium, with the Crowd in the back of the room, as in a balcony overlooking the floor.

Speaker of the Provincial Congress elected

At the end of this session, the Gamemaster will preside over the election of a Speaker for the Congress (any voting member of the Provincial Congress may run). The Gamemaster will ask for self-nominations, and will allow candidates for Speaker one minute each to explain why they should be elected. Other members of Congress and the Crowd may be allowed to ask questions of the candidates at the Gamemaster's discretion. The Speaker is elected by a majority of the members of Congress; if there are three or more candidates such that no one gets a majority, the candidate with the least votes is eliminated and another vote is held. In the event of a tie vote between two candidates, the Gamemaster may break the tie. At that point, the session is over; the elected Speaker will run all Game Sessions to come, and the Gamemaster will retire from the podium.

FIRST PROVINCIAL CONGRESS SESSION (APRIL 1, 1775)

Topics: Resistance to the British Acts; law and order in New York City

1. In response to the Intolerable Acts, the plight of Massachusetts, and the recommendations of the Continental Congress, should New York formally adopt the Association? A text of the Association is provided below; Patriots must include on the blank lines the names of characters in the game who will serve as the official Committee of Inspection to enforce the Association. Patriots may add to or subtract from that text in presenting their proposal to Congress for approval. Amendments may be offered by any character (in or out of Congress) before the final vote.

2. Should the courts in New York City be reopened, and under what conditions, oaths, and laws? Loyalist proponents of such a move should present a proposal indicating how New York would reopen its courts. Amendments may be offered by any character (in or out of Congress) before the final vote.

> **TIP**
>
> In considering whether Manhattan's courts should be reopened, players must consider to whom or to what the members of the court should swear allegiance.

Paper/Speech Topics

This session will consider the Association and the courts in the broad context of the situation New York faces as of April 1775. Students are expected to connect the political theory and arguments from the game book's Core Texts to the circumstances of the time. In particular, papers will focus on the Lockean analysis of property rights and how best to protect property against various threats, as well as the Lockean approach to the fundamental roles of legislatures, courts, consent, and the right of rebellion. But Locke's theory must be combined with the recent facts of colonial life as well as other authors' approaches found in the Core Texts. Normally, papers will be due from these players at this first session. Each of these roles has specific instructions on issues and texts to present for discussion:

From the Patriot faction in the Provincial Congress

- Robert Livingston, who speaks at the podium first and will propose the Association
- Alexander McDougall
- Isaac Sears
- Abraham Brasher

From the Loyalist faction in the Provincial Congress

- James Delancey, who speaks at the podium following Livingston and will present the court proposal
- Frederick Philipse
- James Jauncey

The Speaker of the Congress should open the session by calling upon Livingston first, then Delancey, followed by Patriots and Loyalists in Congress who will come to the podium to present their positions in alternating order. The Speaker will moderate the questioning and debate for each presenter, and all players, in and out of Congress, may pose questions and interject comments during the debate following each oral presentation. Note: the Speaker will not be allowed to call for a vote on any proposal until after these first seven speakers have had their chance at the podium, with full questioning and discussion on each.

WARNING ! *If a mob forms, Congress will immediately suspend its proceedings until the issues raised by the mob have been settled. This rule holds true in all Game Sessions.*

The Association text as approved by the Continental Congress on October 20, 1774 may be found at http://avalon.law.yale.edu/18th_century/contcong_10-20-74.asp. All students should consult the actual documentary text. Below is an abridged version that Patriots may use for their initial proposal that summarizes some (but not all) of the main points that the Continental Congress made in the Association:

THE CONTINENTAL ASSOCIATION

A Proposal for the Provincial Congress of New York, 1775:

In cooperation with our fellow colonies and the recommendations of the Continental Congress, and in response to the British Intolerable Acts, it shall now and henceforth be the policy of the colony of New York to approve and implement the Continental Association. The Association is a policy of non-importation and non-exportation with Great Britain. The Association requires the following actions:

1. *As of the date of adoption, New Yorkers will not import any goods, wares, or merchandise from Great-Britain or Ireland, nor will we import any East-India tea from any part of the world; nor any molasses, syrups, coffee, or pimento, from the British plantations.*

2. *If by September 10, 1775, the acts of the British parliament which we have objected to are not repealed, we will not directly or indirectly export any merchandise or commodity whatsoever to Great-Britain, Ireland, or the West-Indies.*

3. *We will, in our different stations, encourage frugality, economy, and industry, and promote agriculture, arts, and the manufactures of this country, especially that of wool.*

4. *A committee of inspection should be formed by us, the Provincial Congress, whose business it shall be to observe and find out if any violate the Association. If evidence is presented to the satisfaction of a majority of the Provincial Congress that a person is guilty of violating this association, then that person will be publicly known as an enemy of American liberty; and we will break off all dealings with him or her.*

The names of the Committee members are [names/signatures of characters who have agreed to serve on the Committee of Inspection, may be as many or few as desired]:

_____   _____

_____   _____

_____   _____

_____   _____

New Yorkers agree to adhere to this Association until the acts of Parliament that we object to, to wit, the Intolerable Acts, are repealed.

Events caused by outside forces will drive much of the debate in the Provincial Congress once the game begins. These events remain in the cloudy future, so at each session, the Gamemaster will give out news, make sure students know when and on what topics their papers are due, and advance the clock (i.e., move the game time forward in stages through the rest of 1775 and most of 1776). In general, the first papers for remaining characters will come due in the following order, but they may stretch over several class days according to how often the class meets per week and the number of players in the game. Consult your Gamemaster for the game days that characters will have their papers due:

- Remaining Patriot and Loyalist members of Provincial Congress

- John Cuyler's First Newspaper

- Moderate members of Provincial Congress

- Crowd members (laborers, women, and slaves, who are expected to present petitions)

At both the end of a session and at the start of a new session, the Gamemaster will announce and write on the board the current game date (e.g., "It is now August 1775"). Should the current game date advance during a session (e.g., "We have now moved into late fall, 1775"), the Gamemaster will announce this at the appropriate time and change the date on the board accordingly.

Once the Gamemaster has advanced the game time to January 1776, the following reading comes into play and may be cited by all characters:

Required Reading:

- Thomas Paine, *Common Sense*, 1776, p. 160

- James Chalmers, *Plain Truth*, 1776, p. 182

The (probable) sequence of issues for the rest of the game

Among the issues that will arise at various times to come and subsequent sessions are:

Military preparations and their funding; identification of characters who would serve.
Should New York do more than just quarterly militia drills for its defense; if so, should it attach its army/men to those of other colonies for collective defense (which would take New Yorkers away from New York) or should it limit its preparations to a New York army, which would be nearby and under New York command? How will such preparations be paid for—voluntary contributions, taxes, printing money? Amendments may be proposed before the final vote.

Women. Should some women be granted additional political rights such as voting? Petitions are not subject to amendment; they may only be approved or rejected by Congress.

Slaves. Should some or all slaves be freed, and if so, with what conditions? Petitions are not subject to amendment; they may only be approved or rejected by Congress.

Laborers. Should those without property be granted new and improved opportunities for economic advancement? Should all adult white men have the right to vote in elections? Petitions are not subject to amendment; they may only be approved or rejected by Congress.

Debate on independence. Should New York join in calls for declaring independence; if yes, should it approve the draft Declaration of Independence as written?

Debate on reconciliation proposals vis-à-vis the British. If the British make an offer of peace, should New York accept it—that is, what are the dangers and benefits to New York from a full-scale war with the British versus making a deal?

Additional issues and choices will arise throughout the game, and players must adapt their strategies according to the issue, the needs of their faction, and their own personal victory objectives. With the exception of John Cuyler's second newspaper (the Gamemaster will instruct this character on the due date), all second papers will be due at the final session.

DEBRIEFING AND POST-MORTEM

After the game ends, the GM will conduct a debriefing during which players have the opportunity to explain their actions without fear of repercussions. This session is also an opportunity to compare the events in the game with those that happened historically.

ASSIGNMENTS

Written Papers

For this game, everyone must submit two papers. One paper must be submitted before the halfway point; the other must be submitted by the end of the game. Certain characters have their first paper's timing dictated, but otherwise faction members should try to spread out their submissions as much as possible so as to rebut arguments of the other side. Each Gamemaster indicates the time and method of submission for the papers (i.e., professors may ask students to post their papers ahead of a particular Game Session on an electronic discussion board). Professors should also indicate the length of the paper required and the style manual to be used for both writing and attribution.

There are three primary styles to be used for these papers:

1. *The pamphlet.* Pamphlets contained an argument on one or more critical intellectual and ideological points, and were the main literary device used both for and against the revolution. All the attached readings with the exception of Locke were offered in pamphlet form to colonial readers. These readings should not only be read for information to be used in your argument (as a source of examples, evidence, etc.) but also for the organization and style of argument. You need not write as did those in the 1760s and 1770s, but you should internalize their methods while using modern language.

2. *The petition.* Petitions must be submitted humbly, with deference to the majesty of the granting body. Such deference need not be sincere, but it is expected by the elite and should be utilized by the crowd to enhance chances for passage. Those who choose the petition route to the Provincial Congress should look carefully at the recommended Gordon Wood reading in *The Radicalism of the American Revolution*. A petition must begin by identifying the petitioner, contain a short statement at both the beginning and the end of the specific action the petitioner requests Congress to take, and submit a longer analysis/argument for that action as the body of the paper.

3. *The newspaper narrative,* either in the form of a letter to the editor or as a dispatch reporting on events. You may also write a paper in the style of a diary or a narrative, describing the events as you experienced them and what their impact has been on you. John Cuyler will be writing two newspapers, but others may submit their own newspaper articles, either to him to be published, or as self-published material.

Students who serve in the Provincial Congress are expected to write papers that cite Locke (the first one should be devoted almost exclusively to Locke, but analysis of Locke need not be the only thing you include in the second paper—it just has to be somewhere in there). Students who have "dependent" roles (women, slaves, landless laborers) are also expected to cite Locke *if their papers are petitions to the Provincial Congress*. Included in the Core Texts for the Patriots is the most famous Patriot pamphlet—Thomas Paine's *Common Sense*. Pamphlets supporting the positions of Loyalists include those of Samuel Johnson, one of the great wits in the English language, and James Chalmers (a Maryland loyalist opposing Paine). Students should study these for evidence to support their positions and to mimic the style of writing and argument used therein. Finally, students are expected to refer to their knowledge of the social, economic, and political conditions in the colonies, from both the readings and class lectures, and incorporate this material as well.

Oral Participation

Every character in the game must give at least one speech; some Gamemasters may require more than one. Take care to not simply read your speeches. If the exact form of your words is important to you, especially regarding a proposal or petition, you should make copies of that material available to distribute in class as a handout. The fewer notes the better, but a few may be necessary and useful. Properly contextualized quotations from historical documents as well as apt references to speeches and papers produced by other players give strength to speeches. Those who simply read their speeches will lose the interest of their audience. Remember that your job is to persuade the indeterminate moderates as well as the people in the crowd to adopt your position and follow your lead, and if your speech is dull, your audience will become disinterested.

All characters are expected to participate freely in all discussions and debates, whether from the floor of Congress or from the gallery. Even women and slaves are entitled to speak, either to question a speaker or to make points in debate, as well as to make their speech from the podium before the Congress (this is not entirely historically accurate in terms of podium access). The Speaker shall be responsible for running the discussion and the questions following a speech. Additionally, the *podium rule* applies as outlined above under "Rules and Procedures." Anyone may go up to the podium to stand in line behind the speaker at the podium, thereby claiming an absolute right to give the next speech regardless of whether the Speaker of the Congress has recognized that person. This provision is useful if you feel your point of view is not getting a full and fair hearing; all players are entitled to the podium regardless of whether they have already spoken.

Grades

Each Gamemaster shall tell his or her students beforehand how the various elements of this game correspond to the grading scheme for the course. There are three potential elements that may be considered: written papers (two minimum), in-class participation, and game/victory points. The instructor must make clear whether game/victory points, available for achieving certain objectives in the game, will count toward the overall grade in the class.

PART 4: **ROLES AND FACTIONS**

THE PROVINCIAL CONGRESS

Voting in the Provincial Congress

Only elite characters have votes in the Provincial Congress, which is divided into three groups: two factions contending for control of the colony, Patriots and Loyalists, and several Moderates whose preferences are unknown. Each character in Congress has at least two issues to confront—his or her political goals (for which each character has allies) and his or her personal goals (which his or her friends, allies, and business contacts may oppose).

Other non-elite people—principally laborers, women, and slaves—also have a large stake in the outcome of the game and are organized into groups. While they do not have voting power in the Provincial Congress, they will agitate to achieve their objectives by influencing the votes.

Factions in the Provincial Congress

Patriots argue for the most radical opposition to British power, up to and including war and independence. Patriot supporters probably constitute a bare majority in the city, but are certainly not a majority in the New York colony as a whole. There are wealthy men among the Patriots, but such organizations as the Sons of Liberty include men from all walks of life. The Patriots in Congress may include:

Robert Livingston: An extremely wealthy Hudson River landowner, merchant, slaveowner, and leader of the Livingston faction, which has dominated New York politics for generations. He is opposed to the Delancey faction and is a Provincial Court Judge.

Alexander McDougall: From humble beginnings as a poor immigrant child, he commanded two privateering/pirate vessels against the French in the last war, making a fortune and becoming a merchant, a Presbyterian church member, and a member of the Sons of Liberty. He wrote a radical pamphlet in 1769 and was imprisoned for it.

Isaac Sears: Raised a fisherman, he became an intercolonial ship captain at age 16, privateer/pirate against the French in the last war, and subsequently a successful merchant. He is a Sons of Liberty member and defender of the liberty pole through his leadership of mobs. He was recently arrested for calling on all men to arm themselves against the British, but was freed by a mob.

Abraham Brasher: A Manhattan silversmith who started out as an apprentice and then became a journeyman working in other men's shops. He is now the owner of his own silversmith shop employing apprentices, laborers, and slaves. He advocates for free-market opportunities, both within the colony and among the nations of the world.

John Morin Scott: A Manhattan lawyer, raised by a widowed mother, he graduated from Yale at age 16 and established a thriving legal practice at age 22 after an apprenticeship. He is a believer in Enlightenment ideals and helped found New York's first free library. He also acts as a city alderman and is a Sons of Liberty member.

Andrew Reber: He is from Tryon County (one hundred and sixty miles north of Manhattan bordering the Iroquois Confederation), where he is a farmer, small landowner (less than 150 acres), and regular participant at low levels of county government. He is a member of the Anglican Church and is new to New York.

Henry Wisner: He is from Orange County (fifty miles north of Manhattan, on the west side of the Hudson River), where he is a farmer of two hundred acres. He sells farm produce to New York City down the Hudson River.

Loyalists believe that the colonial grievances do not warrant responses such as boycotts and violent resistance. They believe that separation from and war with England would be wrong and foolhardy. Loyalists are generally wealthier and more conservative than Patriots and more fearful of mob violence, which threatens their property and their position in the existing social order. Loyalists in Congress may include:

James Delancey: An extremely wealthy leader of the Delancey faction, which has dominated New York politics for generations and opposes the Livingston faction. He is a merchant/lender, Manhattan landowner, and collection agent for British merchants.

Frederick Philipse: Holding the title of *patroon* (a holder of manorial rights and privileges similar to a feudal lord), he is a wealthy owner of two hundred thousand acres in Westchester (north of Manhattan). His wealth is derived from renting land to hundreds of tenant farmers and his family dates to the Dutch era. His seat in the Assembly (and now the Congress) is the same one that his father held.

James Jauncey: A New York merchant who emigrated from Bermuda thirty-five years ago and runs an import/export business trading with Jamaica and other British colonies in the Caribbean. He is wealthy but suffered recent financial problems due to non-importation and the credit crises.

Robert Murray: A New York merchant and owner of an East River dock, he is a Quaker who recently spent significant time in England and approves of British Parliamentary politics. He is crippled by arthritis and was recently forced to close up his store by a mob enforcing the Association.

Christopher Billop: A Staten Island farmer and owner of ten thousand acres (mostly undeveloped forest and swamp), who sells the produce of his farm in Manhattan for export to the West Indies. He is also a leading member of the Church of England.

John Rapalje: A Brooklyn farmer who owns one hundred and ninety acres and sells surplus farm crops across the East River in Manhattan. He is a leading member of the Dutch Reformed Church.

Moderates are critical to the game's outcome, as their votes and political preferences on the major questions are as yet unknown. Voting members in the Provincial Congress, they are generally sympathetic toward Patriot principles but do not believe those principles contain completely realistic alternatives. They have grave concerns about the practical consequences of going against the British Empire's power and upsetting the established economic and social order. In game terms, they are the swing votes in the Provincial Congress—their choices will depend on the issue and the arguments presented (both ideological and practical). These are men new to the political process, but they hold the balance of power in Congress. Moderates in Congress may include:

John Polhamus: A Queens County (just east of Manhattan) farmer who owns 180 acres and sells farm produce to Manhattan markets. He is a regular purchaser of British goods sold in New York City.

John Cuyler, Jr.: A farmer/merchant from Schenectady (160 miles north of Manhattan) and the publisher of a weekly newspaper for residents of rural Albany County.

Joseph Benedict: A farmer from Westchester (just north of Manhattan), who owns 175 acres with a mortgage and is a first-time representative.

Thomas Tredwell: A farmer and country lawyer born in Smithtown, in Suffolk County, Long Island, he has also practiced law and represented Plattsburgh, near the border with Canada.

Johannes Snyder: A farmer and militia leader from Ulster County, which is up the Hudson River from Manhattan.

John Williams: A young farmer and surgeon, recently emigrated from England, who bought land two years ago near the Massachusetts border.

THE CROWD

Members of the Crowd are not able to vote in elections or serve in Congress at this time. They are composed of three distinct groups.

Laborers are landless poor young white males in New York City in search of a better economic future, younger sons of poor farmers who have migrated in search of opportunity, day laborers, dock workers, and sailors waiting for their next ship. All have great resentment against the wealthy elite, and are ready to join a mob to gain more political rights and better economic prospects. Many of these folk have joined mobs before, in land riots and in the city over the last ten years—but which side can offer them the best chance at land or prosperous steady employment? Laborers may include:

WARNING ! *A laborer strategy that focuses on gaining more land to the west confronts two barriers: the Native Americans who still possess significant numbers and military power, and the British government, which as of 1763 has forbidden colonial settlement west of the Appalachian Mountains. Such opposition is not insuperable, but should be considered.*

Isaac Deane: A son of a former tenant farmer evicted after the land riots in 1766, he worked day labor jobs for nine years to support his widowed mother and four siblings. He is a member of the Sons of Liberty.

George Hewes: A journeyman shoemaker who is extremely short of stature, his father died when he was 7 years old and he was apprenticed to an abusive shoemaker at age 14. He is now 25 years old and working piecemeal for master shoemakers. He is a member of the liberty pole mobs.

John Forster: A sailor since the age of 16, he has crewed on Atlantic vessels since 1756. Now 35, he is recently unemployed due to the economic crisis and is fearful of British impressment.

Women compose roughly half of the colony's population and have made critical forays into political life during the boycotts against the Stamp Act and the Townshend Acts. Women made the substitute products to replace the goods that couldn't be imported (such as clothing); women reported merchants who raised their prices during the shortages; and women took up extra work on their farms and in their shops (especially taverns, which are plentiful in New York City) while their husbands participated in the resistance efforts. Women's participation or refusal to participate in various proposals and actions will affect who controls New York. Women may include:

Margarite de la Montagne: A tavern owner and recent widow of Abraham de la Montagne, she is the mother of one teenaged son and the owner of her tavern and its lot, thanks to her husband's will. She is a clever businesswoman.

Prudence Holman: A 31-year-old wife of a farmer, living roughly one mile north of town in an area now called the Lower East Side. She is the mother of four children born in the last seven years.

Mary Pearsee Willett: Married to cabinetmaker and Sons of Liberty leader Marinus Willett, she is the mother of a 14-year-old son. She runs a salon on the Enlightenment and political disputes.

Slaves composed perhaps 15 percent of New York City's population. They were owned by landowners and merchants, and they worked on farms and on the docks, as laborers, and as domestic servants. Slaves in Manhattan frequent the bars and many can read. Many have heard the rhetoric that Britain is trying to enslave the colonists. Slave revolts, real or feared, led to a merciless slaughter of many slaves in 1712 and 1741, but maybe in the current chaos, there's a chance to gain freedom and a political future.

Joseph Bartlet: A stout young man, son of an enslaved woman imported from Barbados to New York City, apprenticed to a baker, cook for his wealthy owner Gilbert Livingston (distant relative of Robert Livingston). Unmarried, no family, literate, he makes a small amount selling pastries on the side when his master is out of town.

Joseph Collins: A young farm laborer, the only slave owned by Patriot Joseph Kip on a farm just north of the city along the East River (Kip's Bay), field hand, hauler of produce, jack of all trades. Trained by Kip to read the Bible, now a practicing Christian in one of the local black congregations.

Thomas Foster: A strong young man owned by Patriot John Harbeck in Albany, but rented to merchant Evert Bancker for work on his ships and docks in New York City. Single, with disfiguring scars that show he has been in fights.

The Gamemaster will announce how many students are in the class, so all may know the political dynamics of the numbers needed for various actions. The Gamemaster will also announce which particular characters are being used to fill the number of roles in each faction, so all players can know some background on everyone else's role (reread the above section after role sheets are distributed).

Role Allocation Table

ROLE	ALLOCATION BY CLASS SIZE																	
	11	12	13	14	15	16	17	18	19	20	21	22	23	24	25	26	27	28
Patriots (Provincial Congress)	3	3	3	4	4	4	4	5	5	5	5	6	6	6	6	7	7	7
Loyalists (Provincial Congress)	2	2	2	3	3	3	3	4	4	4	4	5	5	5	5	6	6	6
Moderates (Provincial Congress)	2	2	2	3	3	3	3	3	4	4	4	4	5	5	5	5	5	6
Laborers (Crowd)	2	2	2	2	2	2	3	2	2	3	3	3	3	3	3	3	3	3
Women (Crowd)	1	2	2	1	2	2	2	2	2	2	3	2	2	3	3	3	3	3
Slaves (Crowd)	1	1	2	1	1	2	2	2	2	2	2	2	2	2	3	2	3	3
MINIMUM MOB SIZE	4	5	6	4	5	6	7	6	6	7	8	7	7	8	9	8	9	9

PART 5: **CORE TEXTS**

NOTE ON THE TEXTS

In order to play the game well, one must have a grasp of the documents that follow. Editorial comments by the authors of this game book appear in the footnotes and margins. The formatting, grammar, punctuation, and spelling in all of the documents have been silently modernized to facilitate ease of reading and comprehension.

INTRODUCTION TO LOCKE'S *SECOND TREATISE*[1]

John Locke (1632–1704) was a renowned English Enlightenment philosopher whose father was a relatively well-off small landowner and solicitor. He grew up in the midst of the English Civil War. At Westminster school starting at age 14 and then at Oxford in 1652 when he was 20, Locke's intellectual views were shaped by a political storm that shook England to its core. To understand the portion of Locke's thought contained in the document that follows, one must first understand the upheavals of his youth.

The English Civil War began in 1642. Parliament, controlled by radical Puritans, put an army that included Locke's father in the field against King Charles I. Over the next seven years, royalist and Parliamentary armies ravaged England. In 1649 Charles was captured and beheaded, an event followed by eleven years of political and military turmoil under Oliver Cromwell and his "Commonwealth" government. These events forced a reexamination of what constituted legitimate authority. Some blamed Parliament for the turmoil and called for a return to the stability of a monarchy. Two such theorists were Sir Robert Filmer and Thomas Hobbes.

Filmer insisted in *Patriarcha: The Natural Power of Kings* that monarchs were the legitimate rulers of any nation. Their authority had been specified in the Bible; as Adam ruled over his sons, so, too, did all fathers—the descendants of Adam—rule over their sons. Never has patriarchal authority been more explicit: monarchy became the embodiment of paternal authority, writ large. Nearly all nations were ruled by kings because God had ordained it.

But few theorists were satisfied with a theological justification of political institutions. What, in the absence of divine authority, could entitle a government to take one's life and property? What right, in other words, allowed a government to order citizens' imprisonment or tax and confiscate their property?

To answer these questions, political theorists imagined what life would be like in the absence of governmental authority. But this posed immediate problems. If in a modern society all governments were to be abolished, society as it was then known would cease to exist. To cite a current example of government's effect, our modern lives depend on the maintenance of highways and functioning of traffic lights. The point can also be demonstrated in the seventeenth century. Stable government authority, including the coercive power to preserve order and the taxation to ensure it, was necessary to shield the populace from the horrors and insecurities of the English Civil War.

Political theorists therefore attempted to imagine societies at a much simpler and earlier moment in human affairs. These theorists referred to man's prehistorical lifestyle as "a state of nature." The discovery of the Americas in previous centuries had given some sense of the lives of North American Indians in such a state. Accounts of these "noble savages" fueled speculation as to the characteristics of a state of nature for all peoples. What rights, theorists asked, did human beings inherently have in a state of nature? And why did all "advanced" societies move from a state of nature to formal governments?

Political philosopher Thomas Hobbes answered this question in 1651 by asserting that in the state of nature, man's life was "solitary, poor, nasty, brutish, and short." Improving on the state of nature, with its anxieties and fears based in violence, required a government, but which sort? Hobbes insisted that monarchy prevailed not because it was ordained by God, as Filmer maintained, but because people had chosen monarchy as the best system of government. Alluding to the bloody chaos of the English Civil War, Hobbes declared that in the absence of clear and effective government, human beings ran amok, falling prey to criminals and warlords. Fear for their lives prompted people everywhere to surrender their rights and property to a powerful protector—a formidable warlord, perhaps. Eventually this protector became a hereditary king. The people's original surrender of rights was in fact a contract—a "social contract" between the people and their monarch. It was a good deal for all parties: vulnerable individuals acquired the protection of a king, who acquired the people's subservience and support, which could be directed to ensure the security of all. Both contracting parties gained from the arrangement.

But Locke developed a very different outlook starting in the 1660s, shaped by the Enlightenment philosophy that enshrined reason. After the restoration of the monarchy in 1660 under Charles II, Locke became tied to the Whig political opposition in the 1670s and 1680s. The Whigs were attempting to keep Charles II's brother James (the Duke of York, for whom New York is named) from being made heir to the throne. The issue was James's Catholicism; if James became king, the Whigs feared that Protestant England would fall prey to the political influence of the pope and a religion seen as wallowing in superstition and corruption. Their efforts failed: James was crowned king in 1685, and Locke fled in exile to Holland from 1683 to 1689. However, he saw confirmation for his belief that reason could prevail in politics in the "Glorious Revolution" of 1688 that deposed James II. The new English monarchs, Protestants William of Orange and his wife Mary (James's daughter), accepted a bill of rights and joint rule with Parliament.

While in exile Locke wrote *Two Treatises on Government* (1689) which provided the philosophical justification for an end to absolute monarchy. In the *First Treatise*, not included in the game book, Locke dismantled Filmer's argument that absolute monarchy had been endorsed by scripture. The *Second Treatise*, excerpted at length below, was a defense of resistance to the king, of Parliamentary sovereignty, and of the justice of replacing one monarch with another (as in the Glorious Revolution). Locke argued for a limited constitutional state in support of the individual's natural right to private property, an ideology later described as "possessive individualism." Locke contended that the people had a right of revolution, but only in extremely serious situations: when the government failed to perform its functions and invaded the lives, property, and liberties of its people.

Although Locke's *Second Treatise on Government* makes no mention of Hobbes, it was a direct response to that text, beginning with a reconsideration of the "state of nature." Where Hobbes viewed life in a state of nature as "nasty, brutish, and short," Locke held that that human beings naturally lived companionably, aided by reason and common sense. Where Hobbes assumed that, in the absence of an overarching "leviathan" to impose order, people would plunge into chaos, Locke believed that, for the most part, people in a state of nature would get along reasonably well.

Hobbes's and Locke's speculations about the state of nature were intended to ascertain the very nature of humanity; they believed that human beings in civil society—that is, societies in which governmental authority had been instituted—adhered to laws out of fear of punishment. In the absence of the constraint of a state, they assumed, man's true nature would surface more readily. While Hobbes maintained that human beings were inherently aggressive, fractious, and emotional, Locke insisted that they were cooperative, sociable, and reasonable. To support this, Locke, like Filmer, invoked a theological explanation: A benevolent God had provided mankind with the faculties of reason and the abundance of nature.

After the Glorious Revolution, Locke returned safely to England. From 1696 to 1700 he was a member of the Board of Trade, the administrative agency that supervised Britain's American (and other) colonies, and he invested in the sugar colony of the Bahamas. At that time, he evidently saw no contradiction between his principles and the realities of British control over the colonies. Locke also invested in the Royal Africa Company, which was the English company primarily responsible for obtaining slaves from Africa and transporting them to colonies in the West Indies and North America. He was a man of property and interested in protecting it—property that included slaves. Other points that seem directly at odds with Locke's philosophy of equality include his discussion (in parts of the *Second Treatise* not included in this game book) of paternal power and of the power of "a husband over his wife," and his references only to men when speaking of liberty and equality. Issues of equality between men and women, especially in political roles, did not get Locke's attention.[2]

In the American colonies during the revolutionary crisis of the 1760s and 1770s, political debate was done through pamphlets as well as orally. In those pamphlets, Locke was cited repeatedly (more than any other single source) on natural rights and on the social and governmental contracts. The pamphlets often included Locke's sophisticated political analyses, but some quoted from him cavalierly, "as if he could be relied on to support anything the writers happened to be arguing."[3] Loyalists and Patriots alike could invoke Locke, in part because his ideas so powerfully echoed the sentiment of middle-class Englishmen in the eighteenth century. For example, Locke can be used in arguing for the protection of property rights, especially against mobs that seem to be out of control, but also to craft an argument for when resistance is or is not warranted (see section 225, p. 127).

This game is about the legitimacy of political power. Colonists, having transformed the "state of nature" of the New World into a civil society, were eager to understand what authority could secure and maintain legitimacy. The *Second Treatise* was the single most valuable guide for colonial New Yorkers in 1775 seeking solutions to their myriad crises. But it would be well, too, to keep in mind Hobbes's pessimism—and conservatism. Loyalists especially may regard the Patriot agenda as a cataclysm that destroys civil authority and plunges everyone into chaos.

JOHN LOCKE

FROM *Second Treatise of Government*, 1689

Seventeenth- and eighteenth-century texts were somewhat fluid, changing between editions even long after the author was dead. This version is reproduced from the 1764 edition, the sixth publication of the Second Treatise, *a version that would have circulated in the colonies. Italics within the text were not used in the original publication but rather reflect the choice of the editor of a subsequent edition to emphasize particular key words and concepts. Lockean thought is essential to understanding the arguments surrounding the revolution and the questions of political legitimacy addressed by this game. Be sure to read carefully the "Introduction to Locke's* Second Treatise*" section immediately preceding this text. Locke begins the* Second Treatise *by exploring the legitimate and illegitimate uses of political power, moves back in time to consider man in the state of nature, and then jumps forward to reveal how government betters man's condition through the rule of law. Editor's note: This document has been broken into sections and headings have been added to facilitate both reading and referencing.*

SOURCE: *John Locke,* Second Treatise of Government, *edited by C. B. MacPherson (Indianapolis: Hackett Publishing, 1980). Also found at www.constitution.org/jl/2ndtreat.htm*

Chapter I

* * *

3. Political power, then, I take to be a right of making laws, with penalties of death, and consequently all less penalties for the regulating and preserving of *property*, and of employing the force of the community in the execution of such laws, and in the defense of the commonwealth[1] from foreign injury, and all this only for the *public good*.

Chapter II, Of the State of Nature

4. To understand political power aright, and derive it from its original, we must consider what estate all men are naturally in, and that is, a state of perfect freedom to order their actions, and dispose of their possessions and persons as they think fit, within the bounds of the *law of Nature*, without asking leave or depending upon the will of any other man.

A state also of equality, wherein all the power and jurisdiction is reciprocal, no one having more than another, there being nothing more evident than that creatures of the same species and rank, promiscuously born to all the same advantages of Nature, and the use of the same faculties, should also be equal one amongst another, without subordination or subjection, unless the lord and master of them all should, by any manifest declaration of his will, set one above another, and confer on him, by an evident and clear appointment, an undoubted right to dominion and sovereignty.

Locke constructs a thought experiment called "the state of nature," a theoretical state existing before society and governments were invented in which all men are free and equal, but freedom does not allow citizens license to do whatever they want to themselves or others.

5. This equality of men by Nature, the judicious Hooker[2] looks upon as so evident in itself, and beyond all question, that he makes it the foundation of that obligation to mutual love amongst men on which he builds the duties they owe one another, and from whence he derives the great maxims of justice and charity. . . .

6. But though this be a state of liberty, yet it is not a state of license; though man in that state have an uncontrollable liberty to dispose of his person or possessions, yet he has not liberty to destroy himself, or so much as any creature in his possession, but where some nobler use than its bare preservation calls for it. The state of Nature has a law of Nature to govern it, which obliges every one, and

---

1. The term "commonwealth" comes from "common weal," meaning common well-being. It had come to mean in the seventeenth century a state in which supreme power was vested in the people. It could be seen as a provocative term as well, recalling the Commonwealth of England that, under Oliver Cromwell, had executed King Charles I in 1649 and established a form of republic off and on for eleven years.

2. Locke is referring to the Reverend Richard Hooker (1554–1600), a theologian known as one of the fathers of the Anglican (Church of England) faith, combining reason, revelation, and tradition in a defense of Puritan Protestantism.

reason, which is that law, teaches all mankind who will but consult it, that being all equal and independent, no one ought to harm another in his life, health, liberty or possessions; for men being all the workmanship of one omnipotent and infinitely wise Maker; all the servants of one sovereign Master, sent into the world by His order and about His business; they are His property, whose workmanship they are made to last during His, not one another's pleasure. And, being furnished with like faculties, sharing all in one community of Nature, there cannot be supposed any such subordination among us that may authorize us to destroy one another, as if we were made for one another's uses, as the inferior ranks of creatures are for ours. Every one as he is bound to preserve himself, and not to quit his station willfully, so by the like reason, when his own preservation comes not in competition, ought he as much as he can to preserve the rest of mankind, and not unless it be to do justice on an offender, take away or impair the life, or what tends to the preservation of the life, the liberty, health, limb, or goods of another.

7. And that all men may be restrained from invading others' rights, and from doing hurt to one another, and the law of Nature be observed, which wills the peace and preservation of all mankind, the execution of the law of Nature is in that state put into every man's hands, whereby everyone has a right to punish the transgressors of that law to such a degree as may hinder its violation. For the law of Nature would, as all other laws that concern men in this world, be in vain if there were nobody that in the state of Nature had a power to execute that law, and thereby preserve the innocent and restrain offenders; and if anyone in the state of Nature may punish another for any evil he has done, everyone may do so. For in that state of perfect equality, where naturally there is no superiority or jurisdiction of one over another, what any may do in prosecution of that law, everyone must needs have a right to do.

In the state of nature, all have equal rights to restrain or punish those who harm others or take others' property, but the restraint or punishment must be proportionate to the offense.

8. And thus, in the state of Nature, one man comes by a power over another, but yet no absolute or arbitrary power to use a criminal, when he has got him in his hands, according to the passionate heats or boundless extravagancy of his own will, but only to [retaliate against] him so far as calm reason and conscience dictate, what is proportionate to his transgression, which is so much as may serve for reparation and restraint. . . .

* * *

13. To this strange doctrine—viz., That in the state of Nature everyone has the executive power of the law of Nature—I doubt not but it will be objected that it is unreasonable for men to be judges in their own cases, that self-love will make men partial to themselves and their friends; and, on the other side, ill-nature, passion, and revenge will carry them too far in punishing others, and hence nothing but confusion and disorder will follow, and that therefore God has certainly appointed government to restrain the partiality and violence of men. I easily grant that civil

government is the proper remedy for the inconveniences of the state of Nature, which must certainly be great where men may be judges in their own case, since it is easy to be imagined that he who was so unjust as to do his brother an injury will scarce be so just as to condemn himself for it. But I shall desire those who make this objection to remember that absolute monarchs are but men; and if government is to be the remedy of those evils which necessarily follow from men being judges in their own cases, and the state of Nature is therefore not to be endured, I desire to know what kind of government that is, and how much better it is than the state of Nature, where one man commanding a multitude has the liberty to be judge in his own case, and may do to all his subjects whatever he pleases without the least question or control of those who execute his pleasure and in whatsoever he does, whether led by reason, mistake, or passion, must be submitted to. Much better it is in the state of Nature, wherein men are not bound to submit to the unjust will of another. And if he that judges, judges amiss in his own or any other case, he is answerable for it to the rest of mankind.

Due to natural human tendencies, people will rule for themselves if they have the power to judge their own causes. That is why government is needed: to "restrain the partiality and violence of men."

* * *

Chapter IV, Of Slavery

22. The natural liberty of man is to be free from any superior power on earth, and not to be under the will or legislative authority of man, but to have only the law of Nature for his rule. *The liberty of man in society is to be under no other legislative power but that established by consent in the commonwealth, nor under the dominion of any will, or restraint of any law, but what that legislative shall enact according to the trust put in it.* Freedom, then, is not what Sir Robert Filmer[3] tells us: "A liberty for everyone to do what he lists, to live as he pleases, and not to be tied by any laws"; but *freedom of men under government is to have a standing rule to live by, common to every one of that society, and made by the legislative power erected in it.* A liberty to follow my own will in all things where that rule prescribes not, not to be subject to the inconstant, uncertain, unknown, arbitrary will of another man, as freedom of nature is to be under no other restraint but the law of Nature.

Only captives in war can be enslaved legitimately; men cannot violate the principle of natural liberty even by choosing to enslave themselves.

23. This freedom from absolute, arbitrary power is so necessary to, and closely joined with, a man's preservation, that he cannot part with it but by what forfeits his preservation and life together. For a man, not having the power of his own life, cannot by compact or his own consent enslave himself to any one, nor put himself under the absolute, arbitrary power of another to take away his life when he

---

3. Sir Robert Filmer (1588–1653), as noted in the introduction to this text, was a defender of the divine right of kings and the Stuart monarchy.

pleases. Nobody can give more power than he has himself, and he that cannot take away his own life, cannot give another power over it. Indeed, having by his fault forfeited his own life by some act that deserves death, he to whom he has forfeited it may, when he has him in his power, delay to take it, and make use of him to his own service; and he does him no injury by it. For, whenever he finds the hardship of his slavery outweigh the value of his life, it is in his power, by resisting the will of his master, to draw on himself the death he desires.

24. This is the perfect condition of slavery, which is nothing else but the state of war continued between a lawful conqueror and a captive, for if once compact enter between them, and make an agreement for a limited power on the one side, and obedience on the other, the state of war and slavery ceases as long as the compact endures; for, as has been said, no man can by agreement pass over to another that which he has not in himself—a power over his own life. . . .

Chapter V, Of Property

25. Whether we consider natural reason, which tells us that men, being once born, have a right to their preservation, and consequently to meat and drink and such other things as Nature affords for their subsistence, or "revelation," which gives us an account of those grants God made of the world to Adam, and to Noah and his sons, it is very clear that God, as King David says (Psalm 115:16), "has given the earth to the children of men," given it to mankind in common. But, this being supposed, it seems to some a very great difficulty how any one should ever come to have a property in anything, I will not content myself to answer, that, if it be difficult to make out "property" upon a supposition that God gave the world to Adam and his posterity in common, it is impossible that any man but one universal monarch should have any "property" upon a supposition that God gave the world to Adam and his heirs in succession, exclusive of all the rest of his posterity; but I shall endeavor to show how men might come to have a property in several parts of that which God gave to mankind in common, and that without any express compact of all the commoners.

Here Locke posits a labor theory of property rights. This natural right is subject to limits, however, in the case of waste or lack of opportunity.

26. God, who has given the world to men in common, has also given them reason to make use of it to the best advantage of life and convenience. The earth and all that is therein is given to men for the support and comfort of their being. And though all the fruits it naturally produces, and beasts it feeds, belong to mankind in common, as they are produced by the spontaneous hand of Nature, and nobody has originally a private dominion exclusive of the rest of mankind in any of them, as they are thus in their natural state, yet being given for the use of men, there must of necessity be a means to appropriate them some way or other before they can be of any use, or at all beneficial, to any particular men. The fruit or venison which nourishes the wild Indian, who knows no enclosure, and is still a tenant in common, must be his, and so [becomes] his—i.e., a part of him, that another

can no longer have any right to it before it can do him any good for the support of his life.

27. Though the earth and all inferior creatures be common to all men, yet every man has a "property" in his own "person." This nobody has any right to but himself. The "labor" of his body and the "work" of his hands, we may say, are properly his. Whatsoever, then, he removes out of the state that Nature has provided and left it in, he has mixed his labor with it, and joined to it something that is his own, and thereby makes it his property. It being by him removed from the common state Nature placed it in, it has by this labor something annexed to it that excludes the common right of other men. For this "labor" being the unquestionable property of the laborer, no man but he can have a right to what that is once joined to, at least where there is enough, and as good left in common for others.

28. He that is nourished by the acorns he picked up under an oak, or the apples he gathered from the trees in the wood, has certainly appropriated them to himself. Nobody can deny but the nourishment is his. I ask, then, when did they begin to be his? when he digested? or when he ate? or when he boiled? or when he brought them home? or when he picked them up? And it is plain, if the first gathering made them not his, nothing else could. That labor put a distinction between them and common. That added something to them more than Nature, the common mother of all, had done, and so they became his private right. And will anyone say he had no right to those acorns or apples he thus appropriated because he had not the consent of all mankind to make them his? Was it a robbery thus to assume to himself what belonged to all in common? If such a consent as that was necessary, man had starved, notwithstanding the plenty God had given him. We see in commons, which remain so by compact, that it is the taking any part of what is common, and removing it out of the state Nature leaves it in, which begins the property, without which the common is of no use. And the taking of this or that part does not depend on the express consent of all the commoners. Thus, the grass my horse has bit, the turfs my servant has cut, and the ore I have dug in any place, where I have a right to them in common with others, become my property without the assignation or consent of anybody. The labor that was mine, removing them out of that common state they were in, has fixed my property in them.

30. Thus this law of reason makes the deer that Indian's who has killed it; it is allowed to be his goods who has bestowed his labor upon it, though, before, it was the common right of every one. And amongst those who are counted the civilized part of mankind, who have made and multiplied positive laws to determine property, this original law of Nature for the beginning of property, in what was before common, still takes place, and by virtue thereof, what fish any one catches in the ocean, that great and still remaining common of mankind; or what ambergris[4] any one takes up here is by the labor that removes it out of that common state Nature

---

4. Ambergris is found in whales' digestive systems and was used in perfumes.

left it in, made his property who takes that pains about it. And even amongst us, the hare that any one is hunting is thought his who pursues her during the chase. For being a beast that is still looked upon as common, and no man's private possession, whoever has employed so much labour about any of that kind as to find and pursue her has thereby removed her from the state of Nature wherein she was common, and has begun a property.

31. It will, perhaps, be objected to this, that if gathering the acorns or other fruits of the earth, etc., makes a right to them, then any one may engross[5] as much as he will. To which I answer, Not so. The same law of Nature that does by this means give us property, does also bound that property too. "God has given us all things richly." Is the voice of reason confirmed by inspiration? But how far has He given it us—"to enjoy"? As much as anyone can make use of any advantage of life before it spoils, so much he may by his labor fix a property in. Whatever is beyond this is more than his share, and belongs to others.[6] Nothing was made by God for man to spoil or destroy. And thus considering the plenty of natural provisions there was a long time in the world, and the few spenders, and to how small a part of that provision the industry of one man could extend itself and engross it to the prejudice of others, especially keeping within the bounds set by reason of what might serve for his use, there could be then little room for quarrels or contentions about property so established.

32. But the chief matter of property being now not the fruits of the earth and the beasts that subsist on it, but the earth itself, as that which takes in and carries with it all the rest, I think it is plain that property in that too is acquired as the former. As much land as a man tills, plants, improves, cultivates, and can use the product of, so much is his property. He by his labor does, as it were, enclose it from the common. Nor will it invalidate his right to say everybody else has an equal title to it, and therefore he cannot appropriate, he cannot enclose, without the consent of all his fellow-commoners, all mankind. God, when He gave the world in common to all mankind, commanded man also to labor, and the penury of his condition required it of him. God and his reason commanded him to subdue the earth—i.e., improve it for the benefit of life and therein lay out something upon it that was his own, his labor. He that, in obedience to this command of God, subdued, tilled, and sowed any part of it, thereby annexed to it something that was his property, which another had no title to, nor could without injury take from him.

33. Nor was this appropriation of any parcel of land, by improving it, any prejudice to any other man, since there was still enough and as good left, and more than the yet unprovided could use. So that, in effect, there was never the less left for

---

5. To "engross" meant to monopolize, to accumulate so as to deny others access.

6. This principle, against engrossment beyond what one can use oneself, supports an argument for redistribution of wealth.

others because of his enclosure for himself. For he that leaves as much as another can make use of does as good as take nothing at all. Nobody could think himself injured by the drinking of another man, though he took a good draught, who had a whole river of the same water left him to quench his thirst. And the case of land and water, where there is enough of both, is perfectly the same.

34. God gave the world to men in common, but since He gave it them for their benefit and the greatest conveniences of life they were capable to draw from it, it cannot be supposed He meant it should always remain common and uncultivated. He gave it to the use of the industrious and rational (and labor was to be his title to it); not to the fancy or covetousness of the quarrelsome and contentious. He that had as good left for his improvement as was already taken up needed not complain, ought not to meddle with what was already improved by another's labor; if he did it is plain he desired the benefit of another's pains, which he had no right to, and not the ground which God had given him, in common with others, to labor on, and whereof there was as good left as that already possessed, and more than he knew what to do with, or his industry could reach to.

35. . . . And the condition of human life, which requires labor and materials to work on, necessarily introduce private possessions.

36. The measure of property Nature well set, by the extent of men's labor and the convenience of life. No man's labor could subdue or appropriate all, nor could his enjoyment consume more than a small part; so that it was impossible for any man, this way, to entrench upon the right of another or acquire to himself a property to the prejudice of his neighbor, who would still have room for as good and as large a possession (after the other had taken out his) as before it was appropriated. Which measure did confine every man's possession to a very moderate proportion, and such as he might appropriate to himself without injury to anybody in the first ages of the world, when men were more in danger to be lost, by wandering from their company, in the then vast wilderness of the earth than to be [limited] for want of room to plant in.

The natural right of property requires sufficient opportunity, such that no one's acquisitions harm another's chances to gain property. The current world does not lack in such opportunity as a state of nature still exists in America, with land and property available to acquire. There is no reference to Native Americans (Indians) here or to their natural right to this land; throughout, Locke seems to regard America as vacant.

And the same measure may be allowed still, without prejudice to anybody, full as the world seems. For, supposing a man or family, in the state they were at first, peopling of the world by the children of Adam or Noah, let him plant in some inland vacant places of America. We shall find that the possessions he could make himself, upon the measures we have given, would not be very large, nor, even to this day, prejudice the rest of mankind or give them reason to complain or think themselves injured by this man's encroachment, though the race of men have now spread themselves to all the corners of the world, and do infinitely exceed the small number [there] was at the beginning. Nay, the extent of ground is of so little value without labor that I have heard it affirmed that in Spain itself a man may be permitted to plow, sow, and reap, without being disturbed, upon land he has no other title to, but only his making use of it. But, on the contrary, the inhabitants think themselves beholden to him who, by his industry neglected, and consequently waste land, has increased the stock of corn, which they wanted. But be this as it will, which I lay no stress on, this I dare boldly affirm, that the same rule of propriety—viz., that every man should have as much as he could make use of, would hold still in the world, without straitening anybody, since there is land enough in the world to suffice double the inhabitants, had not the invention of money, and the tacit agreement of men to put a value on it, introduced (by consent) larger possessions and a right to them; which, how it has done, I shall by and by show more at large.

* * *

Here Locke starts to explore how men will want to accumulate more and more property, especially after money is invented, and thus need law to provide and protect freedom against the violence of their appetites.[7]

45. Thus labor, in the beginning, gave a right of property, wherever any one was pleased to employ it, upon what was common, which remained a long while, the far greater part, and is yet more than mankind makes use of Men at first, for the most part, contented themselves with what unassisted Nature offered to their necessities; and though afterwards, in some parts of the world, where the increase of people and stock, with the use of money, had made land scarce, and so of some value, the several communities settled the bounds of their distinct territories, and, by laws, within themselves, regulated the properties of the private men of their society, and so, by compact and agreement, settled the property which labor and industry began. And the leagues that have been made between several states and kingdoms, either expressly or tacitly disowning all claim and right to the land in the other's possession, have, by common consent, given up their pretences to their natural common right, which originally they had to those countries; and so have, by positive agreement, settled a property amongst themselves, in distinct parts of the world; yet there are still great tracts of ground to be found, which the inhabitants thereof, not having joined with the rest of mankind in the consent of the use of their common money, lie waste, and are more than the people who dwell on it, do, or can make use of, and so still lie in common; though this can scarce happen amongst that part of mankind that have consented to the use of money.

46. The greatest part of things really useful to the life of man, and such as the necessity of subsisting made the first commoners of the world look after—as it does the Americans now—are generally things of short duration, such as—if they

---

7. C.B. MacPherson summarized Locke's thought as follows: "Man is naturally infinitely desirous; he is rational enough to see that to give that desire full rein he needs to adhere to bargains and contracts; but his exorbitant desire will lead him to disregard his obligations unless there is a superior authority to enforce them. This is what requires the institution of government." John Locke, *Second Treatise of Government*, xviii.

are not consumed by use—will decay and perish of themselves. Gold, silver, and diamonds are things that fancy or agreement has put the value on, more than real use and the necessary support of life. Now of those good things which Nature has provided in common, every one has a right (as has been said) to as much as he could use; and had a property in all he could affect with his labor; all that his industry could extend to, to alter from the state Nature had put it in, was his. He that gathered a hundred bushels of acorns or apples had thereby a property in them; they were his goods as soon as gathered. He was only to look that he used them before they spoiled, else he took more than his share, and robbed others. And, indeed, it was a foolish thing, as well as dishonest, to hoard up more than he could make use of. If he gave away a part to anybody else, so that it perished not uselessly in his possession, these he also made use of. And if he also bartered away plums that would have rotted in a week, for nuts that would last good for his eating a whole year, he did no injury; he wasted not the common stock; destroyed no part of the portion of goods that belonged to others, so long as nothing perished uselessly in his hands. Again, if he would give his nuts for a piece of metal, pleased with its color, or exchange his sheep for shells, or wool for a sparkling pebble or a diamond, and keep those by him all his life, he invaded not the right of others; he might heap up as much of these durable things as he pleased; the exceeding of the bounds of his just property not lying in the largeness of his possession, but the perishing of anything uselessly in it.

47. And thus came in the use of money; some lasting thing that men might keep without spoiling, and that, by mutual consent, men would take in exchange for the truly useful but perishable supports of life.

48. And as different degrees of industry were apt to give men possessions in different proportions, so this invention of money gave them the opportunity to continue and enlarge them. For supposing an island, separate from all possible commerce with the rest of the world, wherein there were but a hundred families, but there were sheep, horses, and cows, with other useful animals, wholesome fruits, and land enough for corn for a hundred thousand times as many, but nothing in the island, either because of its commonness or perishableness, fit to supply the place of money. What reason could anyone have there to enlarge his possessions beyond the use of his family, and a plentiful supply to its consumption, either in what their own industry produced, or they could barter for like perishable, useful commodities with others? Where there is not something both lasting and scarce, and so valuable to be hoarded up, there men will not be apt to enlarge their possessions of land, were it never so rich, never so free for them to take. For I ask, what would a man value ten thousand or an hundred thousand acres of excellent land, ready cultivated and well stocked, too, with cattle, in the middle of the inland parts of America, where he had no hopes of commerce with other parts of the world, to draw money to him by the sale of the product? It would not be worth the enclosing, and we should see him give up again to the wild common of Nature

whatever was more than would supply the conveniences of life, to be had there for him and his family.

49. Thus, in the beginning, all the world was America, and more so than that is now; for no such thing as money was anywhere known. Find out something that has the use and value of money amongst his neighbors, you shall see the same man will begin presently to enlarge his possessions.

50. But, since gold and silver, being little useful to the life of man, in proportion to food, raiment, and carriage, has its value only from the consent of men—whereof labor yet makes in great part the measure—it is plain that the consent of men have agreed to a disproportionate and unequal possession of the earth—I mean out of the bounds of society and compact; for in governments the laws regulate it; they having, by consent, found out and agreed in a way how a man may, rightfully and without injury, possess more than he himself can make use of by receiving gold and silver, which may continue long in a man's possession without decaying for the overplus, and agreeing those metals should have a value.

51. And thus, I think, it is very easy to conceive, without any difficulty, how *labor could at first begin a title of property in the common things of Nature,* and how the spending it upon our uses bounded it; so that there could then be no reason of quarrelling about title, nor any doubt about the largeness of possession it gave. Right and convenience went together. For as a man had a right to all he could employ his labor upon, so he had no temptation to labor for more than he could make use of. This left no room for controversy about the title, nor for encroachment on the right of others. What portion a man carved to himself was easily seen; and it was useless, as well as dishonest, to carve himself too much, or take more than he needed.

* * *

57. The law that was to govern Adam was the same that was to govern all his posterity, the law of reason. But his offspring having another way of entrance into the world, different from him, by a natural birth, that produced them ignorant, and without the use of reason, they were not presently under that law. For nobody can be under a law that is not promulgated to him; and this law being promulgated or made known by reason only, he that is not come to the use of his reason cannot be said to be under this law; and Adam's children being not presently as soon as born under this law of reason, were not presently free. *For law, in its true notion, is not so much the limitation as the direction of a free and intelligent agent to his proper interest, and prescribes no farther than is for the general good of those under that law.* Could they be happier without it, the law, as a useless thing, would of itself vanish; and that ill deserves the name of confinement which hedges us in only from bogs and precipices. *So that however it may be mistaken, the end of law is not to abolish or restrain, but to preserve and enlarge freedom.* For in all the states of created beings, capable of laws, where there is no law there is no freedom. *For liberty is to be free from restraint and violence from others, which cannot be where there is no law; and is not, as we are told,*

"a liberty for every man to do what he lists." For who could be free, when every other man's humor might domineer over him? But a liberty to dispose and order freely as he lists his person, actions, possessions, and his whole property within the allowance of those laws under which he is, and therein not to be subject to the arbitrary will of another, but freely follow his own.

* * *

63. The freedom then of man, and liberty of acting according to his own will, is grounded on his having reason, which is able to instruct him in that law he is to govern himself by, and make him know how far he is left to the freedom of his own will. To turn him loose to an unrestrained liberty, before he has reason to guide him, is not allowing him the privilege of his nature to be free, but to thrust him out amongst brutes, and abandon him to a state as wretched and as much beneath that of a man as theirs.

* * *

Chapter VII, Of Political or Civil Society

87. *Man being born, as has been proved, with a title to perfect freedom and an uncontrolled enjoyment of all the rights and privileges of the law of Nature, equally with any other man,* or number of men in the world, has by nature a power not only to preserve his property—that is, his life, liberty, and estate, against the injuries and attempts of other men, but to judge of and punish the breaches of that law in others, as he is persuaded the offense deserves, even with death itself, in crimes where the heinousness of the fact, in his opinion, requires it. But because no political society can be, nor subsist, without having in itself the power to preserve the property, and in order thereunto punish the offenses of all those of that society, there, and there only, is political society where every one of the members has quitted this natural power, resigned it up into the hands of the community in all cases that exclude him not from appealing for protection to the law established by it. And thus all private judgment of every particular member being excluded, the community comes to be umpire, and by understanding indifferent rules and men authorized by the community for their execution, decides all the differences that may happen between any members of that society concerning any matter of right, and punishes those offences which any member has committed against the society with such penalties as the law has established; whereby it is easy to discern who are, and are not, in political society together. Those who are united into one body, and have a common established law and judicature to appeal to, with authority to decide controversies between them and punish offenders, are in civil society one with another; but those who have no such common appeal, I mean on earth, are still in the state of Nature, each being where there is no other,

Political society is founded when men give up the freedom and equality of the state of nature, exchanging it for the protection offered by numbers of men who can punish transgressions impartially through legislation for the public good.

judge for himself and executioner; which is, as I have before showed it, the perfect state of Nature.

88. And thus the commonwealth comes by a power to set down what punishment shall belong to the several transgressions they think worthy of it, committed amongst the members of that society (which is the power of making laws), as well as it has the power to punish any injury done unto any of its members by any one that is not of it (which is the power of war and peace); and all this for the preservation of the property of all the members of that society, as far as is possible. But though every man entered into society has quitted his power to punish offenses against the law of Nature in prosecution of his own private judgment, yet with the judgment of offenses which he has given up to the legislative, in all cases where he can appeal to the magistrate, he has given up a right to the commonwealth to employ his force for the execution of the judgments of the commonwealth whenever he shall be called to it, which, indeed, are his own judgments, they being made by himself or his representative. And herein we have the original of the legislative and executive power of civil society, which is to judge by standing laws how far offenses are to be punished when committed within the commonwealth; and also by occasional judgments founded on the present circumstances of the fact, how far injuries from without are to be vindicated, and in both these to employ all the force of all the members when there shall be need.

89. *Wherever, therefore, any number of men so unite into one society as to quit everyone his executive power of the law of Nature, and to resign it to the public, there and there only is a political or civil society.* And this is done wherever any number of men, in the state of Nature, enter into society to make one people one body politic under one supreme government: or else when any one joins himself to, and incorporates with any government already made; for hereby he authorizes the society, or which is all one, the legislative thereof, to make laws for him as the public good of the society shall require, to the execution whereof his own assistance (as to his own decrees) is due. And this puts men out of a state of Nature into that of a commonwealth, by setting up a judge on earth with authority to determine all the controversies and redress the injuries that may happen to any member of the commonwealth, which judge is the legislative or magistrates appointed by it. And wherever there are any number of men, however associated, that have no such decisive power to appeal to, there they are still in the state of Nature.

90. And hence it is evident that absolute monarchy, which by some men is counted for the only government in the world, is indeed inconsistent with civil society, and so can be not [a] form of civil government at all. *For the end of civil society being to avoid and remedy those inconveniences of the state of Nature which necessarily follow from every man's being judge in his own case,* by setting up a known authority to which every one of that society may appeal upon any injury received, or controversy that may arise, and which every one of the society ought to obey. Wherever any persons are who have not such an authority to appeal to, and decide

any difference between them there, those persons are still in the state of Nature. And so is every absolute prince in respect of those who are under his dominion.[8]

* * *

Chapter VIII, Of the Beginning of Political Societies

95. *MEN being, as has been said, by nature all free, equal, and independent, no one can be put out of this estate and subjected to the political power of another without his own consent*, which is done by agreeing with other men, to join and unite into a community for their comfortable, safe, and peaceable living, one amongst another, in a secure enjoyment of their properties, and a greater security against any that are not of it. This any number of men may do, because it injures not the freedom of the rest; they are left, as they were, in the liberty of the state of Nature. When any number of men have so consented to make one community or government, they are thereby presently incorporated, and make one body politic, wherein the majority have a right to act and conclude the rest.

Essentials for creating a just political society: 1) that no one can lose his property without giving his consent, and 2) that majority rule grants that consent on behalf of all individuals within the society, even when a person in the minority opposes it.

96. For, when any number of men have, *by the consent of every individual, made a community, they have thereby made that community one body, with a power to act as one body, which is only by the will and determination of the majority.* For that which acts any community, being only the consent of the individuals of it, and it being one body, must move one way, it is necessary the body should move that way whither the greater force carries it, which is the consent of the majority, or else it is impossible it should act or continue one body, one community, which the consent of every individual that united into it agreed that it should; and so everyone is bound by that consent to be concluded by the majority. And therefore we see that in assemblies empowered to act by positive laws where no number is set by that positive law which empowers them, the act of the majority passes for the act of the whole, and of course determines as having, by the law of Nature and reason, the power of the whole.

97. And thus every man, by consenting with others to make one body politic under one government, puts himself under an obligation to every one of that society to submit to the determination of the majority, and to be concluded by it; or else this original compact, whereby he with others incorporates into one society, would signify nothing, and be no compact if he be left free and under no other ties than he was in before in the state of Nature. For what appearance would there be of any compact? What new engagement if he were no farther tied by any decrees of the society than he himself thought fit and did actually consent to? This would be still as great a liberty as he himself had before his compact, or anyone else in

---

8. Consider this section when reading Thomas Paine's indictment of monarchs in general and George III in particular.

the state of Nature, who may submit himself and consent to any acts of it if he thinks fit.

98. For if the consent of the majority shall not in reason be received as the act of the whole, and conclude every individual, nothing but the consent of every individual can make anything to be the act of the whole, which, considering the infirmities of health and avocations of business, which in a number though much less than that of a commonwealth, will necessarily keep many away from the public assembly; and the variety of opinions and [contrary] interests which unavoidably happen in all collections of men, it is next impossible ever to be had. . . . Such a constitution as this would make the mighty leviathan of a shorter duration than the feeblest creatures, and not let it outlast the day it was born in, which cannot be supposed till we can think that rational creatures should desire and constitute societies only to be dissolved. For where the majority cannot conclude the rest, there they cannot act as one body, and consequently will be immediately dissolved again.

99. Whosoever, therefore, out of a state of Nature unite into a community, must be understood to give up all the power necessary to the ends for which they unite into society to the majority of the community, unless they expressly agreed in any number greater than the majority. And this is done by barely agreeing to unite into one political society, which is all the compact that is, or needs be, between the individuals that enter into or make up a commonwealth. And thus, that which begins and actually constitutes any political society is nothing but the consent of any number of freemen capable of majority, to unite and incorporate into such a society. And this is that, and that only, which did or could give beginning to any lawful government in the world.

Thus, not all consent is actual—agreement is not provided by those in the minority or who do not participate—but the majority has legitimate authority nonetheless due to how the civil society was originally formed.

* * *

119. Every man being, as has been showed, naturally free, and nothing being able to put him into subjection to any earthly power, but only his own consent, it is to be considered what shall be understood to be a sufficient declaration of a man's consent to make him subject to the laws of any government. There is a common distinction of an express and a tacit consent, which will concern our present case. Nobody doubts but an express consent of any man, entering into any society, makes him a perfect member of that society, a subject of that government. The difficulty is, what ought to be looked upon as a tacit consent, and how far it binds—i.e., how far anyone shall be looked on to have consented, and thereby submitted to any government, where he has made no expressions of it at all. And to this I say, *that every man that has any possession or enjoyment of any part of the dominions of any government does hereby give his tacit consent, and is as far forth obliged to obedience to the laws of that government, during such*

Consent exists not merely when one participates through affirmative acts such as voting, but when one possesses and enjoys property within a jurisdiction. This is called "tacit consent," and can always be revoked by leaving.

enjoyment, as anyone under it, whether this his possession be of land to him and his heirs forever, or a lodging only for a week; or whether it be barely travelling freely on the highway; and, in effect, it reaches as far as the very being of anyone within the territories of that government.

120. To understand this the better, it is fit to consider that every man when he at first incorporates himself into any commonwealth, he, by his uniting himself thereunto, annexes also, and submits to the community those possessions which he has, or shall acquire, that do not already belong to any other government. For it would be a direct contradiction for anyone to enter into society with others for the securing and regulating of property, and yet to suppose his land, whose property is to be regulated by the laws of the society, should be exempt from the jurisdiction of that government to which he himself, and the property of the land, is a subject. By the same act, therefore, whereby anyone unites his person, which was before free, to any commonwealth, by the same he unites his possessions, which were before free, to it also; and they become, both of them, person and possession, subject to the government and dominion of that commonwealth as long as it has a being. Whoever therefore, from thenceforth, by inheritance, purchases permission, or otherwise enjoys any part of the land so annexed to, and under the government of that commonweal, must take it with the condition it is under—that is, of submitting to the government of the commonwealth, under whose jurisdiction it is, as far forth as any subject of it.

121. But since the government has a direct jurisdiction only over the land and reaches the possessor of it (before he has actually incorporated himself in the society) only as he dwells upon and enjoys that, the obligation anyone is under by virtue of such enjoyment to submit to the government begins and ends with the enjoyment; so that whenever the owner, who has given nothing but such a tacit consent to the government will, by donation, sale or otherwise, quit the said possession, he is at liberty to go and incorporate himself into any other commonwealth, or agree with others to begin a new one in *vacuis locis,*[9] in any part of the world they can find free and unpossessed; whereas he that has once, by actual agreement and any express declaration, given his consent to be of any commonweal, is perpetually and indispensably obliged to be, and remain unalterably a subject to it, and can never be again in the liberty of the state of Nature, unless by any calamity the government he was under comes to be dissolved.

122. But submitting to the laws of any country, living quietly and enjoying privileges and protection under them, makes not a man a member of that society; it is only a local protection and homage due to and from all those who, not being in a state of war, come within the territories belonging to any government, to all parts whereof the force of its law extends. But this no more makes a man a member of that society, a perpetual subject of that commonwealth, than it would make a

---

9. "In empty places" (Latin).

man a subject to another in whose family he found it convenient to abide for some time, though, while he continued in it, he were obliged to comply with the laws and submit to the government he found there. And thus we see that foreigners, by living all their lives under another government, and enjoying the privileges and protection of it, though they are bound, even in conscience, to submit to its administration as far forth as any denizen, yet do not thereby come to be subjects or members of that commonwealth. Nothing can make any man so but his actually entering into it by positive engagement and express promise and compact. This is that which, I think, concerning the beginning of political societies, and that consent which makes any one a member of any commonwealth.

Chapter IX, Of the Ends of Political Society and Government

123. IF man in the state of Nature be so free as has been said, if he be absolute lord of his own person and possessions, equal to the greatest and subject to nobody, why will he part with his freedom, this empire, and subject himself to the dominion and control of any other power? To which it is obvious to answer, that though in the state of Nature he has such a right, yet the enjoyment of it is very uncertain and constantly exposed to the invasion of others; for all being kings as much as he, every man his equal, and the greater part no strict observers of equity and justice, the enjoyment of the property he has in this state is very unsafe, very insecure. This makes him willing to quit this condition which, however free, is full of fears and continual dangers; and it is not without reason that he seeks out and is willing to join in society with others who are already united, or have a mind to unite for the mutual preservation of their lives, liberties and estates, which I call by the general name—property.

The main end of political society is the preservation of property. This goal is "very uncertain and constantly exposed to the invasion of others" in the state of nature. There are three ways in which governments are better than the state of nature at protecting property.

124. The great and chief end, therefore, of men uniting into commonwealths, and putting themselves under government, is the preservation of their property; to which in the state of Nature there are many things wanting.

First, there wants an established, settled, known law, received and allowed by common consent to be the standard of right and wrong, and the common measure to decide all controversies between them. For though the law of Nature be plain and intelligible to all rational creatures, yet men, being biased by their interest, as well as ignorant for want of study of it, are not apt to allow of it as a law binding to them in the application of it to their particular cases.[10]

125. Secondly, in the state of Nature there wants a known and indifferent judge, with authority to determine all differences according to the established law. For every one in that state being both judge and executioner of the law of Nature,

---

10. This point is a variation on that found in Section 13 and the next two sections, which maintain that human nature, flawed by self-interest and bias, leads them to ignore the law of nature and thus ruin the state of nature.

men being partial to themselves, passion and revenge is very apt to carry them too far, and with too much heat in their own cases, as well as negligence and unconcernedness, make them too remiss in other men's.

126. Thirdly, in the state of Nature there often wants power to back and support the sentence when right, and to give it due execution. They who by any injustice offended will seldom fail where they are able by force to make good their injustice. Such resistance many times makes the punishment dangerous, and frequently destructive to those who attempt it.

127. Thus mankind, notwithstanding all the privileges of the state of Nature, being but in an ill condition while they remain in it are quickly driven into society. Hence it comes to pass, that we seldom find any number of men live any time together in this state. The inconveniencies that they are therein exposed to by the irregular and uncertain exercise of the power every man has of punishing the transgressions of others, make them take sanctuary under the established laws of government, and therein seek the preservation of their property. It is this that makes them so willingly give up every one his single power of punishing to be exercised by such alone as shall be appointed to it amongst them, and by such rules as the community, or those authorized by them to that purpose, shall agree on. And in this we have the original right and rise of both the legislative and executive power as well as of the governments and societies themselves.

128. For in the state of Nature to omit the liberty he has of innocent delights, a man has two powers. The first is to do whatsoever he thinks fit for the preservation of himself and others within the permission of the law of Nature; by which law, common to them all, he and all the rest of mankind are one community, make up one society distinct from all other creatures, and were it not for the corruption and viciousness of degenerate men, there would be no need of any other, no necessity that men should separate from this great and natural community, and associate into lesser combinations. The other power a man has in the state of Nature is the power to punish the crimes committed against that law. Both these he gives up when he joins in a private, if I may so call it, or particular political society, and incorporates into any commonwealth separate from the rest of mankind.

129. The first power—viz., of doing whatsoever he thought fit for the preservation of himself and the rest of mankind, he gives up to be regulated by laws made by the society, so far forth as the preservation of himself and the rest of that society shall require; which laws of the society in many things confine the liberty he had by the law of Nature.

130. Secondly, the power of punishing he wholly gives up, and engages his natural force, which he might before employ in the execution of the law of Nature, by his own single authority, as he thought fit, to assist the executive power of the society as the law thereof shall require. For being now in a new state, wherein he is to enjoy many conveniences from the labor, assistance, and society of others in the same community, as well as protection from its whole strength, he is to part also with as much of his natural liberty, in providing for himself, as the good,

Locke sets up a standard against which to measure a government (does it do better in preserving life, liberty, and property than the state of nature?), leaving for later an exploration of how the people can act if the government is found wanting.

prosperity, and safety of the society shall require, which is not only necessary but just, since the other members of the society do the like.

131. But though *men when they enter into society give up the equality, liberty, and executive power they had in the state of Nature into the hands of the society*, to be so far disposed of by the legislative as the good of the society shall require, yet it being only with an *intention in every one the better to preserve himself, his liberty and property* (for no rational creature can be supposed to change his condition with an intention to be worse), the power of the society or legislative constituted by them can never be supposed to extend farther than the common good, but is obliged to secure every one's property by providing against those three defects above mentioned that made the state of Nature so unsafe and uneasy. And so, whoever has the legislative or supreme power of any commonwealth, is bound to govern by established standing laws, promulgated and known to the people, and not by extemporary decrees, by indifferent and upright judges, who are to decide controversies by those laws; and to employ the force of the community at home only in the execution of such laws, or abroad to prevent or redress foreign injuries and secure the community from inroads and invasion. And all this to be directed to no other end but the peace, safety, and public good of the people.

* * *

Chapter XI, Of the Extent of the Legislative Power

134. THE great end of men's entering into society being the enjoyment of their properties in peace and safety, and the great instrument and means of that being the laws established in that society, the first and fundamental positive law of all commonwealths is the establishing of the legislative power, as the first and fundamental natural law which is to govern even the legislative itself is the preservation of the society and (as far as will consist with the public good) of every person in it.

The legislature is the key element of government; in this chapter Locke illustrates what a legislature should do (serve only the public good; tax only with the consent of the majority) and should not do (issue arbitrary decrees; take property without consent).

This legislative is not only the supreme power of the commonwealth, but sacred and unalterable in the hands where the community has once placed it. Nor can any edict of anybody else, in what form soever conceived, or by what power soever backed, have the force and obligation of a law which has not its sanction from that legislative which the public has chosen and appointed; for without this the law could not have that which is absolutely necessary to its being a law, the consent of the society, over whom nobody can have a power to make laws[11] but by their own consent and by authority received from them . . .

---

11. In a portion of the treatise not included here, Locke quotes Hooker at length on whether past generations of legislation have any sway in the present. Locke argues that the current legislature can always revoke old laws; thus the current legislature is said to consent to the old laws by its silence.

135. Though the legislative . . . be the supreme power in every commonwealth, yet, first, it is not, nor can possibly be, absolutely arbitrary over the lives and fortunes of the people. For it being but the joint power of every member of the society given up to that person or assembly which is legislator, it can be no more than those persons had in a state of Nature before they entered into society, and gave it up to the community. For nobody can transfer to another more power than he has in himself, and nobody has an absolute arbitrary power over himself, or over any other, to destroy his own life, or take away the life or property of another. A man, as has been proved, cannot subject himself to the arbitrary power of another; and having, in the state of Nature, no arbitrary power over the life, liberty, or possession of another, but only so much as the law of Nature gave him for the preservation of himself and the rest of mankind, this is all he does, or can give up to the commonwealth, and by it to the legislative power. . . . It is limited to the public good of the society. It is a power that has no other end but preservation, and therefore can never have a right to destroy, enslave, or designedly to impoverish the subjects; the obligations of the law of Nature cease not in society, but only in many cases are drawn closer, and have, by human laws, known penalties annexed to them to enforce their observation. Thus the law of Nature stands as an eternal rule to all men, legislators as well as others. The rules that they make for, other men's actions must, as well as their own and other men's actions, be conformable to the law of Nature—i.e., to the will of God, of which that is a declaration, and the fundamental law of Nature being the preservation of mankind, no human sanction can be good or valid against it.

136. Secondly, *the legislative or supreme authority cannot assume to itself a power to rule by extemporary arbitrary decrees,* but is bound to dispense justice and decide the rights of the subject by promulgated standing laws, and known authorized judges. . . . To avoid these inconveniences which disorder men's properties in the state of Nature, men unite into societies that they may have the united strength of the whole society to secure and defend their properties, and may have standing rules to bound it by which every one may know what is his. To this end it is that men give up all their natural power to the society they enter into, and the community put the legislative power into such hands as they think fit, with this trust, that they shall be governed by declared laws, or else their peace, quiet, and property will still be at the same uncertainty as it was in the state of Nature.

No matter how much they desire to serve the public good, legislatures must still use standing laws and known judges to avoid exerting arbitrary power and instances of men judging their own cases.

137. Absolute arbitrary power, or governing without settled standing laws, can neither of them consist with the ends of society and government, which men would not quit the freedom of the state of Nature for . . . This were to put [men] into a worse condition than the state of Nature, wherein they had a liberty to defend their right against the injuries of others, and were upon equal terms of force to maintain it, whether invaded by a single man or many in combination. Whereas by supposing they have given up themselves to the absolute arbitrary power and will of a legislator, they have disarmed themselves, and armed him to make a prey

of them when he pleases . . . And, therefore, whatever form the commonwealth is under, the ruling power ought to govern by declared and received laws, and not by extemporary dictates and undetermined resolutions, for then mankind will be in a far worse condition than in the state of Nature if they shall have armed one or a few men with the joint power of a multitude, to force them to obey at pleasure the exorbitant and unlimited decrees of their sudden thoughts, or unrestrained, and till that moment, unknown wills, without having any measures set down which may guide and justify their actions.

* * *

138. *Thirdly, the supreme power cannot take from any man any part of his property without his own consent.* For the preservation of property being the end of government, and that for which men enter into society, it necessarily supposes and requires that the people should have property, without which they must be supposed to lose that by entering into society which was the end for which they entered into it; too gross an absurdity for any man to own. Men, therefore, in society having property, they have such a right to the goods, which by the law of the community are theirs, that nobody has a right to take them, or any part of them, from them without their own consent; without this they have no property at all. For I have truly no property in that which another can by right take from me when he pleases against my consent. Hence it is a mistake to think that the supreme or legislative power of any commonwealth can do what it will, and dispose of the estates of the subject arbitrarily, or take any part of them at pleasure.

Taxation must be done by legislative majority according to the rule forbidding property to be taken without consent. It remains to be resolved who may give such consent—Parliament or the colonial legislature—in New York in 1775.

139. But government, into whatsoever hands it is put, being as I have before shown, entrusted with this condition, and for this end, that men might have and secure their properties, the prince or senate, *however it may have power to make laws for the regulating of property between the subjects one amongst another, yet can never have a power to take to themselves the whole, or any part of the subjects' property, without their own consent; for this would be in effect to leave them no property at all.* And to let us see that even absolute power, where it is necessary, is not arbitrary by being absolute, but is still limited by that reason and confined to those ends which required it in some cases to be absolute, we need look no farther than the common practice of martial discipline. For the preservation of the army, and in it of the whole commonwealth, requires an absolute obedience to the command of every superior officer, and it is justly death to disobey or dispute the most dangerous or unreasonable of them; but yet we see that neither the sergeant that could command a soldier to march up to the mouth of a cannon, or stand in a breach where he is almost sure to perish, can command that soldier to give him one penny of his money; nor the general that can condemn him to death for deserting his post, or not obeying the most desperate orders, cannot yet with all his absolute power of life and death dispose of

one farthing of that soldier's estate, or seize one jot of his goods; whom yet he can command anything, and hang for the least disobedience. Because such a blind obedience is necessary to that end for which the commander has his power—viz., the preservation of the rest, but the disposing of his goods has nothing to do with it.

140. It is true governments cannot be supported without great charge, and it is fit every one who enjoys his share of the protection should pay out of his estate his proportion for the maintenance of it. But still it must be with his own consent—i.e., the consent of the majority, giving it either by themselves or their representatives chosen by them; for if any one shall claim a power to lay and levy taxes on the people by his own authority, and without such consent of the people, he thereby invades the fundamental law of property, and subverts the end of government.[12] For what property have I in that which another may by right take when he pleases to himself?

141. Fourthly. The legislative cannot transfer the power of making laws to any other hands, for it being but a delegated power from the people, they who have it cannot pass it over to others. The people alone can appoint the form of the commonwealth, which is by constituting the legislative, and appointing in whose hands that shall be. . . .

142. These are the bounds which the trust that is put in them by the society and the law of God and Nature have set to the legislative power of every commonwealth, in all forms of government. First: They are to govern by promulgated established laws, not to be varied in particular cases, but to have one rule for rich and poor, for the favorite at Court, and the countryman at plough. Secondly: These laws also ought to be designed for no other end ultimately but the *good of the people.* Thirdly: *They must not raise taxes on the property of the people without the consent of the people given by themselves or their deputies.* . . . Fourthly: Legislative neither must nor can transfer the power of making laws to anybody else, or place it anywhere but where the people have.

* * *

Chapter XIII, Of the Subordination of the Powers of the Commonwealth

149. THOUGH in a constituted commonwealth standing upon its own basis and acting according to its own nature—that is, acting for the preservation of the community, there can be but one supreme power, which is the legislative, to which all

---

12. Here and in the summary in section 142 is the whole of Locke's discussion of taxation, needed by government, proper if done with the consent of the majority (even if only the majority of legislators), and illegitimate if done without such consent. A true Lockean would say "no taxation without consent" rather than "no taxation without representation," a phrase that has often been used in this debate.

Popular sovereignty, the final and unalterable power of the people to remove or change a legislature when the legislature acts contrary to the people's trust, is claimed here. But when is the appropriate time to use this power for the good of the people?

the rest are and must be subordinate, yet the legislative being only a fiduciary[13] power to act for certain ends, there remains still in the people a supreme power to remove or alter the legislative, when they find the legislative act contrary to the trust reposed in them. For all power given with trust for the attaining an end being limited by that end, whenever that end is manifestly neglected or opposed, the trust must necessarily be forfeited, and the power devolve into the hands of those that gave it, who may place it anew where they shall think best for their safety and security. And thus the community perpetually retains a supreme power of saving themselves from the attempts and designs of anybody, even of their legislators, whenever they shall be so foolish or so wicked as to lay and carry on designs against the liberties and properties of the subject. . . .

158. *Salus populi suprema lex*[14] is certainly so just and fundamental a rule, that he who sincerely follows it cannot dangerously err. . . . Whenever the people shall choose their representatives upon just and undeniably equal measures, suitable to the original frame of the government, it cannot be doubted to be the will and act of the society, whoever permitted or proposed to them so to do.

* * *

Chapter XV, Of Paternal, Political and Despotical Power, Considered Together

172. Thirdly, despotical power is an absolute, arbitrary power one man has over another, to take away his life whenever he pleases; and this is a power which neither Nature gives, for it has made no such distinction between one man and another, nor compact can convey. For man, not having such an arbitrary power over his own life, cannot give another man such a power over it, but it is the effect only of forfeiture which the aggressor makes of his own life when he puts himself into the state of war with another. For having quitted reason, which God has given to be the rule betwixt man and man, and the peaceable ways which that teaches, and made use of force to compass his unjust ends upon another where he has no right,

---

13. "Fiduciary" means to act in trust for another person, or in this case, for the people. A fiduciary's responsibility is to serve the interests of the principle party (here, the people); it is the highest standard of duty the law imposes on a relationship. Locke maintains that if the fiduciary (the legislature) is seen to breach the trust, the people can cancel the relationship. He concludes from this, startlingly, that the people have the supreme power to overthrow the government.

14. "The good of the people is the supreme law" (Latin), a phrase widely known in political circles.

he renders himself liable to be destroyed by his adversary whenever he can, as any other noxious and brutish creature that is destructive to his being. And thus captives, taken in a just and lawful war, and such only, are subject to a despotical power, which, as it arises not from compact, so neither is it capable of any, but is the state of war continued. For what compact can be made with a man that is not master of his own life? What condition can he perform? And if he be once allowed to be master of his own life, the despotical, arbitrary power of his master ceases. He that is master of himself and his own life has a right, too, to the means of preserving it; so that as soon as compact enters, slavery ceases, and he so far quits his absolute power and puts an end to the state of war who enters into conditions with his captive.

Locke argues that paternal power (such as that claimed by a king) can be applied to children only before they reach the ability to reason, which does not describe adult males in a civil society.

173. Nature gives the first of these—viz., paternal power to parents for the benefit of their children during their minority, to supply their want of ability and understanding how to manage their property. (By property I must be understood here, as in other places, to mean that property which men have in their persons as well as goods.) Voluntary agreement gives the second—viz., political power to governors, for the benefit of their subjects, to secure them in the possession and use of their properties. And forfeiture gives the third—despotical power to lords for their own benefit over those who are stripped of all property.

174. He that shall consider the distinct rise and extent, and the different ends of these several powers, will plainly see that paternal power comes as far short of that of the magistrate as despotical exceeds it; and that absolute dominion, however placed, is so far from being one kind of civil society that it is as inconsistent with it as slavery is with property. Paternal power is only where minority makes the child incapable to manage his property; political where men have property in their own disposal; and despotical over such as have no property at all.

* * *

Chapter XIX, Of the Dissolution of Government

211. HE that will, with any clearness, speak of the dissolution of government, ought in the first place to distinguish between the dissolution of the society and the dissolution of the government. That which makes the community, and brings men out of the loose state of Nature into one politic society, is the agreement which everyone has with the rest to incorporate and act as one body, and so be one distinct commonwealth. *The usual, and almost only way whereby this union is dissolved, is the inroad of foreign force making a conquest upon them.* For in that case (not being able to maintain and support themselves as one entire and independent body) the union belonging to that body, which consisted therein, must necessarily cease, and so everyone return to the state he was in before, with a liberty to shift for himself

and provide for his own safety, as he thinks fit, in some other society. Whenever the society is dissolved, it is certain the government of that society cannot remain. Thus conquerors' swords often cut up governments by the roots, and mangle societies to pieces, separating the subdued or scattered multitude from the protection of and dependence on that society which ought to have preserved them from violence. The world is too well instructed in, and too forward to allow of this way of dissolving of governments, to need any more to be said of it; and there wants not much argument to prove that where the society is dissolved, the government cannot remain; that being as impossible as for the frame of a house to subsist when the materials of it are scattered and displaced by a whirlwind, or jumbled into a confused heap by an earthquake.

212. Besides this overturning from without, governments are dissolved from within:

. . . *When the legislative is altered* . . . ; it is in their legislative that the members of a commonwealth are united and combined together into one coherent living body. This is the soul that gives form, life, and unity to the commonwealth; from hence the several members have their mutual influence, sympathy, and connection; and therefore when the legislative is broken, or dissolved, dissolution and death follows. For the essence and union of the society consisting in having one will, the legislative, when once established by the majority, has the declaring and, as it were, keeping of that will. . . . *When any one, or more, shall take upon them to make laws whom the people have not appointed so to do, they make laws without authority, which the people are not therefore bound to obey*; by which means they come again to be out of subjection, and may constitute to themselves a new legislative, as they think best, being in full liberty to resist the force of those who, without authority, would impose anything upon them. Everyone is at the disposure of his own will, when those who had, by the delegation of the society, the declaring of the public will, are excluded from it, and others usurp the place who have no such authority or delegation.

Locke establishes the conditions under which a government can be considered tyrannical—and the conditions under which the people may, or may not, exercise their sovereign power to overthrow that government.

213. This being usually brought about by such in the commonwealth, who misuse the power they have, it is hard to consider it [correctly], and know at whose door to lay it, without knowing the form of government in which it happens. Let us suppose, then, the legislative placed in the concurrence of three distinct persons:— First, a single hereditary person having the constant, supreme, executive power, and with it the power of convoking and dissolving the other two within certain periods of time. Secondly, an assembly of hereditary nobility. Thirdly, an assembly of representatives chosen, pro tempore,[15] by the people. Such a form of government supposed, it is evident:

---

15. "For the time being" (Latin).

214. First, that *when such a single person or prince sets up his own arbitrary will in place of the laws which are the will of the society declared by the legislative, then the legislative is changed.* . . . Whoever introduces new laws, not being thereunto authorized, by the fundamental appointment of the society, or subverts the old, disowns and overturns the power by which they were made, and so sets up a new legislative.

215. Secondly, *when the prince hinders the legislative from assembling in its due time,* or from acting freely, pursuant to those ends for which it was constituted, the legislative is altered. . . . [S]o that he who takes away the freedom, or hinders the acting of the legislative in its due seasons, in effect takes away the legislative, and puts an end to the government.

216. Thirdly, when, by the arbitrary power of the prince, the electors or *ways of election are altered without the consent and contrary to the common interest of the people,* there also the legislative is altered. . . .

217. Fourthly, the delivery also of the people into the subjection of a foreign power, either by the prince or by the legislative, is certainly a change of the legislative, and so a dissolution of the government. For the end why people entered into society being to be preserved one entire, free, independent society to be governed by its own laws, this is lost whenever they are given up into the power of another.

Patriots claim that the Coercive Acts, passed by Parliament and implemented by the king through his army, fit the situation described in the following sections. Does this situation describe New York?

* * *

219. There is one way more whereby such a government may be dissolved, and that is: *When he who has the supreme executive power neglects and abandons that charge, so that the laws already made can no longer be put in execution*; this is demonstratively to reduce all to anarchy, and so effectively to dissolve the government. . . . Where there is no longer the administration of justice for the securing of men's rights, nor any remaining power within the community to direct the force, or provide for the necessities of the public, there certainly is no government left. Where the laws cannot be executed it is all one as if there were no laws, and a government without laws is, I suppose, a mystery in politics inconceivable to human capacity, and inconsistent with human society.

220. *In these, and the like cases, when the government is dissolved, the people are at liberty to provide for themselves by erecting a new legislative differing from the other by the change of persons, or form, or both, as they shall find it most for their safety and good.* For the society can never, by the fault of another, lose the native and original right it has to preserve itself, which can only be done by a settled legislative and a fair and impartial execution of the laws made by it. But the state of mankind is not so miserable that they are not capable of using this remedy till it be too late to look for any. To tell people they may provide for themselves by erecting a new legislative, when, by oppression, artifice, or being delivered over to a foreign power, their old one is gone, is only to tell them they may expect relief when it is too late, and the evil is past cure. This is, in effect, no more than to bid them first be slaves, and then

to take care of their liberty, and, when their chains are on, tell them they may act like free men. This, if barely so, is rather mockery than relief, and men can never be secure from tyranny if there be no means to escape it till they are perfectly under it; and, therefore, it is that they have not only a right to get out of it, but to prevent it.

In the following sections, New Yorkers must ask: has Parliament or the king invaded their property, or become arbitrary destroyers of life, liberty, or fortunes in such a way that power has reverted to the people?

221. There is, therefore, secondly, *another way whereby governments are dissolved, and that is, when the legislative, or the prince, either of them act contrary to their trust.* For the legislative acts against the trust reposed in them when they endeavor to invade the property of the subject, and to make themselves, or any part of the community, masters or arbitrary disposers of the lives, liberties, or fortunes of the people.

222. The reason why men enter into society is the preservation of their property; and the end while they choose and authorize a legislative is that there may be laws made, and rules set, as guards and fences to the properties of all the society, to limit the power and moderate the dominion of every part and member of the society. For since it can never be supposed to be the will of the society that the legislative should have a power to destroy that which everyone designs to secure by entering into society, and for which the people submitted themselves to legislators of their own making: *whenever the legislators endeavor to take away and destroy the property of the people, or to reduce them to slavery under arbitrary power, they put themselves into a state of war with the people,* who are thereupon absolved from any farther obedience, and are left to the common refuge which God has provided for all men against force and violence. Whensoever, therefore, the legislative shall transgress this fundamental rule of society, and either by ambition, fear, folly, or corruption, endeavor to grasp themselves, or put into the hands of any other, an absolute power over the lives, liberties, and estates of the people, *by this breach of trust they forfeit the power the people had put into their hands for quite contrary ends, and it devolves to the people, who have a right to resume their original liberty, and by the establishment of a new legislative (such as they shall think fit), provide for their own safety and security, which is the end for which they are in society.* What I have said here concerning the legislative in general holds true also concerning the supreme executor,[16] who having a double trust put in him, both to have a part in the legislative and the supreme execution of the law, acts against both, when he goes about to set up his own arbitrary will as the law of the society. He acts also contrary to his trust when he employs the force, treasure, and offices of the society to corrupt the representatives and gain them

---

16. Meaning the executive branch, the king in a constitutional monarchy. In the remainder of this section, Locke details the common methods used in the 1600s and 1700s by kings to corrupt the legislature to their will and control Parliament.

to his purposes, when he openly pre-engages the electors, and prescribes, to their choice, such whom he has, by solicitation, threats, promises, or otherwise, won to his designs, and employs them to bring in such who have promised beforehand what to vote and what to enact. . . .

223. To this, perhaps, it will be said that the people being ignorant and always discontented, to lay the foundation of government in the unsteady opinion and uncertain humor of the people, is to expose it to certain ruin; and no government will be able long to subsist if the people may set up a new legislative whenever they take offense at the old one. To this I answer, quite the contrary. People are not so easily got out of their old forms as some are apt to suggest. They are hardly to be prevailed with to amend the acknowledged faults in the frame they have been accustomed to. And if there be any original defects, or adventitious ones introduced by time or corruption, it is not an easy thing to get them changed, even when all the world sees there is an opportunity for it. This slowness and aversion in the people to quit their old constitutions has in the many revolutions [that] have been seen in this kingdom, in this and former ages, still kept us to, or after some interval of fruitless attempts, still brought us back again to, our old legislative of king, lords and commons; and whatever provocations have made the crown be taken from some of our princes' heads, they never carried the people so far as to place it in another line.

224. But it will be said this hypothesis lays a ferment for frequent rebellion. To which I answer:

First: no more than any other hypothesis. For when the people are made miserable, and find themselves exposed to the ill usage of arbitrary power, cry up their governors as much as you will for sons of Jupiter, let them be sacred and divine, descended or authorized from Heaven; give them out for whom or what you please, the same will happen. The people generally ill treated, and contrary to right, will be ready upon any occasion to ease themselves of a burden that sits heavy upon them. They will wish and seek for the opportunity, which in the change, weakness, and accidents of human affairs, seldom delays long to offer itself. He must have lived but a little while in the world, who has not seen examples of this in his time; and he must have read very little who cannot produce examples of it in all sorts of governments in the world.

225. Secondly: I answer, such revolutions happen not upon every little mismanagement in public affairs. Great mistakes in the ruling part, many wrong and inconvenient laws, and all the slips of human frailty will be borne by the people without mutiny or murmur. But if a long train of abuses, prevarications, and artifices, all tending the same way, make the design visible to the people, and they cannot but feel what they lie under, and see whither they are going, it is not to be wondered that they should then rouse themselves, and endeavor to put the rule into such hands which may secure to them the ends for which government was at first erected, and without which, ancient names and specious forms are so far from

Carefully scrutinize sections 225 to 230 in light of the history of British actions from 1763 to 1775; are recent events "mismanagement," "mistakes," or part of a "design"?

being better, that they are much worse than the state of Nature or pure anarchy; the inconveniences being all as great and as near, but the remedy farther off and more difficult.

226. Thirdly: I answer, that this power in the people of providing for their safety anew by a new legislative when their legislators have acted contrary to their trust by invading their property, is the best fence against rebellion, and the probable means to hinder it. For rebellion being an opposition, not to persons, but authority, which is founded only in the constitutions and laws of the government: those, whoever they be, who, by force, break through, and, by force, justify their violation of them, are truly and properly rebels. For when men, by entering into society and civil government, have excluded force, and introduced laws for the preservation of property, peace, and unity amongst themselves, those who set up force again in opposition to the laws, do rebel are—that is, bring back again the state of war, and are properly rebels, which they who are in power, by the pretence they have to authority, the temptation of force they have in their hands, and the flattery of those about them being likeliest to do, the proper way to prevent the evil is to show them the danger and injustice of it who are under the greatest temptation to run into it.

227. In both the aforementioned cases, when either the legislative is changed, or the legislators act contrary to the end for which they were constituted, those who are guilty are guilty of rebellion. For if any one by force takes away the established legislative of any society, and the laws by them made, pursuant to their trust, he thereby takes away the umpirage which everyone had consented to for a peaceable decision of all their controversies, and a bar to the state of war amongst them. They who remove or change the legislative take away this decisive power, which nobody can have but by the appointment and consent of the people, and so destroying the authority which the people did, and nobody else can, set up, and introducing a power which the people have not authorized, actually introduce a state of war, which is that of force without authority; and thus by removing the legislative established by the society, in whose decisions the people acquiesced and united as to that of their own will, they untie the knot, and expose the people anew to the state of war. And if those, who by force take away the legislative, are rebels, the legislators themselves, as has been shown, can be no less esteemed so, when they who were set up for the protection and preservation of the people, their liberties and properties shall by force invade and endeavor to take them away; and so they putting themselves into a state of war with those who made them the protectors and guardians of their peace, are properly, and with the greatest aggravation, rebellantes, rebels.

228. But if they who say it lays a foundation for rebellion mean that it may occasion civil wars or intestine broils to tell the people they are absolved from obedience when illegal attempts are made upon their liberties or properties, and may oppose the unlawful violence of those who were their magistrates when they

invade their properties, contrary to the trust put in them, and that, therefore, this doctrine is not to be allowed, being so destructive to the peace of the world; they may as well say, upon the same ground, that honest men may not oppose robbers or pirates, because this may occasion disorder or bloodshed. If any mischief comes in such cases, it is not to be charged upon him who defends his own right, but on him that invades his neighbor's. If the innocent honest man must quietly quit all he has for peace sake to him who will lay violent hands upon it, I desire it may be considered what kind of a peace there will be in the world which consists only in violence and rapine, and which is to be maintained only for the benefit of robbers and oppressors. Who would not think it an admirable peace betwixt the mighty and the mean, when the lamb, without resistance, yielded his throat to be torn by the imperious wolf? . . .

229. The end of government is the good of mankind; and which is best for mankind, that the people should be always exposed to the boundless will of tyranny, or that the rulers should be sometimes liable to be opposed when they grow exorbitant in the use of their power, and employ it for the destruction, and not the preservation, of the properties of their people?

230. Nor let anyone say that mischief can arise from hence as often as it shall please a busy head or turbulent spirit to desire the alteration of the government. It is true such men may stir whenever they please, but it will be only to their own just ruin and perdition. For till the mischief be grown general, and the ill designs of the rulers become visible, or their attempts sensible to the greater part, the people, who are more disposed to suffer than right themselves by resistance, are not apt to stir. The examples of particular injustice or oppression of here and there an unfortunate man moves them not. But if they universally have a persuasion grounded upon manifest evidence that designs are carrying on against their liberties, and the general course and tendency of things cannot but give them strong suspicions of the evil intention of their governors, who is to be blamed for it? Who can help it if they, who might avoid it, bring themselves into this suspicion? . . .

231. That subjects or foreigners attempting by force on the properties of any people may be resisted with force is agreed on all hands; but that magistrates doing the same thing may be resisted, has of late been denied; as if those who had the greatest privileges and advantages by the law had thereby a power to break those laws by which alone they were set in a better place than their brethren; whereas their offence is thereby the greater, both as being ungrateful for the greater share they have by the law, and breaking also that trust which is put into their hands by their brethren.

The logic here is that if you can use force and violence against a foreign invader to protect property and rights, you can use the same force against your own government; political violence, often considered to be treason, may constitute self-defense instead.

232. Whosoever uses force without right—as everyone does in society who does it without law—puts himself into a state of war with those against whom he so uses it, and in that state all former ties are cancelled, all other

rights cease, and everyone has a right to defend himself, and to resist the aggressor. This is so evident that Barclay[17] himself—that great assertor of the power and sacredness of kings—is forced to confess that it is lawful for the people, in some cases, to resist their king, and that, too, in a chapter wherein he pretends to show that the Divine law shuts up the people from all manner of rebellion.

* * *

240. Here it is like the common question will be made: Who shall be judge whether the prince or legislative act contrary to their trust? This, perhaps, ill-affected and factious men may spread amongst the people, when the prince only makes use of his due prerogative. To this I reply, *The people shall be judge*; for who shall be judge whether his trustee or deputy acts well and according to the trust reposed in him, but he who deputes him and must, by having deputed him, have still a power to discard him when he fails in his trust?[18] If this be reasonable in particular cases of private men, why should it be otherwise in that of the greatest moment, where the welfare of millions is concerned and also where the evil, if not prevented, is greater, and the redress very difficult, dear, and dangerous?

> The people have the final decision on whether there has been an abuse of trust. This defines popular sovereignty for American constitutional theory.

241. But, farther, this question, Who shall be judge? cannot mean that there is no judge at all. For where there is no judicature on earth to decide controversies amongst men, God in heaven is judge. He alone, it is true, is judge of the right. But every man is judge for himself, as in all other cases so in this, whether another has put himself into a state of war with him, and whether he should appeal to the supreme judge, as Jephtha did.

242. If a controversy arise betwixt a prince and some of the people in a matter where the law is silent or doubtful, and the thing be of great consequence, I should think *the proper umpire in such a case should be the body of the people*. For in such cases where the prince has a trust reposed in him, and is dispensed from the common, ordinary rules of the law, there, if any men find themselves aggrieved, and think the prince acts contrary to, or beyond that trust, who so proper to judge as the body of the people (who at first lodged that trust in him) how far they meant it should extend? But if the prince, or whoever they be in the administration, decline that way of determination, the appeal then lies nowhere but to Heaven. Force between either persons who have no known superior on earth or, which permits no appeal to a judge on earth, being properly a state of war, wherein the appeal lies only to heaven; and in that state the injured party must judge for himself when he will think fit to make use of that appeal and put himself upon it.

---

17. William Barclay (1546–1608), Scottish jurist and advocate for the divine right of kings.

18. Locke again uses the language of fiduciary duty here to support his argument for the people's sovereignty.

243. To conclude. The power that every individual gave the society when he entered into it can never revert to the individuals again, as long as the society lasts, but will always remain in the community; because without this there can be no community—no commonwealth, which is contrary to the original agreement; so also when the society has placed the legislative in any assembly of men, to continue in them and their successors, with direction and authority for providing such successors, the legislative can never revert to the people whilst that government lasts: because, having provided a legislative with power to continue forever, they have given up their political power to the legislative, and cannot resume it. But if they have set limits to the duration of their legislative, and made this supreme power in any person or assembly only temporary; or else when, by the miscarriages of those in authority, it is forfeited; *upon the forfeiture of their rulers, or at the determination of the time set, it reverts to the society, and the people have a right to act as supreme, and continue the legislative in themselves or place it in a new form, or new hands, as they think good.*[19]

19. But how can the people's decision be assessed? Many contend that the "people" are those who demonstrate in the streets in large numbers, expressing their will en masse. Others contend that such mob action is akin to anarchy.

DANIEL DULANY

"Considerations on the Propriety of Imposing Taxes in the British Colonies for the Purpose of Raising a Revenue, by Act of Parliament," 1765

Daniel Dulany represented Frederick County in the Maryland General Assembly and was a member of the Maryland Governor's Council during the crisis over the Stamp Act. His writings opposing the Stamp Act were widely distributed, in the colonies as well as in England. Dulany's argument is primarily grounded in geography—that no part of the colonies is or can be represented in Parliament for the purpose of taxing the colonies to raise revenue. This pamphlet is valuable to Patriot arguments, despite the fact that by 1775 Dulany had become a leading Loyalist in Maryland; opposition to British acts did not lead automatically to a desire for revolution.

SOURCE: *AMDOCS Documents for the Study of American History,* www.let.rug.nl/usa/documents /1751-1775/daniel-dulany-considerations-october-1765.php

I shall undertake to disprove the supposed similarity of situation, whence the same kind of Representation is deduced of the inhabitants of the colonies, and of the British non-electors; and, if I succeed, the Notion of a virtual representation[1] of the colonies must fail, which, in Truth is a mere cob-web, spread to catch the unwary, and entangle the weak. I would be understood. I am upon a question of propriety, not of power; and though some may be inclined to think it is to little purpose to discuss the one, when the other is irresistible, yet are they different considerations; and, at the same time that I invalidate the claim upon which it is founded, I may very consistently recommend a submission to the law, whilst it endures.

Lessees for years, copyholders, proprietors of the public funds, inhabitants of Birmingham, Leeds, Halifax and Manchester, merchants of the City of London, or members of the corporation of the East India Company, are, as such, under no personal incapacity to be electors; for they may acquire the right of election, and there are *actually* not only a considerable number of electors in each of the classes of lessees for years etc., but in many of them, if not all, even members of Parliament. The interests therefore of the nonelectors, the electors, and the representatives, are individually the same; to say nothing of the connection among neighbors, friends and relations. The security of the non-electors against oppression, is that their oppression will fall also upon the electors and the representatives. The one can't be injured and the other indemnified.

Further, if the nonelectors should not be taxed by the British Parliament, they would not be taxed *at all*; and it would be iniquitous, as well as a solecism in the political system, that they should partake of all the benefits resulting from the imposition and application of taxes, and derive an immunity from the circumstances of not being qualified to vote. Under this Constitution then, a double or virtual representation may be reasonably supposed.

There is not that intimate and inseparable relation between the electors of Great-Britain and the inhabitants of the colonies, which must inevitably involve both in the same taxation; on the contrary, not a single actual elector in England, might be immediately affected by a taxation in America, imposed by a statute which would have a general operation and effect, upon the properties of the inhabitants of the colonies . . . wherefore the relation between the British Americans, and the English electors, is a knot too infirm to be relied on. . . .

---

1. Virtual representation was the argument that, though many (in fact, the vast majority of adult men, and all women) in England could not vote (non-electors), they still consented through representation in Parliament.

It appears to me, that there is a clear and necessary Distinction between an Act imposing a tax for the *single purpose of revenue*, and those Acts which have been made for the *regulation of trade*, and have produced some revenue in consequence of their effect and operation as regulations of trade.[2]

The colonies claim the privileges of British subjects. It has been proved to be inconsistent with those privileges, to tax them without their own consent, and it has been demonstrated that a tax imposed by Parliament, is a tax without their consent.

The subordination of the colonies, and the authority of Parliament to preserve it, have been fully acknowledged. Not only the welfare, but perhaps the existence of the mother country, as an independent kingdom, may depend upon her trade and navigation, and these so far upon her intercourse with the colonies, that if this should be neglected, there would soon be an end to that commerce, whence her greatest wealth is derived, and upon which her maritime power is principally founded. From these considerations, the right of the *British Parliament to regulate the trade of the colonies, may be justly deduced*; a denial of it would contradict the admission of the subordination, and of the authority to preserve it, resulting from the nature of the relation between the mother country and her colonies. It is a common, and frequently the most proper method to regulate trade by duties on imports and exports. The authority of the mother country to regulate the trade of the colonies being unquestionable, what regulations are the most proper, are to be of course submitted to the determination of the Parliament; and if an *incidental revenue*, should be produced by such regulations; these are not therefore unwarrantable.

A right to impose an internal tax on the colonies, without their consent for the single purpose of revenue, is denied, a right to regulate their trade without their consent is admitted. The imposition of a duty may, in some instances, be the proper regulation. If the claims of the mother country and the colonies should seem on such an occasion to interfere, and the point of right to be doubtful, (which I take to be otherwise) it is easy to guess that the determination will be on the side of power, and the inferior will be constrained to submit.

---

2. This point is made to distinguish the Navigation Acts, which had existed for decades and which most colonists recognized as legitimate, from measures such as the Stamp Act tax.

SOAME JENYNS

"The Objections to the Taxation of our American Colonies by the Legislature of Great Britain, briefly consider'd," 1765

Soame Jenyns was a member of the British Parliament as well as of the Board of Trade and Plantations (the colonies' administrators) when he wrote this pamphlet to defend the constitutionality of the Stamp Act (and Parliamentary taxation of the colonies in general). Jenyns mocks the argument about colonists needing to consent to such taxes and relies on the facts of taxation in Britain (only one in twenty could vote) to deny colonists their claim. Jenyns thus advocates a position known as the "virtual representation" theory of consent to taxes.

SOURCE: *AMDOCS Documents for the Study of American History, www.vlib.us/amdocs/texts /objectio.htm*

The right of the Legislature of Great-Britain to impose taxes on her American Colonies, and the expediency of exerting that right in the present conjuncture, are propositions so indisputably clear, that I should never have thought it necessary to have undertaken their defense, had not many arguments been lately flung out, both in papers and conversation, which with insolence equal to their absurdity deny them both. As these are usually mixed-up with several patriotic and favorite words such as Liberty, Property, Englishmen, etc., which are apt to make strong impressions on that more numerous part of mankind, who have ears but no understanding, it will not, I think, be improper to give them some answers: to this, therefore, I shall singly confine myself, and do it in as few words as possible, being sensible that the fewest will give least trouble to myself and probably most information to my reader.

The *great capital argument . . . is this; that no Englishman is, or can be taxed, but by his own consent: by which must be meant one of these three propositions; either that no Englishman can be taxed without his own consent as an individual; or that no Englishman can be taxed without the consent of the persons he chooses to represent him; or that no Englishman can be taxed without the consent of the majority of all those, who are elected by himself and others of his fellow-subjects to represent them.* Now let us impartially consider, whether any one of these propositions are in fact true: if not, then this wonderful structure which has been erected upon them, falls at once to the ground, and like another Babel, perishes by a confusion of words, which the builders themselves are unable to understand.

First then, that no Englishman is or can be taxed but by his own consent as an individual: this is so far from being true, that it is the very reverse of truth; for no man that I know of is taxed by his own consent[1]; and an Englishman, I believe, is as little likely to be so taxed, as any man in the world.

Secondly, that no Englishman is or can be taxed but by the consent of those persons whom he has chose to represent him; for the truth of this I shall appeal only to the candid representatives of those unfortunate counties which produce cider,[2] and shall willingly acquiesce under their determination.

Lastly, that no Englishman is, or can be taxed, without the consent of the majority of those, who are elected by himself, and others of his fellow-subjects, to represent them. This is certainly as false as the other two; *for every Englishman is taxed, and not one in twenty represented*[3]: copyholders, leaseholders, and all men possessed of personal property only, choose no representatives; Manchester, Birmingham, and many more of our richest and most flourishing trading towns send no members to parliament, consequently cannot consent by their representatives, *because they choose none to represent them; yet are they not Englishmen? or are they not taxed?* I am well aware, that I shall hear Locke, Sidney, Selden, and many other great names quoted to prove that every Englishman, whether he has a right to vote for a representative, or not, is still represented in the British Parliament; in which opinion they all agree: on what principle of common sense this opinion is founded I comprehend not, but on the authority of such respectable names I shall acknowledge its truth; but then I will ask one question, and on that I will rest the whole merits of the cause: Why does not this imaginary representation extend to America, as well as over the whole island of Great-Britain? If it can travel three hundred miles, why not three thousand? If it can jump over rivers and mountains, why cannot it sail over the ocean? *If the towns of Manchester and Birmingham sending no representatives to Parliament, are notwithstanding there represented, why are not the cities of Albany and Boston equally represented in that assembly? Are they not alike British subjects? are they not Englishmen?* or are they only Englishmen when they solicit for protection, but not Englishmen when taxes are required to enable this country to protect them?

But it is urged, that the Colonies are by their charters placed under distinct Governments, each of which has a legislative power within itself, by which alone it ought to be taxed; that if this privilege is once given up, that liberty which every Englishman has a right to, is torn from them, they are all slaves, and all is lost.

---

1. In the sense that no one likes to have money taken from him by taxes.

2. In 1763–64, Parliament proposed and passed a heavy tax on alcoholic cider, despite the uniform opposition of the members of Parliament from cider-producing areas.

3. This limitation of the franchise to roughly 5 percent of the adult males (women were barred from voting and are excluded entirely from Jenyns' pamphlet) was primarily due to land ownership being required for voting.

The liberty of an Englishman . . . cannot mean; that is, an exemption from taxes imposed by the authority of the Parliament of Great Britain; nor is there any charter, that ever pretended to grant such a privilege to any colony in America; and had they granted it, it could have had no force; their charters being derived from the Crown, and no charter from the Crown can possibly supersede the right of the whole legislature: their charters are undoubtedly no more than those of all corporations, which empower them to make by-laws, and raise duties for the purposes of their own police, forever subject to the superior authority of parliament; and in some of their charters, the manner of exercising these powers is specified in these express words, "according to the course of other corporations in Great-Britain": and therefore they can have no more pretense to plead an exemption from this parliamentary authority, than any other corporation in England.

It has been moreover alleged, that, though Parliament may have power to impose taxes on the Colonies, they have no right to use it, because it would be an unjust tax; and no supreme or legislative power can have a right to enact any law in its nature unjust: to this, I shall only make this short reply, that if Parliament can impose no taxes but what are equitable, and [if] the persons taxed are to be the judges of that equity, they will in effect have no power to lay any tax at all. No tax can be imposed exactly equal on all, and if it is not equal, it cannot be just: and if it is not just, no power whatever can impose it; by which short syllogism, all taxation is at an end; but why it should not be used by Englishmen on this side the Atlantic, as well as by those on the other, I do not comprehend. . . .

SAMUEL JOHNSON

"Taxation No Tyranny," 1775

Samuel Johnson (1709–1784) was one of the great essayists, critics, and dictionary writers in the English language. He was a staunch supporter of Tory (conservative) politicians in England, and a defender of Parliamentary rights and privileges. In this pamphlet, Johnson defends the Coercive Acts of 1774 and writes a rejoinder to the Declaration of Rights promulgated by the Continental Congress of 1774 in protest of those Intolerable Acts. He supports the theory of virtual representation in denying the colonial grievances. This pamphlet today is most remembered for its barbed quip about American slaveowners' hypocrisy regarding liberty, found near the end of the pamphlet. A copy of the Continental Congress Declaration may be found at http://avalon.law.yale.edu/18th_century/resolves.asp. Editor's note: This document has been broken into sections and headings have been added to facilitate both reading and referencing.

SOURCE: *Samuel Johnson*, The Works of Samuel Johnson, *volume 14 (Troy: Pafraets and Company, 1913), 93–144. Also at www.samueljohnson.com/tnt.html*

*J*n all the parts of human knowledge, whether terminating in science merely speculative, or operating upon life, private or civil, are admitted some fundamental principles, or common axioms, which, being generally received, are little doubted, and, being little doubted, have been rarely proved. . . .

Of this kind is the position, that "the supreme power of every community has the right of requiring, from all its subjects, such contributions as are necessary to the public safety or public prosperity," which was considered, by all mankind, as comprising the primary and essential condition of all political society, till it became disputed by those zealots of anarchy, who have denied, to the parliament of Britain the right of taxing the American colonies.

In favor of this exemption of the Americans from the authority of their lawful sovereign, and the dominion of their mother-country, very loud clamors have been raised, and many wild assertions advanced, which, by such as borrow their opinions from the reigning fashion, have been admitted as arguments; and, what is strange, though their tendency is to lessen English honor and English power, have been heard by Englishmen, with a wish to find them true. Passion has, in its first violence, controlled interest, as the eddy for awhile runs against the stream. . . .

Section 1. Summary of the American arguments

The nation is, sometimes, to be mollified by a tender tale of men, who fled from tyranny to rocks and deserts, and is persuaded to lose all claims of justice, and all sense of dignity, in compassion for a harmless people, who, having worked hard for bread in a wild country, and obtained, by the slow progression of manual industry, the accommodations of life, are now invaded by unprecedented oppression, and plundered of their properties by the harpies of taxation.[1]

---

1. Sarcasm, Johnson's prime rhetorical weapon, is brilliantly wielded here.

We are told how their industry is obstructed by unnatural restraints, and their trade confined by rigorous prohibitions; how they are forbidden to enjoy the products of their own soil, to manufacture the materials which nature spreads before them, or to carry their own goods to the nearest market; and surely the generosity of English virtue will never heap new weight upon those that are already overladen; will never delight in that dominion, which cannot be exercised, but by cruelty and outrage.

But, while we are melting in silent sorrow, and, in the transports of delirious pity, dropping both the sword and balance from our hands, another friend of the Americans thinks it better to awaken another passion, and tries to alarm our interest, or excite our veneration, by accounts of their greatness and their opulence, of the fertility of their land, and the splendor of their towns. We then begin to consider the question with more evenness of mind, are ready to conclude that those restrictions are not very oppressive, which have been found consistent with this speedy growth of prosperity; and begin to think it reasonable, that they who thus flourish under the protection of our government, should contribute something toward its expense.

But we are soon told, that the Americans, however wealthy, cannot be taxed; that they are the descendants of men who left all for liberty, and that they have constantly preserved the principles and stubbornness of their progenitors; that they are too obstinate for persuasion, and too powerful for constraint; that they will laugh at argument, and defeat violence; that the continent of North America contains three millions, not of men merely, but of whigs[2] fierce for liberty, and disdainful of dominion; that they multiply with the fecundity of their own rattlesnakes, so that every quarter of a century doubles their numbers.

Men accustomed to think themselves masters do not love to be threatened. This talk is, I hope, commonly thrown away, or raises passions different from those which it was intended to excite. Instead of terrifying the English hearer to tame acquiescence, it disposes him to hasten the experiment of bending obstinacy, before it is become yet more obdurate, and convinces him that it is necessary to attack a nation thus prolific, while we may yet hope to prevail. When he is told, through what extent of territory we must travel to subdue them, he recollects how far, a few years ago, we travelled in their defense.[3] When it is urged, that they will shoot up, like the hydra, he naturally considers how the hydra was destroyed.

Nothing dejects a trader like the interruption of his profits. A commercial people, however magnanimous, shrinks at the thought of declining traffic and an

---

2. Whig refers to a political faction as well as a belief system in favor of liberty within constitutional monarchy; Whigs were the party primarily responsible for the Glorious Revolution of 1688 against James II, and they continued to see threats to liberty in the 1700s from governments corrupted by the king and his ministers.

3. This refers to the British military efforts in North America during the French and Indian War (1754–63).

unfavorable balance.[4] The effect of this terror has been tried. We have been stunned with the importance of our American commerce, and heard of merchants, with warehouses that are never to be emptied, and of manufacturers starving for want of work.

That our commerce with America is profitable, however less than ostentatious or deceitful estimates have made it, and that it is our interest to preserve it, has never been denied; but, surely, it will most effectually be preserved, by being kept always in our own power. Concessions may promote it for a moment, but superiority only can ensure its continuance. There will always be a part, and always a very large part of every community, that have no care but for themselves, and whose care for themselves reaches little further than impatience of immediate pain, and eagerness for the nearest good. The blind are said to feel with peculiar nicety. They who look but little into [the] future, have, perhaps, the quickest sensation of the present. A merchant's desire is not of glory, but of gain; not of public wealth, but of private emolument; he is, therefore, rarely to be consulted about war and peace, or any designs of wide extent and distant consequence.

Yet this, like other general characters, will sometimes fail. The traders of Birmingham have rescued themselves from all imputation of narrow selfishness, by a manly recommendation to parliament of the rights and dignity of their native country.

To these men I do not intend to ascribe an absurd and enthusiastic contempt of interest, but to give them the rational and just praise of distinguishing real from seeming good; of being able to see through the cloud of interposing difficulties, to the lasting and solid happiness of victory and settlement. . . .

Johnson is referring here to the impact of American boycotts of trade, both in the past regarding the Stamp and Townshend Acts as well as currently with the Association.

Section 2. An evaluation of the American principles regarding taxation

But terrors and pity are not the only means by which the taxation of the Americans is opposed. There are those, who profess to use them only as auxiliaries to reason and justice; who tell us, that to tax the colonies is usurpation and oppression, an invasion of natural and legal rights, and a violation of those principles which support the constitution of English government.

This question is of great importance. That the Americans are able to bear taxation, is indubitable; that their refusal may be overruled, is highly probable; but power is no sufficient evidence of truth. Let us examine our own claim, and the

---

4. It was the boycotts of the 1760s in response to the Stamp and Townshend Acts that hurt the British merchants with "declining traffic" and "unfavorable balances"—more imports than exports, more losses than profits—and which shocked Johnson and the British as to their vulnerability to the Americans.

objections of the recusants, with caution proportioned to the event of the decision, which must convict one part of robbery, or the other of rebellion.

A tax is a payment, exacted by authority, from part of the community, for the benefit of the whole. From whom, and in what proportion such payment shall be required, and to what uses it shall be applied, those only are to judge to whom government is entrusted. In the British dominions taxes are apportioned, levied, and appropriated by the states assembled in parliament.

Of every empire all the subordinate communities[5] are liable to taxation, because they all share the benefits of government, and, therefore, ought all to furnish their proportion of the expense.

This the Americans have never openly denied. That it is their duty to pay the costs of their own safety, they seem to admit; nor do they refuse their contribution to the exigencies, whatever they may be, of the British empire; but they make this participation of a public burden a duty of very uncertain extent, and imperfect obligation, a duty temporary, occasional, and elective, of which they reserve to themselves the right of settling the degree, the time, and the duration; of judging when it may be required, and when it has been performed.

They allow to the supreme power[6] nothing more than the liberty of notifying to them its demands or its necessities. Of this notification they profess to think for themselves, how far it shall influence their counsels; and of the necessities alleged, how far they shall endeavor to relieve them. They assume the exclusive power of settling not only the mode, but the quantity, of this payment. They are ready to cooperate with all the other dominions of the king; but they will cooperate by no means which they do not like, and at no greater charge than they are willing to bear.

This claim, wild as it may seem; this claim, which supposes dominion without authority, and subjects without subordination, has found among the libertines of policy, many clamorous and hardy vindicators. The laws of nature, the rights of humanity, the faith of charters, the danger of liberty, the encroachments of usurpation, have been thundered in our ears, sometimes by interested faction, and sometimes by honest stupidity. . . .

Section 3. Sovereignty: Colonies' histories deny them sovereign power

In sovereignty there are no gradations. There may be limited royalty, there may be limited consulship; but there can be no limited government. There must, in every society, be some power or other, from which there is no appeal, which admits

---

5. "Subordinate communities" here means the American colonies, as well as other British colonies. Johnson argues that benefits of empire require, nay demand, sharing of burdens through taxation.

6. Parliament, or the king-in-Parliament, is the supreme power for Johnson within the British Empire.

no restrictions, which pervades the whole mass of the community, regulates and adjusts all subordination, enacts laws or repeals them, erects or annuls judicatures, extends or contracts privileges, exempt itself from question or control, and bounded only by physical necessity.

By this power, wherever it subsists, all legislation and jurisdiction is animated and maintained. From this all legal rights are emanations, which, whether equitably or not, may be legally recalled. It is not infallible, for it may do wrong; but it is irresistible, for it can be resisted only by rebellion, by an act which makes it questionable, what shall be thenceforward the supreme power.

An English colony is a number of persons, to whom the king grants a charter, permitting them to settle in some distant country, and enabling them to constitute a corporation enjoying such powers as the charter grants, to be administered in such forms as the charter prescribes. As a corporation, they make laws for themselves; but as a corporation, subsisting by a grant from higher authority, to the control of that authority they continue subject. . . .

To their charters the colonies owe, like other corporations, their political existence. The solemnities of legislation, the administration of justice, the security of property, are all bestowed upon them by the royal grant. Without their charter, there would be no power among them, by which any law could be made, or duties enjoined; any debt recovered, or criminal punished. . . .

A colony is to the mother-country,[7] as a member to the body, deriving its action and its strength from the general principle of vitality; receiving from the body, and communicating to it, all the benefits and evils of health and disease; liable, in dangerous maladies, to sharp applications, of which the body, however, must partake the pain; and exposed, if incurably tainted, to amputation, by which the body, likewise, will be mutilated.

The mother-country always considers the colonies, thus connected, as parts of itself; the prosperity or unhappiness of either, is the prosperity or unhappiness of both; not, perhaps, of both in the same degree, for the body may subsist, though less commodiously, without a limb, but the limb must perish, if it be parted from the body.

Our colonies, therefore, however distant, have been, hitherto, treated as constituent parts of the British empire. The inhabitants incorporated by English charters are entitled to all the rights of Englishmen. They are governed by English laws, entitled to English dignities, regulated by English counsels, and protected by English arms; and it seems to follow, by consequence not easily avoided, that they are subject to English government, and chargeable by English taxation.

To him that considers the nature, the original, the progress, and the constitution of the colonies, who remembers that the first discoverers had commissions

---

7. Note the mixed metaphors: the mother-child metaphor of imperialism, but also the empire as a single body, controlled by the head/mother, with the colonies as extremities.

from the crown, that the first settlers owe to a charter their civil forms and regular magistracy, and that all personal immunities and legal securities, by which the condition of the subject has been, from time to time, improved, have been extended to the colonists, it will not be doubted, but the parliament of England has a right to bind them by statutes, and to bind them in all cases whatsoever; and has, therefore, a natural and constitutional power of laying upon them any tax or impost, whether external or internal, upon the product of land, or the manufactures of industry, in the exigencies of war, or in the time of profound peace, for the defense of America, for the purpose of raising a revenue, or for any other end beneficial to the empire.

Section 4. Sovereign power of King-In-Parliament includes taxing colonies

There are some, and those not inconsiderable for number, nor contemptible for knowledge, who except the power of taxation from the general dominion of parliament, and hold, that whatever degrees of obedience may be exacted, or whatever authority may be exercised in other acts of government, there is still reverence to be paid to money, and that legislation passes its limits when it violates the purse.

Johnson summarizes the claims of the lack of consent by colonists due to their lack of representation. Johnson echoes Locke in saying that by accepting government protection, men consent virtually or tacitly, as they do to institutions formed long before they were born.

Of this exception, which, by a head not fully impregnated with politics, is not easily comprehended, it is alleged, as an unanswerable reason, that the colonies send no representatives to the House of Commons.

It is, say the American advocates, the natural distinction of a freeman, and the legal privilege of an Englishman, that he is able to call his possessions his own, that he can sit secure in the enjoyment of inheritance or acquisition, that his house is fortified by the law, and that nothing can be taken from him but by his own consent. This consent is given for every man by his representative in parliament. The Americans, unrepresented, cannot consent to English taxations, as a corporation, and they will not consent, as individuals.

Of this argument, it has been observed by more than one, that its force extends equally to all other laws, for a freeman is not to be exposed to punishment, or be called to any onerous service, but by his own consent. The congress has extracted a position from the fanciful Montesquieu[8] that, "in a free state, every man, being a free agent, ought to be concerned in his own government." Whatever is true of taxation, is true of every other law, that he who is bound by it, without his consent, is not free, for he is not concerned in his own government.

He that denies the English parliament the right of taxation, denies it, likewise, the right of making any other laws, civil or criminal, yet this power over the colonies was never yet disputed by themselves. They have always admitted statutes for

---

8. Baron Montesquieu (1689–1755), French Enlightenment lawyer and political philosopher, noted for his advocacy of separation of powers in government.

the punishment of offences, and for the redress or prevention of inconveniencies; and the reception of any law draws after it, by a chain which cannot be broken, the unwelcome necessity of submitting to taxation.

That a freeman is governed by himself, or by laws to which he has consented, is a position of mighty sound; but every man that utters it, with whatever confidence, and every man that hears it, with whatever acquiescence, if consent be supposed to imply the power of refusal, feels it to be false. We virtually and implicitly allow the institutions of any government, of which we enjoy the benefit, and solicit the protection. In wide extended dominions, though power has been diffused with the most even hand, yet a very small part of the people are either primarily or secondarily consulted in legislation. The business of the public must be done by delegation. The choice of delegates is made by a select number, and those who are not electors stand idle and helpless spectators of the commonweal, "wholly unconcerned in the government of themselves."

Of the electors the hap is but little better. They are often far from unanimity in their choice; and where the numbers approach to equality, almost half must be governed not only without, but against their choice.

How any man can have consented to institutions established in distant ages, it will be difficult to explain. In the most favorite residence of liberty, the consent of individuals is merely passive; a tacit admission, in every community, of the terms which that community grants and requires. As all are born the subjects of some state or other, we may be said to have been all born consenting to some system of government. Other consent than this the condition of civil life does not allow. It is the unmeaning clamor of the pedants of policy, the delirious dream of republican fanaticism.

But hear, ye sons and daughters of liberty, the sounds which the winds are wafting from the western continent. The Americans are telling one another, what, if we may judge from their noisy triumph, they have but lately discovered, and what yet is a very important truth: "That they are entitled to life, liberty, and property; and that they have never ceded to any sovereign power whatever a right to dispose of either without their consent." . . .

Their next resolution[9] declares, that "Their ancestors, who first settled the colonies, were, at the time of their emigration from the mother-country, entitled to all the rights, liberties, and immunities of free and natural-born subjects within the realm of England."

This, likewise, is true; but when this is granted, their boast of original rights is at an end; they are no longer in a state of nature.[10] These lords of themselves, these

---

9. Johnson is quoting from the Declaration and Resolves of the First Continental Congress (October 14, 1774).

10. Note the echoes of the colonial Lockean argument, based on rights found in the statue of nature. Johnson refutes those principles here, as well as noting that colonists left a place where they might vote—England—for better opportunities in America.

kings of ME, these demigods of independence sink down to colonists, governed by a charter. If their ancestors were subjects, they acknowledged a sovereign; if they had a right to English privileges, they were accountable to English laws; and, what must grieve the lover of liberty to discover, had ceded to the king and parliament, whether the right or not, at least, the power of disposing, "without their consent, of their lives, liberties, and properties." It, therefore, is required of them to prove, that the parliament ever ceded to them a dispensation from that obedience, which they owe as natural-born subjects, or any degree of independence or immunity, not enjoyed by other Englishmen.

They say, that by such emigration, they by no means forfeited, surrendered, or lost any of those rights; but, that "they were, and their descendants now are, entitled to the exercise and enjoyment of all such of them, as their local and other circumstances enable them to exercise and enjoy."

That they who form a settlement by a lawful charter, having committed no crime, forfeit no privileges, will be readily confessed; but what they do not forfeit by any judicial sentence, they may lose by natural effects. As man can be but in one place, at once, he cannot have the advantages of multiplied residence. He that will enjoy the brightness of sunshine, must quit the coolness of the shade. He who goes voluntarily to America, cannot complain of losing what he leaves in Europe. He, perhaps, had a right to vote for a knight or burgess; by crossing the Atlantic, he has not nullified his right; but he has made its exertion no longer possible. By his own choice he has left a country, where he had a vote and little property, for another, where he has great property, but no vote. But as this preference was deliberate and unconstrained, he is still "concerned in the government of himself;" he has reduced himself from a voter, to one of the innumerable multitude that have no vote. He has truly "ceded his right," but he still is governed by his own consent; because he has consented to throw his atom of interest into the general mass of the community. Of the consequences of his own act he has no cause to complain; he has chosen, or intended to choose, the greater good; he is represented, as himself desired, in the general representation. . . .

"They inherit," they say, "from their ancestors, the right which their ancestors possessed, of enjoying all the privileges of Englishmen." That they inherit the right of their ancestors is allowed; but they can inherit no more. Their ancestors left a country, where the representatives of the people were elected by men particularly qualified, and where those who wanted qualifications, or who did not use them, were bound by the decisions of men, whom they had not deputed.

The colonists are the descendants of men, who either had no vote in elections, or who voluntarily resigned them for something, in their opinion, of more estimation; they have, therefore, exactly what their ancestors left them, not a vote in making laws, or in constituting legislators, but the happiness of being protected by law, and the duty of obeying it.

What their ancestors did not carry with them, neither they nor their descendants have since acquired. They have not, by abandoning their part in one legislature, obtained the power of constituting another, exclusive and independent, any more than the multitudes, who are now debarred from voting, have a right to erect a separate parliament for themselves. . . .

Section 5. Virtual representation in England

The necessary connection of representatives with taxes, seems to have sunk deep into many of those minds, that admit sounds, without their meaning.

Our nation is represented in parliament by an assembly as numerous as can well consist with order and dispatch, chosen by persons so differently qualified in different places, that the mode of choice seems to be, for the most part, formed by chance, and settled by custom. Of individuals, far the greater part have no vote, and, of the voters, few have any personal knowledge of him to whom they entrust their liberty and fortune.

Yet this representation has the whole effect expected or desired, that of spreading so wide the care of general interest, and the participation of public counsels, that the advantage or corruption of particular men can seldom operate with much injury to the public.

For this reason many populous and opulent towns neither enjoy nor desire particular representatives: they are included in the general scheme of public administration, and cannot suffer but with the rest of the empire.

It is urged, that the Americans have not the same security, and that a British legislator may wanton with their property; yet, if it be true, that their wealth is our wealth, and that their ruin will be our ruin, the parliament has the same interest in attending to them, as to any other part of the nation. The reason why we place any confidence in our representatives is that they must share in the good or evil which their counsels shall produce. Their share is, indeed, commonly consequential and remote; but it is not often possible that any immediate advantage can be extended to such numbers as may prevail against it. We are, therefore, as secure against intentional depravations of government, as human wisdom can make us, and upon this security the Americans may venture to repose. . . .

It must always be remembered, that they are represented by the same virtual representation as the greater part of Englishmen; and that, if by change of place, they have less share in the legislature than is proportionate to their opulence, they, by their removal, gained that opulence, and had originally, and have now, their choice of a vote at home, or riches at a distance. . . .

The friends of the Americans are of different opinions. Some think, that, being unrepresented, they ought to tax themselves; and others, that they ought to have representatives in the British parliament.

If they are to tax themselves, what power is to remain in the supreme legislature? That they must settle their own mode of levying their money is supposed. May the British parliament tell them how much they shall contribute? If the sum may be prescribed, they will return few thanks for the power of raising it; if they are at liberty to grant or to deny, they are no longer subjects.

There were 558 members of the House of Commons in the 1700s, with 489 from England, 45 from Scotland, and 24 from Wales. Johnson now looks at the math of representation explain why the colonists have not asked for seats in Parliament in the current dispute.

If they are to be represented, what number of these western orators are to be admitted? This, I suppose, the parliament must settle; yet, if men have a natural and unalienable right to be represented, who shall determine the number of their delegates? Let us, however, suppose them to send twenty-three, half as many as the kingdom of Scotland, what will this representation avail them? To pay taxes will be still a grievance. The love of money will not be lessened, nor the power of getting it increased.

Whither will this necessity of representation drive us? Is every petty settlement to be out of the reach of government, till it has sent a senator to parliament; or may two of them, or a greater number, be forced to unite in a single deputation? What, at last, is the difference between him that is taxed, by compulsion, without representation, and him that is represented, by compulsion, in order to be taxed?

For many reigns the House of Commons was in a state of fluctuation: new burgesses were added, from time to time, without any reason now to be discovered; but the number has been fixed for more than a century and a half, and the king's power of increasing it has been questioned. It will hardly be thought fit to new-model the constitution in favor of the planters, who, as they grow rich, may buy estates in England, and, without any innovation, effectually represent their native colonies.

The friends of the Americans, indeed, ask for them what they do not ask for themselves. This inestimable right of representation they have never solicited. They mean not to exchange solid money for such airy honor. They say, and say willingly, that they cannot conveniently be represented; because their inference is, that they cannot be taxed. They are too remote to share the general government, and, therefore, claim the privilege of governing themselves.

Section 6. Political conditions of intimidation in America

Of the principles contained in the resolutions of the congress,[11] however wild, indefinite, and obscure, such has been the influence upon American understanding, that, from New England to South Carolina, there is formed a general combination of all the provinces against their mother-country. The madness of independence

---

11. First Continental Congress, 1774.

has spread from colony to colony, till order is lost, and government despised; and all is filled with misrule, uproar, violence, and confusion. To be quiet is disaffection, to be loyal is treason.

The congress of Philadelphia, an assembly convened by its own authority, has promulgated a declaration, in compliance with which the communication between Britain and the greatest part of North America, is now suspended. They ceased to admit the importation of English goods, in December, 1774, and determine to permit the exportation of their own no longer than to November, 1775.[12]

This might seem enough; but they have done more: they have declared, that they shall treat all as enemies who do not concur with them in disaffection and perverseness; and that they will trade with none that shall trade with Britain.

They threaten to stigmatize, in their gazette, those who shall consume the products or merchandise of their mother-country, and are now searching suspected houses for prohibited goods.

These hostile declarations they profess themselves ready to maintain by force. They have armed the militia of their provinces, and seized the public stores of ammunition. They are, therefore, no longer subjects, since they refuse the laws of their sovereign, and, in defense of that refusal, are making open preparations for war.

Section 7. Coercive acts analyzed and defended

When they apply to our compassion, by telling us, that they are to be carried from their own country to be tried for certain offences, we are not so ready to pity them, as to advise them not to offend. While they are innocent they are safe.[13]

When they tell of laws made expressly for their punishment, we answer, that tumults and sedition were always punishable, and that the new law prescribes only the mode of execution.

When it is said, that the whole town of Boston is distressed for a misdemeanor of a few, we wonder at their shamelessness; for we know that the town of Boston and all the associated provinces, are now in rebellion to defend or justify the criminals.[14]

If frauds in the imposts of Boston are tried by commission without a jury, they are tried here in the same mode; and why should the Bostonians expect from us more tenderness for them than for ourselves?

If they are condemned unheard, it is because there is no need of a trial. The crime is manifest and notorious. All trial is the investigation of something

---

12. The Association, approved by the Continental Congress, and sent to the colonies for ratification and enforcement.

13. Johnson is referring to the Administration of Justice Act, part of the Coercive Acts.

14. Johnson is referring to the Boston Port Act, part of the Coercive Acts, which closed Boston's port in response to the Tea Party.

doubtful. An Italian philosopher observes that no man desires to hear what he has already seen.

If their assemblies have been suddenly dissolved, what was the reason? Their deliberations were indecent, and their intentions, seditious. The power of dissolution is granted and reserved for such times of turbulence. Their best friends have been lately soliciting the king to dissolve his parliament; to do what they so loudly complain of suffering.[15]

That the same vengeance involves the innocent and guilty, is an evil to be lamented; but human caution cannot prevent it, nor human power always redress it. To bring misery on those who have not deserved it, is part of the aggregated guilt of rebellion.

That governors have been sometimes given them, only that a great man might get ease from importunity, and that they have had judges, not always of the deepest learning, or the purest integrity, we have no great reason to doubt, because such misfortunes happen to ourselves. Whoever is governed, will, sometimes, be governed ill, even when he is most "concerned in his own government."

That improper officers or magistrates are sent is the crime or folly of those that sent them. When incapacity is discovered, it ought to be removed; if corruption is detected, it ought to be punished. No government could subsist for a day, if single errors could justify defection.

One of their complaints is not such as can claim much commiseration from the softest bosom. They tell us, that we have changed our conduct, and that a tax is now laid, by parliament, on those who were never taxed by parliament before. To this, we think, it may be easily answered, that the longer they have been spared, the better they can pay. It is certainly not much their interest to represent innovation as criminal or invidious; for they have introduced into the history of mankind a new mode of disaffection, and have given, I believe, the first example of a proscription published by a colony against the mother-country.

To what is urged of new powers granted to the courts of admiralty, or the extension of authority conferred on the judges, it may be answered, in a few words, that they have themselves made such regulations necessary; that they are established for the prevention of greater evils; at the same time, it must be observed, that these powers have not been extended since the rebellion in America.

Section 8. The colonial fear of a slavery plot and its absurdity

One mode of persuasion their ingenuity has suggested, which it may, perhaps, be less easy to resist. That we may not look with indifference on the American contest, or imagine that the struggle is for a claim, which, however decided, is of small

---

15. Johnson is referring to the Massachusetts Government Act, part of the Coercive Acts.

importance and remote consequence, the Philadelphian congress has taken care to inform us, that they are resisting the demands of parliament, as well for our sakes as their own.

Their keenness of perspicacity has enabled them to pursue consequences to a greater distance; to see through clouds impervious to the dimness of European sight; and to find, I know not how, that when they are taxed, we shall be enslaved.

That slavery is a miserable state we have been often told, and, doubtless, many a Briton will tremble to find it so near as in America; but how it will be brought hither the congress must inform us. The question might distress a common understanding; but the statesmen of the other hemisphere can easily resolve it. "Our ministers," they say, "are our enemies, and if they should carry the point of taxation, may, with the same army, enslave us. It may be said, we will not pay them; but remember," say the western sages, "the taxes from America, and, we may add, the men, and particularly the Roman catholics of this vast continent, will then be in the power of your enemies. Nor have you any reason to expect, that, after making slaves of us, many of us will refuse to assist in reducing you to the same abject state." . . .

In this last terrific paragraph are two positions, that, if our fears do not overpower our reflection, may enable us to support life a little longer. We are told by these croakers of calamity, not only that our present ministers design to enslave us, but that the same malignity of purpose is to descend through all their successors; and that the wealth to be poured into England by the Pactolus[16] of America, will, whenever it comes, be employed to purchase the "remains of liberty." . . .

There is no plot against liberty; the British actions are the only available options for confronting the rebels, unless the British give up and give the colonies independence.

When subordinate communities oppose the decrees of the general legislature with defiance thus audacious, and malignity thus acrimonious, nothing remains but to conquer or to yield; to allow their claim of independence, or to reduce them, by force, to submission and allegiance.

The argument of the irregular troops of controversy, stripped of its colors, and turned out naked to the view, is no more than this. Liberty is the birthright of man, and where obedience is compelled, there is no liberty. The answer is equally simple. Government is necessary to man, and where obedience is not compelled, there is no government. . . .

If the subject refuses to obey, it is the duty of authority to use compulsion. Society cannot subsist but by the power, first of making laws, and then of enforcing them.

---

16. Ancient river of gold, allegedly formed by King Midas washing himself in the river.

Section 9: The hypocritical and false colonial rhetoric of being "enslaved"

It has been, of late, a very general practice to talk of slavery among those who are setting at defiance every power that keeps the world in order. If the learned author of the Reflections on Learning has rightly observed, that no man ever could give law to language, it will be vain to prohibit the use of the word slavery; but I could wish it more discreetly uttered: it is driven, at one time, too hard into our ears by

Johnson finds ridiculous the idea of giving the colonists more liberty and not trying to enforce British regulations. He does not wish to concede independence to America without a fight.

the loud hurricane of Pennsylvanian eloquence, and, at another, glides too cold into our hearts by the soft conveyance of a female patriot, bewailing the miseries of her friends and fellow-citizens.

Such has been the progress of sedition, that those who, a few years ago, disputed only our right of laying taxes, now question the validity of every act of legislation. They consider themselves as emancipated from obedience, and as being no longer the subjects of the British crown. They leave us no choice, but of yielding or conquering, of resigning our dominion or maintaining it by force. . . .

Others persuade us to give them more liberty, to take off restraints, and relax authority; and tell us what happy consequences will arise from forbearance; how their affections will be conciliated, and into what diffusions of beneficence their gratitude will luxuriate. They will love their friends. They will reverence their protectors. They will throw themselves into our arms, and lay their property at our feet; they will buy from no other what we can sell them; they will sell to no other what we wish to buy.

That any obligations should overpower their attention to profit, we have known them long enough not to expect. It is not to be expected from a more liberal people. With what kindness they repay benefits, they are now showing us, who, as soon as we have delivered them from France, are defying and proscribing us.

But if we will permit them to tax themselves, they will give us more than we require. If we proclaim them independent, they will, during pleasure, pay us a subsidy. The contest is not now for money, but for power. The question is not, how much we shall collect, but, by what authority the collection shall be made.

Those who find that the Americans cannot be shown, in any form, that may raise love or pity, dress them in habiliments of terror, and try to make us think them formidable. The Bostonians can call into the field ninety thousand men. While we conquer all before us, new enemies will rise up behind, and our work will be always to begin. If we take possession of the towns, the colonists will retire into the inland regions, and the gain of victory will be only empty houses, and a wide extent of waste and desolation. If we subdue them for the present, they will universally revolt in the next war, and resign us, without pity, to subjection and destruction.

To all this it may be answered, that between losing America, and resigning it, there is no great difference; that it is not very reasonable to jump into the sea, because the ship is leaky. All those evils may befall us, but we need not hasten them.

The dean of Gloucester has proposed, and seems to propose it seriously, that we should, at once, release our claims, declare them masters of themselves, and whistle them down the wind. His opinion is, that our gain from them will be the same, and our expense less. What they can have most cheaply from Britain, they will still buy; what they can sell to us at the highest price, they will still sell.

It is, however, a little hard, that, having so lately fought and conquered for their safety, we should govern them no longer. By letting them loose before the war, how many millions might have been saved. One wild proposal is best answered by another. Let us restore to the French what we have taken from them. We shall see our colonists at our feet, when they have an enemy so near them. Let us give the Indians arms, and teach them discipline, and encourage them, now and then, to plunder a plantation. Security and leisure are the parents of sedition.

Johnson proposes freeing and arming American slaves, and suggests (sarcastically) that the American colonists, as lovers of liberty, will applaud such an act.

While these different opinions are agitated, it seems to be determined, by the legislature, that force shall be tried. Men of the pen have seldom any great skill in conquering kingdoms, but they have strong inclination to give advice. I cannot forbear to wish, that this commotion may end without bloodshed, and that the rebels may be subdued by terror rather than by violence; and, therefore, recommend such a force as may take away, not only the power, but the hope of resistance, and, by conquering without a battle, save many from the sword.

If their obstinacy continues, without actual hostilities, it may, perhaps, be mollified, by turning out the soldiers to free quarters, forbidding any personal cruelty or hurt. It has been proposed, that the slaves should be set free, an act, which, surely, the lovers of liberty cannot but commend. If they are furnished with firearms for defense, and utensils for husbandry, and settled in some simple form of government within the country, they may be more grateful and honest than their masters. . . .

Since the Americans have made it necessary to subdue them, may they be subdued with the least injury possible to their persons and their possessions! When they are reduced to obedience, may that obedience be secured by stricter laws and stronger obligations!

Nothing can be more noxious to society, than that erroneous clemency, which, when a rebellion is suppressed, exacts no forfeiture, and establishes no securities, but leaves the rebels in their former state. Who would not try the experiment, which promises advantage without expense? If rebels once obtain a victory, their wishes are accomplished; if they are defeated, they suffer little, perhaps less than their conquerors; however often they play the game, the chance is always in their favor. In the mean time, they are growing rich by victualling the troops that we have sent against them, and, perhaps, gain more by the residence of the army than they lose by the obstruction of their port.

Their charters, being now, I suppose, legally forfeited, may be modeled, as shall appear most commodious to the mother-country. Thus the privileges which are found, by experience, liable to misuse, will be taken away, and those who now bellow as patriots, bluster as soldiers, and domineer as legislators, will sink into sober merchants and silent planters, peaceably diligent, and securely rich.

But there is one writer, and, perhaps, many who do not write, to whom the contraction of these pernicious privileges appears very dangerous, and who startle at the thoughts of "England free, and America in chains." Children fly from their own shadow, and rhetoricians are frighted by their own voices. Chains is, undoubtedly, a dreadful word; but, perhaps, the masters of civil wisdom may discover some gradations between chains and anarchy. Chains need not be put upon those who will be restrained without them. This contest may end in the softer phrase of English superiority and American obedience.

This paragraph's concluding line is the one for which this essay is most noted, a classic attack on the hypocrisy of the colonial rhetoric versus the actual practice of slavery.

We are told, that the subjection of Americans may tend to the diminution of our own liberties; an event, which none but very perspicacious politicians are able to foresee. If slavery be thus fatally contagious, how is it that we hear the loudest yelps for liberty among the drivers of negroes?

But let us interrupt awhile this dream of conquest, settlement, and supremacy. Let us remember, that being to contend, according to one orator, with three millions of whigs, and, according to another, with ninety thousand patriots of Massachusetts bay, we may possibly be checked in our career of reduction. We may be reduced to peace upon equal terms, or driven from the western continent, and forbidden to violate, a second time, the happy borders of the land of liberty. The time is now, perhaps, at hand, which Sir Thomas Browne predicted, between jest and earnest:

"When America should no more send out her treasure, But spend it at home in American pleasure."

IF WE ARE ALLOWED, UPON OUR DEFEAT, TO STIPULATE CONDITIONS, I HOPE THE TREATY OF BOSTON WILL PERMIT US TO IMPORT INTO THE CONFEDERATED CANTONS SUCH PRODUCTS AS THEY DO NOT RAISE, AND SUCH MANUFACTURES AS THEY DO NOT MAKE, AND CANNOT BUY CHEAPER FROM OTHER NATIONS, PAYING, LIKE OTHERS, THE APPOINTED CUSTOMS; THAT, IF AN ENGLISH SHIP SALUTES A FORT WITH FOUR GUNS, IT SHALL BE ANSWERED, AT LEAST, WITH TWO; AND THAT, IF AN ENGLISHMAN BE INCLINED TO HOLD A PLANTATION, HE SHALL ONLY TAKE AN OATH OF ALLEGIANCE TO THE REIGNING POWERS, AND BE SUFFERED, WHILE HE LIVES INOFFENSIVELY, TO RETAIN HIS OWN OPINION OF ENGLISH RIGHTS, UNMOLESTED IN HIS CONSCIENCE BY AN OATH OF ABJURATION.

SAMUEL SEABURY

"Free Thoughts on the Proceedings of the Continental Congress in a Letter to the Farmer," November 16, 1774

Samuel Seabury, born in 1729, was ordained a priest in the Church of England in 1753. He was the rector of St. Peter's, in what is now the Bronx but was then part of Westchester County, when he wrote a series of four letters reflecting the Loyalist position. After the Revolution, he became the first Episcopal bishop in the United States. This letter was published pseudonymously, as was often the case in colonial political debates, but students should refer to it as "Seabury's." Editor's note: This document has been broken into sections and headings have been added to facilitate both reading and referencing.

SOURCE: *Clarence H. Vance, ed.,* Letters of a Westchester Farmer by Samuel Seabury, *in* Publications of the Westchester County Historical Society *(1930), 8:43–62. Also available at http://anglicanhistory.org /usa/seabury/farmer/01.html.

*P*ERMIT me to address you upon a subject, which, next to your eternal welfare in a future world, demands your most serious and dispassionate consideration. The American Colonies are unhappily involved in a scene of confusion and discord. The bands of civil society are broken; the authority of government weakened, and in some instances taken away: Individuals are deprived of their liberty; their property is frequently invaded by violence, and not a single Magistrate has had courage or virtue enough to interpose. From this distressed situation it was hoped, that the wisdom and prudence of the Congress lately assembled at Philadelphia, would have delivered us. The eyes of all men were turned to them. We ardently expected that some prudent scheme of accommodating our unhappy disputes with the Mother-Country, would have been adopted and pursued. But alas! they are broken up without ever attempting it: they have taken no one step that tended to peace: they have gone on from bad to worse, and have either ignorantly misunderstood, carelessly neglected, or basely betrayed the interests of all the Colonies.

[M]y first business shall be to point out to you some of the consequences that will probably follow from the Non-importation, Non-exportation, and Non-consumption Agreements, which they have adopted, and which they have ordered to be enforced in the most arbitrary manner, and under the severest penalties.[1] On this subject, I choose to address myself principally to You the Farmers of the Province of New-York, because I am most nearly connected with you, being one of your number, and having no interest in the country but in common with you; and also, because the interest of the farmers in general will be more sensibly affected, and more deeply injured by these agreements, than the interest of any other body of people on the continent. . . .

Section 1: Consequences of the association for the British Empire

Let us now consider the probable consequences of these agreements, supposing they should take place, and be exactly adhered to. The first I shall mention is clamors, discord, confusion, mobs, riots, insurrections, rebellions, in Great-Britain, Ireland, and the West-Indies. This consequence does not indeed immediately affect You, the Farmers of New-York; nor do I think it a probable one: But the Congress certainly intended it should happen in some degree, or the effect they propose from these agreements cannot possibly take place. They intend to distress the manufacturers in Great-Britain, by depriving them of employment—to distress the inhabitants of Ireland, by depriving them of flax-seed, and of a vent for their linens,—to distress the West-India people, by with-holding provisions and lumber from them, and by stopping the market for their produce. And they hope, by these means, to force them all to join their clamors with ours, to get the acts complained of, repealed. This was the undoubted design of the Congress when these agreements were framed; and this is the avowed design of their warm supporters and partisans, in common conversation.

But where is the justice, where is the policy of this procedure? The manufacturers of Great-Britain, the inhabitants of Ireland, and of the West-Indies, have done us no injury. They have been no ways instrumental in bringing our distresses upon us. Shall we then revenge ourselves upon them? Shall we endeavor to starve them into a compliance with our humors? Shall we, without any provocation, tempt or force them into riots and insurrections, which must be attended with the ruin of many—probably with the death of some of them? Shall we attempt to unsettle the whole British Government—to throw all into confusion, because our self-will is not complied with? Because the ill-projected, ill-conducted, abominable scheme of some of the colonists, to form a republican government independent of Great-Britain, cannot otherwise succeed?—Good God! can we look forward to the ruin, destruction, and desolation of the whole British Empire, without one relenting thought? Can we contemplate it with pleasure; and promote it with all our might and vigor, and at the same time call ourselves his Majesty's most dutiful and loyal subjects? Whatever the Gentlemen of the Congress may think of the matter, the spirit that dictated such a measure was not the spirit of humanity.

---

1. The Association, passed by the Continental Congress in October, 1774, but yet to be ratified in New York.

Section 2: Consequences of non-importation on the colonists' consumption due to inflation

Next let us consider the policy, or rather impolicy of this measure. Instead of conciliating, it will alienate the affections of the people of Great-Britain. Of friends it will make them our enemies; it will excite the resentment of the government at home against us; and their resentment will do us no good, but, on the contrary, much harm. . . .

The first distress will fall on ourselves: it will be more severely felt by us, than by any part of all his Majesty's dominions; and it will affect us the longest. The fleets of Great-Britain command respect throughout the globe. Her influence extends to every part of the earth. Her manufactures are equal to any, superior to most in the world. Her wealth is great. Her people enterprising, and persevering in their attempts to extend and enlarge and protect her trade. The total loss of our trade would be felt only for a time. Her merchants would turn their attention another way. New sources of trade and wealth would be opened: New schemes pursued. She would soon find a vent for all her manufactures in spite of all we could do. Our malice would hurt ourselves only. Should our schemes distress some branches of her trade, it could be only for a time; and there is ability and humanity enough in the nation to relieve those that are distressed by us, and to put them in some other way of getting their living.

The case is very different with us. We have no trade but under the protection of Great-Britain. We can trade nowhere but where she pleases. We have no influence abroad, no ambassadors, no consuls, no fleet to protect our ships in passing the seas, nor our merchants and people in foreign countries. Should our mad schemes take place, our sailors, ship-carpenters, cartmen, sail-makers, riggers, miners, smelters, forge-men, and workers in bar-iron, &c. would be immediately out of employ; and we should have twenty mobs and riots in our own country, before one would happen in Britain or Ireland.

* * *

The next thing I shall take notice of, is the advanced prices of goods,[2] which will, not only probably, but necessarily, follow, as soon as the non-importation from Great Britain, &c. shall take effect. This is a consequence that most nearly concerns you; nor can you prevent it. You are obliged to buy many articles of clothing. You cannot make them yourselves; or you cannot make them so cheap as you can buy them. You want woollens for your winter clothing. Few of you have wool enough to answer the purpose. For notwithstanding the boasts of some ignorant, hot-headed men, there is not wool enough on the continent, taking all the colonies together, to supply the inhabitants with stockings. Notwithstanding all the home-spun you can make, many of you find it difficult, at the year's end, to pay the

---

2. Inflation.

shop-keeper for what the necessities of your families have obliged you to take up. What will you do when the prices of goods are advanced a quarter, for instance, or a half? To say that the prices of goods will not be raised betrays your ignorance and folly. The price of any commodity always rises in proportion to the demand for it; and the demand always increases in proportion to its scarcity. As soon as the importation ceases in New-York, the quantity of goods will be daily lessened, by daily consumption; and the prices will gradually rise in proportion. "But the merchants of New-York have declared that, they will demand only a reasonable profit." Who is to judge what a reasonable profit is? Why, the merchants. Will they expose their invoices, and the secrets of their trade to you, that you may judge whether their profits are reasonable or not? Certainly they will not. And if they did, you cannot understand them; and, consequently, can form no judgment about them. You have therefore nothing to trust to in this case but the honor of the merchants. Let us then consider how far we have reason to trust to their honor.

Not to raise the price of a commodity when it is scarce, and in demand, is contrary to the principles and practice of merchants. Their maxim is, to buy as cheap, and sell as dear, as they can. Will they let you have a piece of goods for twenty shillings, which will fetch twenty-five? When the stores and shops are full, and a price is demanded which you think unreasonable, you will ask an abatement. If you are refused, you will look elsewhere. But when there are few goods and many buyers, no abatement can be expected. If you won't give the price, your neighbor perhaps is in greater necessity, and must give it. Besides, the merchant knows that no more goods can be imported. He knows that the necessities of the country are increasing, and that what you refuse now at twenty shillings, you will be obliged to take, by and by, at twenty-five. . . .

Section 3: Consequences of non-exportation on farmers' income

Look well to yourselves, I beseech you. From the day that the exports from this province are stopped, the farmers may date the commencement of their ruin. Can you live without money? Will the shop-keeper give you his goods? Will the weaver, shoemaker, blacksmith, carpenter, work for you without pay? If they will, it is more than they will do for me. And unless you can sell your produce, how are you to get money? Nor will the case be better, if you are obliged to sell your produce at an under-rate; for then it will not pay you for the labor and expense of raising it. But this is the least part of the distress that will come upon you.

Unhappily, many of you are in debt, and obliged to pay the enormous interest of seven pounds on the hundred,[3] for considerable sums. It matters not whether

---

3. 7 percent interest, a historically high rate.

your debts have been contracted through necessity, or carelessness: You must pay them, at least the interest, punctually; the usurer will not wait long; indeed you cannot expect he should: You have had his money, and are obliged, in justice, to pay him the principal and interest, according to agreement. But without selling your produce, you can neither pay the one, nor the other; the consequence will be that after a while, a process of law will be commenced against you, and your farms must be sold by execution; and then you will have to pay not only principal and interest, but Sheriffs fees, Lawyers fees, and a long list of et ceteras.

Nor, under these circumstances, will your farms fetch half what they cost you. What is a farm good for, the produce of which cannot be sold? Had matters continued in their old course, some one of your neighbors, who knew the value of your farm, might have been willing and able to have given you a reasonable price for it, had you been disposed, or obliged to sell; but he has more wit than to buy a farm, when he cannot sell its produce. Your creditor then, or some rich merchant, or usurer, must take it at their own price: To you it is of no consequence who takes it; for you are ruined, stripped of your farm, and very probably of the means of subsistence for yourself and family. Glorious effect of Non-exportation! Think a little, and then tell me—when the Congress adopted this cursed scheme, did they in the least consider your interest? No, impossible! they ignorantly misunderstood, carelessly neglected, or basely betrayed you. . . .

Section 4: Consequences of using the association to enforce non-importation and non-exportation, bypassing the court system

Rouse, my friends, rouse from your stupid lethargy. Mark the men who shall dare to impede the course of justice. Brand them as the infamous betrayers of the rights of their country. The grand security of the property, the liberty, the lives of Englishmen, consists in the due administration of justice. While the courts are duly attended to, and fairly conducted, our property is safe. As soon as they are shut, everything is precarious: for neither property, nor liberty, have any foundation to stand upon.

Tell me not of Delegates, Congresses, Committees, Riots, Mobs, Insurrections, Associations,—a plague on them all.—Give me the steady, uniform, unbiased influence of the Courts of Justice. I have been happy under their protection, and I trust in God, I shall be so again.

But after all, some of you, I fear, look forward with pleasure to those halcyon days of security, when the Courts shall be shut. Undisturbed by the clamors of creditors, undismayed by the sight of the Sheriff, you think to pass your lives in quietness and peace. But ah! my friends! trust not the fatal, the ill-judged security. You would not, I hope, be so dishonest as not to do your utmost endeavor to pay your debts; besides, while the Courts of Justice are shut, you will be apt to be careless.

You will neglect paying your interest, your debts will accumulate, your creditors will be irritated; and as soon as a legal process can be commenced, you will be ruined before you can look about you.

Some of you are indebted to the loan-office. You have your money, it is true, at a low rate: You pay only five per centum: But if you cannot sell your produce, you can no more pay five per cent, than seven. The shutting up of the Courts of Justice can here give you no relief. By virtue of the act which regulates the Loan-Office, your farms, if you fail to pay the interest, will be sold in a limited time, without any judicial process at all.

Some of you, also, are tenants at will; and if you fail in paying your rents, you may be turned off, with little or no warning.

Consider now the situation you will be in, if Great-Britain, provoked by your Non-Importation Agreement, should shut up our ports; or should the Non-Exportation agreed to by the Congress, take effect. In that case you will not be able to sell your produce: you cannot pay even the interest of the money you are indebted for: your farms must be sold, and you and your families turned out, to beggary and wretchedness. Blessed fruits of Non-Importation and Non-Exportation! The farmer that is in debt, will be ruined: the farmer that is clear in the world, will be obliged to run in debt, to support his family: and while the proud merchant, and the forsworn smuggler, riot in their ill-gotten wealth; the laborious farmers, the grand support of every well-regulated country, must all go to the dogs together.— Vile! Shamefull! Diabolical Device!

Section 5: Consequences of the boycott and the committees to enforce it upon colonial personal freedom

Let us now attend a little to the Non-Consumption Agreement, which the Congress, in their Association, has imposed upon us. After the first of March we are not to purchase or use any East-India Tea whatsoever; nor any goods, wares, or merchandize from Great-Britain or Ireland, imported after the first day of December next: nor any molasses, syrups, &c. from the British plantations in the West-Indies, or from Dominica; nor wine from Madeira, or the Western Islands; nor foreign indigo.

Will you submit to this slavish regulation? You must. Our sovereign Lords and Masters, the High and Mighty Delegates, in Grand Continental Congress assembled, have ordered and directed it. They have directed the Committees[4] in the respective colonies, to establish such further regulations as they may think proper, for carrying their association, of which this Non-consumption agreement is a part, into execution. . . . The business of the Committee so chosen is to be, to inspect the conduct of the inhabitants, and see whether they violate the Association. Among

---

4. Committees of Inspection, established in each locale to enforce the Association.

other things, whether they drink any Tea or wine in their families, after the first of March; or wear any British or Irish manufactures; or use any English molasses, &c. imported after the first day of December next. If they do, their names are to be published in the Gazette, that they may be publicly known, and universally contemned, as foes to the Rights of British America, and enemies of American Liberty. And then the parties of the said Association will respectively break off all dealings with him or her. In plain English, they shall be considered as Out-laws, unworthy of the protection of civil society, and delivered over to the vengeance of a lawless, outrageous mob, to be tarred, feathered, hanged, drawn, quartered, and burnt.—O rare American Freedom!

Probably, [the New York Committee leader] will issue his Mandate to the supervisors in the several counties, as he did about the choice of Delegates, and direct them to have Committees chosen in their respective districts, for the same laudable purpose.

Will you be instrumental in bringing the most abject slavery on yourselves? Will you choose such Committees? Will you submit to them, should they be chosen by the weak, foolish, turbulent part of the country people? Do as you please: but, by HIM that made me, I will not. No, if I must be enslaved, let it be by a KING at least, and not by a parcel of upstart lawless Committee-men. If I must be devoured, let me be devoured by the jaws of a lion, and not gnawed to death by rats and vermin.

Did you choose your supervisors for the purpose of enslaving you? What right have they to fix up advertisements to call you together, for a very different purpose from that for which they were elected? Are our supervisors our masters? And should half a dozen foolish people meet together again, in consequence of their advertisements, and choose themselves to be a Committee, as they did in many districts, in the affair of choosing Delegates, are we obliged to submit to such a Committee? You ought, my friends, to assert your own freedom. Should such another attempt be made upon you, assemble yourselves together: tell your supervisor, that he has exceeded his commission: That you will have no such Committees: That you are Englishmen, and will maintain your rights and privileges, and will eat, and drink, and wear, whatever the public laws of your country permit, without asking leave of any illegal, tyrannical Congress or Committee on earth.

But however, as I said before, do as you please: If you like it better, choose your Committee, or suffer it to be chosen by half a dozen Fools in your neighborhood, open your doors to them, let them examine your tea-canisters, and molasses-jugs, and your wives and daughters petty-coats, bow, and cringe, and tremble, and quake, fall down and worship our sovereign Lord the Mob. But I repeat it, By H—n, I will not. No, my house is my castle: as such I will consider it, as such I will defend it, while I have breath. No King's officer shall enter it without my permission, unless supported by a warrant from a magistrate. And shall my house be entered, and my mode of living enquired into, by a domineering Committee-man? Before I submit, I will die: live you, and be slaves.

Seabury, "Free Thoughts on the Proceedings," 1774

THOMAS PAINE

FROM *Common Sense*, 1776

Thomas Paine was a recent immigrant to the colonies, having arrived in 1774 after several years of agitating in England for better pay for himself and other excise officials. Benjamin Franklin encouraged his emigration to Philadelphia and provided him with letters of introduction that led Paine first to an editorial job and then to polemical writing. The appearance of this pamphlet caused a popular sensation, and advanced the cause of American independence six months before the Declaration was approved. Thus began Paine's life as a writer for revolutions on both sides of the Atlantic. This pamphlet's arguments were anticipated by many others, but only Paine phrased them in language and style clear enough for the average reader to comprehend (as opposed to the convoluted arguments based in Locke, law, and political theories of sovereignty). The pamphlet officially sold one hundred thousand copies in three months and was reprinted unofficially hundreds of thousands of times more. Proportionally, Paine's readership would equal anywhere from fifteen to fifty million people today. Editor's note: This version of Common Sense has been abridged and annotated. The document has been broken into sections and headings have been added to facilitate both reading and referencing.

SOURCE: *Thomas Paine*, Common Sense, *Project Gutenberg, www.gutenberg.org/ebooks/147*

Section 1: No advantages from the English constitution

SOME writers have so confounded society with government, as to leave little or no distinction between them; whereas they are not only different, but have different origins. Society is produced by our wants, and government by our wickedness; the former promotes our happiness POSITIVELY by uniting our affections, the latter NEGATIVELY by restraining our vices. The one encourages intercourse, the other creates distinctions. The first is a patron, the last a punisher.

Society in every state is a blessing, but government even in its best state is but a necessary evil in its worst state an intolerable one; for when we suffer, or are exposed to the same miseries BY A GOVERNMENT, which we might expect in a country WITHOUT GOVERNMENT, our calamities is heightened by reflecting that we furnish the means by which we suffer! Government, like dress, is the badge of lost innocence; the palaces of kings are built on the ruins of the bowers of paradise. For were the impulses of conscience clear, uniform, and irresistibly obeyed, man would need no other lawgiver; but that not being the case, he finds it necessary to surrender up a part of his property to furnish means for the protection of the rest; and this he is induced to do by the same prudence which in every other case advises him out of two evils to choose the least. WHEREFORE, security being the true design and end of government, it unanswerably follows that whatever FORM thereof appears most likely to ensure it to us, with the least expense and greatest benefit, is preferable to all others.

Note that Paine begins here as Locke does, with a return to human origins: a state of nature and the first legislature.

In order to gain a clear and just idea of the design and end of government, let us suppose a small number of persons settled in some sequestered part of the earth, unconnected with the rest, they will then represent the first peopling of any country, or of the world. In this state of natural liberty, society will be their first thought. A thousand motives will excite them thereto, the strength of one man is so unequal to his wants, and his mind so unfitted for perpetual solitude, that he is soon obliged to seek assistance and relief of another, who in his turn requires the same. Four or five united would be able to raise a tolerable dwelling in the midst of a wilderness, but one man might labor out the common period of life without accomplishing anything; when he had felled his timber he could not remove it, nor erect it after it was removed; hunger in the mean time would urge him from his work, and every different want call him a different way. Disease, nay even misfortune would be death, for though neither might be mortal, yet either would disable him from living, and reduce him to a state in which he might rather be said to perish than to die.

Thus necessity, like a gravitating power, would soon form our newly arrived emigrants into society, the reciprocal blessings of which, would supersede, and render the obligations of law and government unnecessary while they remained perfectly just to each other; but as nothing but heaven is impregnable to vice, it will unavoidably happen, that in proportion as they surmount the first difficulties of emigration, which bound them together in a common cause, they will begin to relax in their duty and attachment to each other; and this remissness, will point out the necessity, of establishing some form of government to supply the defect of moral virtue.[1]

---

1. Paine's view of human nature parallels that of Locke, but for Paine it is not man's greed or self-interest that forces him to create a government. It is man's tendency to relax and slide into bad habits (or vice).

Some convenient tree will afford them a State-House, under the branches of which, the whole colony may assemble to deliberate on public matters. It is more than probable that their first laws will have the title only of REGULATIONS, and be enforced by no other penalty than public disesteem. In this first parliament every man, by natural right will have a seat.

But as the colony increases, the public concerns will increase likewise, and the distance at which the members may be separated, will render it too inconvenient for all of them to meet on every occasion as at first, when their number was small, their habitations near, and the public concerns few and trifling. This will point out the convenience of their consenting to leave the legislative part to be managed by a select number chosen from the whole body, who are supposed to have the same concerns at stake which those who appointed them, and who will act in the same manner as the whole body would act were they present. If the colony continue increasing, it will become necessary to augment the number of the representatives, and that the interest of every part of the colony may be attended to, it will be found best to divide the whole into convenient parts, each part sending its proper number; and that the ELECTED might never form to themselves an interest separate from the ELECTORS, prudence will point out the propriety of having elections often; because as the ELECTED might by that means return and mix again with the general body of the ELECTORS in a few months, their fidelity to the public will be secured by the prudent reflection of not making a rod for themselves. And as this frequent interchange will establish a common interest with every part of the community, they will mutually and naturally support each other, and on this (not on the unmeaning name of king) depends the STRENGTH OF GOVERNMENT, AND THE HAPPINESS OF THE GOVERNED.

Here then is the origin and rise of government; namely, a mode rendered necessary by the inability of moral virtue to govern the world[2]; here too is the design and end of government, viz., freedom and security. And however our eyes may be dazzled with snow, or our ears deceived by sound; however prejudice may warp our wills, or interest darken our understanding, the simple voice of nature and of reason will say, it is right.

I draw my idea of the form of government from a principle in nature, which no art can overturn, viz., that the more simple any thing is, the less liable it is to be disordered, and the easier repaired when disordered; and with this maxim in view, I offer a few remarks on the so much boasted constitution of England. That it was noble for the dark and slavish times in which it was erected is granted. When the world was overrun with tyranny the least therefrom was a glorious rescue. But that it is imperfect, subject to convulsions, and incapable of producing what it seems to promise, is easily demonstrated.

---

2. Classical republican thought required the moral virtue of citizens in order to succeed. Paine is using Lockean reasoning to create a liberal republican ideology based on self-interest.

Absolute governments (though the disgrace of human nature) have this advantage with them, that they are simple; if the people suffer, they know the head from which their suffering springs, know likewise the remedy, and are not bewildered by a variety of causes and cures. But the constitution of England is so exceedingly complex, that the nation may suffer for years together without being able to discover in which part the fault lies, some will say in one and some in another, and every political physician will advise a different medicine.

I know it is difficult to get over local or long standing prejudices, yet if we will suffer ourselves to examine the component parts of the English constitution, we shall find them to be the base remains of two ancient tyrannies, compounded with some new republican materials.

Section 2: Defining the three-part British "mixed" government as tyrannical

FIRST.—The remains of monarchical tyranny in the person of the king.

SECONDLY.—The remains of aristocratical tyranny in the persons of the peers.

THIRDLY.—The new republican materials, in the persons of the commons, on whose virtue depends the freedom of England.[3]

The two first, by being hereditary, are independent of the people; wherefore in a CONSTITUTIONAL SENSE they contribute nothing towards the freedom of the state.

To say that the constitution of England is a UNION of three powers reciprocally CHECKING each other, is farcical, either the words have no meaning, or they are flat contradictions.

To say that the commons is a check upon the king, presupposes two things.

FIRST.—That the king is not to be trusted without being looked after, or in other words, that a thirst for absolute power is the natural disease of monarchy.

SECONDLY.—That the commons, by being appointed for that purpose, are either wiser or more worthy of confidence than the crown.

But as the same constitution which gives the commons a power to check the king by withholding the supplies, gives afterwards the king a power to check the commons, by empowering him to reject their other bills; it again supposes that the king is wiser than those whom it has already supposed to be wiser than him. A mere absurdity!

---

3. The three parts of the British mixed government were: the king (monarchy) and two houses in Parliament: the House of Lords (aristocracy) and the House of Commons (democracy, or the people). The term democracy is a misnomer, however, as only 5 percent of the adult males possessed sufficient property to vote. In this period, the king and the prime minister were able to control many of the outcomes of the Commons votes through informal means (bribery, control of seats representing areas where nobody lived, etc.).

There is something exceedingly ridiculous in the composition of monarchy; it first excludes a man from the means of information, yet empowers him to act in cases where the highest judgment is required. The state of a king shuts him from the world, yet the business of a king requires him to know it thoroughly; wherefore the different parts, unnaturally opposing and destroying each other, prove the whole character to be absurd and useless.

Some writers have explained the English constitution thus; the king, say they, is one, the people another; the peers are a house in behalf of the king; the commons in behalf of the people; but this has all the distinctions of a house divided against itself; and though the expressions be pleasantly arranged, yet when examined they appear idle and ambiguous; and it will always happen, that the nicest construction that words are capable of, when applied to the description of something which either cannot exist, or is too incomprehensible to be within the compass of description, will be words of sound only, and though they may amuse the ear, they cannot inform the mind, for this explanation includes a previous question, viz. HOW CAME THE KING BY A POWER WHICH THE PEOPLE ARE AFRAID TO TRUST, AND ALWAYS OBLIGED TO CHECK? Such a power could not be the gift of a wise people, neither can any power, WHICH NEEDS CHECKING, be from God; yet the provision, which the constitution makes, supposes such a power to exist.

But the provision is unequal to the task; the means either cannot or will not accomplish the end, and the whole affair is a *felo de se*[4]; for as the greater weight will always carry up the less, and as all the wheels of a machine are put in motion by one, it only remains to know which power in the constitution has the most weight, for that will govern; and though the others, or a part of them, may clog, or, as the phrase is, check the rapidity of its motion, yet so long as they cannot stop it, their endeavors will be ineffectual; the first moving power will at last have its way, and what it wants in speed is supplied by time.

Paine is refuting the idea and value of representation in Parliament in its entirety, stating that the king is still in charge, not the people.

That the crown is this overbearing part in the English constitution needs not be mentioned, and that it derives its whole consequence merely from being the giver of places [and] pensions is self evident, wherefore, though we have [been] wise enough to shut and lock a door against absolute monarchy, we at the same time have been foolish enough to put the crown in possession of the key.

The prejudice of Englishmen, in favor of their own government by king, lords, and commons, arises as much or more from national pride than reason. Individuals are undoubtedly safer in England than in some other countries, but the WILL of the king is as much the LAW of the land in Britain as in France, with this difference, that instead of proceeding directly from his mouth, it is handed to the people

---

4. Suicide (Latin).

under the most formidable shape of an act of parliament. For the fate of Charles the First has only made kings more subtle not more just.

Wherefore, laying aside all national pride and prejudice in favor of modes and forms, the plain truth is, that IT IS WHOLLY OWING TO THE CONSTITUTION OF THE PEOPLE, AND NOT TO THE CONSTITUTION OF THE GOVERNMENT that the crown is not as oppressive in England as in Turkey.

An inquiry into the constitutional errors in the English form of government is at this time highly necessary; for as we are never in a proper condition of doing justice to others, while we continue under the influence of some leading partiality, so neither are we capable of doing it to ourselves while we remain fettered by any obstinate prejudice. And as a man, who is attached to a prostitute, is unfitted to choose or judge of a wife, so any prepossession in favor of a rotten constitution of government will disable us from discerning a good one.[5]

OF MONARCHY AND HEREDITARY SUCCESSION

Section 3: Ending affection for the monarchy, and for George III

MANKIND being originally equals[6] in the order of creation, the equality could only be destroyed by some subsequent circumstance; the distinctions of rich, and poor, may in a great measure be accounted for, and that without having recourse to the harsh, ill-sounding names of oppression and avarice. Oppression is often the CONSEQUENCE, but seldom or never the MEANS of riches; and though avarice will preserve a man from being necessarily poor, it generally makes him too timorous to be wealthy.

But there is another and greater distinction for which no truly natural or religious reason can be assigned, and that is, the distinction of men into KINGS and SUBJECTS. Male and female are the distinctions of nature, good and bad the distinctions of heaven; but how a race of men came into the world so exalted above the rest, and distinguished like some new species, is worth enquiring into, and whether they are the means of happiness or of misery to mankind.

In the early ages of the world, according to the scripture chronology, there were no kings; the consequence of which was there were no wars; it is the pride of kings which throw mankind into confusion. Holland without a king has enjoyed more peace for this last century than any of the monarchial governments in Europe. Antiquity favors the same remark; for the quiet and rural lives of the first patriarchs has a happy something in them, which vanishes away when we come to the history of Jewish royalty. . . .

---

5. Note how neatly Paine compares the British constitution to a whore, without ever using the word.

6. Here and below, Paine echoes Locke on the equality of man.

To the evil of monarchy we have added that of hereditary succession; and as the first is a degradation and lessening of ourselves, so the second, claimed as a matter of right, is an insult and an imposition on posterity. For all men being originally equals, no ONE by BIRTH could have a right to set up his own family in perpetual preference to all others for ever, and though himself might deserve some decent degree of honors of his contemporaries, yet his descendants might be far too unworthy to inherit them. One of the strongest NATURAL proofs of the folly of hereditary right in kings, is, that nature disapproves it, otherwise she would not so frequently turn it into ridicule by giving mankind an ASS FOR A LION.

Secondly, as no man at first could possess any other public honors than were bestowed upon him, so the givers of those honors could have no power to give away the right of posterity, and though they might say, "We choose you for OUR head," they could not, without manifest injustice to their children, say, "that your children and your children's children shall reign over OURS forever." Because such an unwise, unjust, unnatural compact might (perhaps) in the next succession put them under the government of a rogue or a fool. Most wise men, in their private sentiments, have ever treated hereditary right with contempt; yet it is one of those evils, which when once established is not easily removed; many submit from fear, others from superstition, and the more powerful part shares with the king the plunder of the rest.

England, since the conquest, has known some few good monarchs, but groaned beneath a much larger number of bad ones, yet no man in his senses can say that their claim under William the Conqueror is a very honorable one. A French bastard landing with an armed banditti, and establishing himself king of England against the consent of the natives, is in plain terms a very paltry rascally original. It certainly has no divinity in it.[7] However, it is needless to spend much time in exposing the folly of hereditary right, if there are any so weak as to believe it, let them promiscuously worship the ass and lion, and welcome. I shall neither copy their humility, nor disturb their devotion. . . .

As to usurpation, no man will be so hardy as to defend it; and that William the Conqueror was a usurper is a fact not to be contradicted. The plain truth is that the antiquity of English monarchy will not bear looking into. . . .

But it is not so much the absurdity as the evil of hereditary succession which concerns mankind. Did it ensure a race of good and wise men it would have the seal of divine authority, but as it opens a door to the FOOLISH, the WICKED; and the IMPROPER, it has in it the nature of oppression. Men who look upon themselves born to reign, and others to obey, soon grow insolent; selected from the rest of mankind their minds are early poisoned by importance; and the world they act in differs so materially from the world at large, that they have but little opportunity

---

7. Quickly skewering the theory of the divine right of kings through analysis of William the Conqueror.

of knowing its true interests, and when they succeed to the government are frequently the most ignorant and unfit of any throughout the dominions. . . .

In short, monarchy and succession have laid, not this or that kingdom only, but the world in blood and ashes. 'Tis a form of government which the word of God bears testimony against, and blood will attend it. . . .

Since Parliament cannot control the king, and the monarchy inevitably is disastrous, there is only one form of government, a republic, that can succeed.

The nearer any government approaches to a republic, the less business there is for a king. It is somewhat difficult to find a proper name for the government of England. Sir William Meredith calls it a republic; but in its present state it is unworthy of the name, because the corrupt influence of the crown, by having all the places in its disposal, has so effectually swallowed up the power, and eaten out the virtue of the house of commons (the republican part in the constitution) that the government of England is nearly as monarchical as that of France or Spain. Men fall out with names without understanding them. For it is the republican and not the monarchical part of the constitution of England which Englishmen glory in, viz., the liberty of choosing a house of commons from out of their own body—and it is easy to see that when the republican virtue fails, slavery ensues. Why is the constitution of England sickly, but because monarchy has poisoned the republic, the crown has engrossed the commons?

In England a king has little more to do than to make war and give away places; which in plain terms, is to impoverish the nation and set it together by the ears. A pretty business indeed for a man to be allowed eight hundred thousand sterling a year for, and worshipped into the bargain! Of more worth is one honest man to society, and in the sight of God, than all the crowned ruffians that ever lived.

THOUGHTS OF THE PRESENT STATE OF AMERICAN AFFAIRS

Section 4: The multiple grounds for independence

IN the following pages I offer nothing more than simple facts, plain arguments, and common sense; and have no other preliminaries to settle with the reader, than that he will divest himself of prejudice and prepossession, and suffer his reason and his feelings to determine for themselves; that he will put ON, or rather that he will not put OFF the true character of a man, and generously enlarge his views beyond the present day.

Volumes have been written on the subject of the struggle between England and America. Men of all ranks have embarked in the controversy, from different motives, and with various designs; but all have been ineffectual, and the period of debate is closed. Arms, as the last resource, decide the contest; the appeal was the choice of the king, and the continent has accepted the challenge. . . .

The sun never shined on a cause of greater worth. 'Tis not the affair of a city, a country, a province, or a kingdom, but of a continent—of at least one eighth part of the habitable globe. 'Tis not the concern of a day, a year, or an age; posterity are virtually involved in the contest, and will be more or less affected, even to the end of time, by the proceedings now. Now is the seed time of continental union, faith and honor. The least fracture now will be like a name engraved with the point of a pin on the tender rind of a young oak; The wound will enlarge with the tree, and posterity read it in full grown characters.

Section 4a: War has begun

By referring the matter from argument to arms, a new area for politics is struck; a new method of thinking has arisen. All plans, proposals, &c. prior to the nineteenth of April,[8] i.e., to the commencement of hostilities, are like the almanacs of the last year; which, though proper then, are superseded and useless now. Whatever was advanced by the advocates on either side of the question then, terminated in one and the same point, viz., a union with Great Britain; the only difference between the parties was the method of effecting it; the one proposing force, the other friendship; but it has so far happened that the first has failed, and the second has withdrawn her influence.

As much has been said of the advantages of reconciliation, which, like an agreeable dream, has passed away and left us as we were, it is but right, that we should examine the contrary side of the argument, and inquire into some of the many material injuries which these colonies sustain, and always will sustain, by being connected with, and dependant on Great Britain. To examine that connection and dependence, on the principles of nature and common sense, to see what we have to trust to, if separated, and what we are to expect, if dependant.

Section 4b: Free trade with the world

I have heard it asserted by some, that as America has flourished under her former connection with Great Britain, that the same connection is necessary towards her future happiness, and will always have the same effect. Nothing can be more fallacious than this kind of argument. We may as well assert, that because a child has thrived upon milk, that it is never to have meat; or that the first twenty years of our lives is to become a precedent for the next twenty. But even this is admitting more than is true, for I answer roundly, that America would have flourished as much, and probably much more, had no European power had anything to do with her. The commerce by which she has enriched herself are the necessaries of life, and will always have a market while eating is the custom of Europe.

But she has protected us, say some. That she has engrossed us is true, and defended the continent at our expense as well as her own is admitted, and she would have defended Turkey from the same motive, viz., the sake of trade and dominion.

---

8. Battles of Lexington and Concord, April 19, 1775, the previous year.

Alas! we have been long led away by ancient prejudices and made large sacrifices to superstition. We have boasted the protection of Great Britain, without considering, that her motive was INTEREST not ATTACHMENT; that she did not protect us from OUR ENEMIES on OUR ACCOUNT, but from HER ENEMIES on her OWN ACCOUNT, from those who had no quarrel with us on any OTHER ACCOUNT, and who will always be our enemies on the same account. Let Britain wave her pretensions to the continent, or the continent throw off the dependence, and we should be at peace with France and Spain were they at war with Britain. The miseries of Hanover[9] last war ought to warn us against connections.

It has lately been asserted in parliament, that the colonies have no relation to each other but through the parent country, i.e., that Pennsylvania and the Jerseys, and so on for the rest, are sister colonies by the way of England; this is certainly a very roundabout way of proving relationship, but it is the nearest and only true way of proving enemyship, if I may so call it. France and Spain never were, nor perhaps ever will be our enemies as AMERICANS, but as our being the subjects of GREAT BRITAIN.

Section 4c: Freedom from an abusive parent

But Britain is the parent country, say some. Then the more shame upon her conduct. Even brutes do not devour their young; nor savages make war upon their families; wherefore the assertion, if true, turns to her reproach; but it happens not to be true, or only partly so, and the phrase PARENT or MOTHER COUNTRY has been jesuitically adopted by the king and his parasites, with a low papistical design of gaining an unfair bias on the credulous weakness of our minds.[10] Europe, and not England, is the parent country of America. This new world has been the asylum for the persecuted lovers off civil and religious liberty from EVERY PART of Europe. Hither have they fled, not from the tender embraces of the mother, but from the cruelty of the monster; and it is so far true of England, that the same tyranny which drove the first emigrants from home pursues their descendants still.

In this extensive quarter of the globe, we forget the narrow limits of three hundred and sixty miles (the extent of England) and carry our friendship on a larger scale; we claim brotherhood with every European Christian, and triumph in the generosity of the sentiment. . . .

Not one third of the inhabitants, even of this province, are of English descent. Wherefore, I [deny] the phrase of parent or mother country applied to England only, as being false, selfish, narrow and ungenerous.

This argument undermines the emotional power of the mother-child metaphor, as well as providing historical, ideological, and pragmatic grounds for leaving the British Empire.

---

9. The British king was also king of the German province of Hanover, and in the European theater of the French and Indian War (called the Seven Years' War in Europe), Hanover along with many other German territories suffered battles, death, and destruction.

10. Use of terms such as "papistically" and "jesuitically" indicates that Britain and the king are like Catholics, who were roundly hated and distrusted by the vast majority of colonists.

But admitting that we were all of English descent, what does it amount to? Nothing. Britain, being now an open enemy, extinguishes every other name and title: And to say that reconciliation is our duty, is truly farcical. The first king of England, of the present line (William the Conqueror) was a Frenchman, and half the peers of England are descendants from the same country; wherefore by the same method of reasoning, England ought to be governed by France.

Much has been said of the united strength of Britain and the colonies, that in conjunction they might bid defiance to the world. But this is mere presumption; the fate of war is uncertain, neither do the expressions mean anything; for this continent would never suffer itself to be drained of inhabitants to support the British arms in either Asia, Africa, or Europe.

Section 4d: Self-interest and free markets are sufficient to create American prosperity

Besides, what have we to do with setting the world at defiance? Our plan is commerce, and that, well attended to, will secure us the peace and friendship of all Europe; because it is the interest of all Europe to have America a FREE PORT. Her trade will always be a protection, and her barrenness of gold and silver secure her from invaders.

I challenge the warmest advocate for reconciliation, to show, a single advantage that this continent can reap, by being connected with Great Britain. I repeat the challenge, not a single advantage is derived. Our corn will fetch its price in any market in Europe, and our imported goods must be paid for buy them where we will.

But the injuries and disadvantages we sustain by that connection, are without number; and our duty to mankind at large, as well as to ourselves, instruct us to renounce the alliance: Because, any submission to, or dependence on Great Britain, tends directly to involve this continent in European wars and quarrels; and sets us at variance with nations, who would otherwise seek our friendship, and against whom, we have neither anger nor complaint. As Europe is our market for trade, we ought to form no partial connection with any part of it. It is the true interest of America to steer clear of European contentions, which she never can do, while by her dependence on Britain, she is made the make-weight in the scale of British politics.

Europe is too thickly planted with kingdoms to be long at peace, and whenever a war breaks out between England and any foreign power, the trade of America goes to ruin, BECAUSE OF HER CONNECTION WITH BRITAIN. The next war may not turn out like the Past, and should it not, the advocates for reconciliation now will be wishing for separation then, because, neutrality in that case, would be a safer convoy than a man of war. Everything that is right or natural pleads for separation. The blood of the slain, the weeping voice of nature cries, 'TIS TIME TO PART. Even the distance at which the Almighty has placed England and

America, is a strong and natural proof, that the authority of the one, over the other, was never the design of Heaven. The time likewise at which the continent was discovered, adds weight to the argument, and the manner in which it was peopled increases the force of it. The reformation was preceded by the discovery of America, as if the Almighty graciously meant to open a sanctuary to the persecuted in future years, when home should afford neither friendship nor safety.

The authority of Great Britain over this continent is a form of government, which sooner or later must have an end: And a serious mind can draw no true pleasure by looking forward, under the painful and positive conviction, that what he calls "the present constitution" is merely temporary. As parents, we can have no joy, knowing that THIS GOVERNMENT is not sufficiently lasting to ensure anything which we may bequeath to posterity: And by a plain method of argument, as we are running the next generation into debt, we ought to do the work of it, otherwise we use them meanly and pitifully. In order to discover the line of our duty rightly, we should take our children in our hand, and fix our station a few years farther into life; that eminence will present a prospect, which a few present fears and prejudices conceal from our sight.

Section 4e: The impossibility and futility of reconciliation

Though I would carefully avoid giving unnecessary offence, yet I am inclined to believe, that all those who espouse the doctrine of reconciliation, may be included within the following descriptions: Interested men, who are not to be trusted; weak men who CANNOT see; prejudiced men who WILL NOT see; and a certain set of moderate men, who think better of the European world than it deserves; and this last class by an ill-judged deliberation, will be the cause of more calamities to this continent than all the other three.

It is the good fortune of many to live distant from the scene of sorrow; the evil is not sufficiently brought to their doors to make them feel the precariousness with which all American property is possessed. But let our imaginations transport us for a few moments to Boston, that seat of wretchedness will teach us wisdom, and instruct us forever to renounce a power in whom we can have no trust. The inhabitants of that unfortunate city, who but a few months ago were in ease and affluence, have now no other alternative than to stay and starve, or turn out to beg. Endangered by the fire of their friends if they continue within the city, and plundered by the soldiery if they leave it. In their present condition they are prisoners without the hope of redemption, and in a general attack for their relief, they would be exposed to the fury of both armies.

Men of passive tempers look somewhat lightly over the offenses of Britain, and, still hoping for the best, are apt to call out, COME WE SHALL BE FRIENDS AGAIN FOR ALL THIS. But examine the passions and feelings of mankind. Bring the doctrine of reconciliation to the touchstone of nature, and then tell me, whether you

Paine emotionally recalls the military actions the British have taken and the casualties they have inflicted, demanding action against the abusive and evil parent.

can hereafter love, honor, and faithfully serve the power that has carried fire and sword into your land? If you cannot do all these, then are you only deceiving yourselves, and by your delay bringing ruin upon posterity. Your future connection with Britain, whom you can neither love nor honor, will be forced and unnatural, and being formed only on the plan of present convenience, will in a little time fall into a relapse more wretched than the first. But if you say, you can still pass the violations over, then I ask, Has your house been burnt? Has your property been destroyed before your face? Are your wife and children destitute of a bed to lie on, or bread to live on? Have you lost a parent or a child by their hands, and yourself the ruined and wretched survivor? If you have not, then are you not a judge of those who have. But if you have, and can still shake hands with the murderers, then are you unworthy the name of husband, father, friend, or lover, and whatever may be your rank or title in life, you have the heart of a coward, and the spirit of a sycophant.

This is not inflaming or exaggerating matters, but trying them by those feelings and affections which nature justifies, and without which, we should be incapable of discharging the social duties of life, or enjoying the felicities of it. I mean not to exhibit horror for the purpose of provoking revenge, but to awaken us from fatal and unmanly slumbers, that we may pursue determinately some fixed object. It is not in the power of Britain or of Europe to conquer America, if she does not conquer herself by DELAY and TIMIDITY. The present winter is worth an age if rightly employed, but if lost or neglected, the whole continent will partake of the misfortune; and there is no punishment which that man will not deserve, be he who, or what, or where he will, that may be the means of sacrificing a season so precious and useful.

It is repugnant to reason, to the universal order of things, to all examples from the former ages, to suppose, that this continent can longer remain subject to any external power. The most sanguine in Britain does not think so. The utmost stretch of human wisdom cannot, at this time compass a plan short of separation, which can promise the continent even a year's security. Reconciliation is *now* a fallacious dream. Nature has deserted the connection, and Art cannot supply her place. For, as Milton wisely expresses, "never can true reconcilement grow where wounds of deadly hate have pierced so deep."[11]

Every quiet method for peace has been ineffectual. Our prayers have been rejected with disdain; and only tended to convince us, that nothing flatters vanity, or confirms obstinacy in kings more than repeated petitioning—and nothing has contributed more than that very measure to make the kings of Europe absolute: Witness Denmark and Sweden. Wherefore since nothing but blows will do, for God's sake, let us come to a final separation, and not leave the next generation to be cutting throats, under the violated unmeaning names of parent and child.

---

11. John Milton, renowned English writer of the seventeenth century, in his book *Paradise Lost*.

To say, they will never attempt it again is idle and visionary, we thought so at the repeal of the stamp act, yet a year or two undeceived us; as well we may suppose that nations, which have been once defeated, will never renew the quarrel.

As to government matters, it is not in the powers of Britain to do this continent justice: The business of it will soon be too weighty, and intricate, to be managed with any tolerable degree of convenience, by a power, so distant from us, and so very ignorant of us; for if they cannot conquer us, they cannot govern us. To be always running three or four thousand miles with a tale or a petition, waiting four or five months for an answer, which when obtained requires five or six more to explain it in, will in a few years be looked upon as folly and childishness—there was a time when it was proper, and there is a proper time for it to cease.

Small islands not capable of protecting themselves, are the proper objects for kingdoms to take under their care; but there is something very absurd, in supposing a continent to be perpetually governed by an island. In no instance has nature made the satellite larger than its primary planet, and as England and America, with respect to each Other, reverses the common order of nature, it is evident they belong to different systems: England to Europe—America to itself.

I am not induced by motives of pride, party, or resentment to espouse the doctrine of separation and independence; I am clearly, positively, and conscientiously persuaded that it is the true interest of this continent to be so; that everything short of that is mere patchwork, that it can afford no lasting felicity,—that it is leaving the sword to our children, and shrinking back at a time, when, a little more, a little farther, would have rendered this continent the glory of the earth.

As Britain has not manifested the least inclination towards a compromise, we may be assured that no terms can be obtained worthy the acceptance of the continent, or any ways equal to the expense of blood and treasure we have been already put to.

The object contended for, ought always to bear some just proportion to the expense. The removal of the North [government],[12] or the whole detestable junto, is a matter unworthy [of] the millions we have expended. A temporary stoppage of trade, was an inconvenience, which would have sufficiently balanced the repeal of all the acts complained of, had such repeals been obtained; but if the whole continent must take up arms, if every man must be a soldier, it is scarcely worth our while to fight against a contemptible ministry only. Dearly, dearly, do we pay for the repeal of the acts, if that is all we fight for; for in a just estimation, it is as great a folly to pay a Bunker Hill price for law, as for land. As I have always considered the independency of this continent, as an event, which sooner or later must arrive, so from the late rapid progress of the continent to maturity, the event could not be far off. Wherefore, on the breaking out of hostilities, it was not worth the while to have disputed a matter, which time would have finally redressed, unless

---

12. Lord North, prime minister at the time.

we meant to be in earnest; otherwise, it is like wasting an estate of a suit at law, to regulate the trespasses of a tenant, whose lease is just expiring. No man was a warmer wisher for reconciliation than myself, before the fatal nineteenth of April, 1775 (Massacre at Lexington), but the moment the event of that day was made known, I rejected the hardened, sullen tempered Pharaoh of England for ever; and disdain the wretch, that with the pretended title of FATHER OF HIS People, can unfeelingly hear of their slaughter, and composedly sleep with their blood upon his soul.

Section 4f: Reconciliation with Britain would predictably destroy the colonies' freedom

But admitting that matters were now made up, what would be the event? I answer, the ruin of the continent. And that for several reasons:

FIRST. The powers of governing still remaining in the hands of the king, he will have a negative over the whole legislation of this continent. And as he has shown himself such an inveterate enemy to liberty, and discovered such a thirst for arbitrary power, is he, or is he not, a proper man to say to these colonies, "YOU SHALL MAKE NO LAWS BUT WHAT I PLEASE?" And are there any inhabitants in America so ignorant, as not to know, that according to what is called the PRESENT CONSTITUTION, that this continent can make no laws but what the king gives leave to? and is there any man so unwise, as not to see, that (considering what has happened) he will suffer no Law to be made here, but such as suit his purpose? We may be as effectually enslaved by the want of laws in America, as by submitting to laws made for us in England. After matters are made up (as it is called) can there be any doubt but the whole power of the crown will be exerted, to keep this continent as low and humble as possible? Instead of going forward we shall go backward, or be perpetually quarrelling or ridiculously petitioning. We are already greater than the king wishes us to be, and will he not hereafter endeavor to make us less? To bring the matter to one point. Is the power who is jealous of our prosperity, a proper power to govern us? Whoever says No to this question is an INDEPENDENT, for independency means no more, than, whether we shall make our own laws, or whether the king, the greatest enemy this continent hath, or can have, shall tell us, "THERE SHALL BE NO LAWS BUT SUCH AS I LIKE."

But the king you will say has a negative in England; the people there can make no laws without his consent. In point of right and good order, there is something very ridiculous, that a youth of twenty-one (which has often happened) shall say to several millions of people, older and wiser than himself, I forbid this or that act of yours to be law. But in this place I decline this sort of reply, though I will never cease to expose the absurdity of it, and only answer, that England being the king's residence, and America not so, make quite another case. The king's negative HERE is ten times more dangerous and fatal than it can be in England, for there he will scarcely refuse his consent to a bill for putting England into as strong a state of defense as possible, and in America he would never suffer such a bill to be passed.

America is only a secondary object in the system of British politics—England consults the good of THIS country, no farther than it answers her OWN purpose. Wherefore, her own interest leads her to suppress the growth of ours in every case which does not promote her advantage, or in the least interfere with it. A pretty state we should soon be in under such a second-hand government, considering what has happened! Men do not change from enemies to friends by the alteration of a name; and in order to show that reconciliation now is a dangerous doctrine, I affirm, THAT IT WOULD BE POLICY IN THE KINGDOM AT THIS TIME, TO REPEAL THE ACTS FOR THE SAKE OF REINSTATING HIMSELF IN THE GOVERNMENT OF THE PROVINCES; in order, that he MAY ACCOMPLISH BY CRAFT AND SUBTLETY, IN THE LONG RUN, WHAT HE CANNOT DO BY FORCE AND VIOLENCE IN THE SHORT ONE. Reconciliation and ruin are nearly related.

SECONDLY. That as even the best terms, which we can expect to obtain, can amount to no more than a temporary expedient, or a kind of government by guardianship, which can last no longer than till the colonies come of age, so the general face and state of things, in the interim, will be unsettled and unpromising. Emigrants of property will not choose to come to a country whose form of government hangs but by a thread, and who is every day tottering on the brink of commotion and disturbance; and numbers of the present inhabitants would lay hold of the interval, to dispose of their effects, and quit the continent.

But the most powerful of all arguments, is, that nothing but independence, i.e., a continental form of government, can keep the peace of the continent and preserve it inviolate from civil wars. I dread the event of a reconciliation with Britain now, as it is more than probable, that it will be followed by a revolt somewhere or other, the consequences of which may be far more fatal than all the malice of Britain.

Thousands are already ruined by British barbarity; (thousands more will probably suffer the same fate.) Those men have other feelings than us who have nothing suffered. All they NOW possess is liberty, what they before enjoyed is sacrificed to its service, and having nothing more to lose, they disdain submission. Besides, the general temper of the colonies, towards a British government, will be like that of a youth, who is nearly out of his time, they will care very little about her. And a government which cannot preserve the peace is no government at all, and in that case we pay our money for nothing; and pray what is it that Britain can do, whose power will be wholly on paper, should a civil tumult break out the very day after reconciliation? I have heard some men say, many of whom I believe spoke without thinking, that they dreaded independence, fearing that it would produce civil wars. It is but seldom that our first thoughts are truly correct, and that is the case here; for there are ten times more to dread from a patched up connection than from independence. I make the sufferers case my own, and I protest, that were I driven from house and home, my property destroyed, and my circumstances ruined, that as man, sensible of injuries, I could never relish the doctrine of reconciliation, or consider myself bound thereby.

Section 5: An American republic, stable and effective government

The colonies have manifested such a spirit of good order and obedience to continental government, as is sufficient to make every reasonable person easy and happy on that head. No man can assign the least pretence for his fears, on any other grounds, that such as are truly childish and ridiculous, viz., that one colony will be striving for superiority over another.

Where there are no distinctions there can be no superiority, perfect equality affords no temptation. The republics of Europe are all (and we may say always) in peace. Holland and Switzerland are without wars, foreign or domestic; monarchical governments, it is true, are never long at rest: the crown itself is a temptation to enterprising ruffians at HOME; and that degree of pride and insolence ever attendant on regal authority swells into a rupture with foreign powers, in instances where a republican government, by being formed on more natural principles, would negotiate the mistake.

If there is any true cause of fear respecting independence it is because no plan is yet laid down. Men do not see their way out; wherefore, as an opening into that business I offer the following hints; at the same time modestly affirming, that I have no other opinion of them myself, than that they may be the means of giving rise to something better. Could the straggling thoughts of individuals be collected, they would frequently form materials for wise and able men to improve to useful matter.

Let the assemblies be annual, with a President only. The representation more equal. Their business wholly domestic, and subject to the authority of a continental congress . . .

Here Paine foreshadows the Constitutional Convention of 1787 in order to address the issue of how to express popular sovereignty over Congress. Note the elements that he discusses that ultimately appear in the Constitution or Bill of Rights eleven years later.

But as there is a peculiar delicacy, from whom, or in what manner, this business must first arise, and as it seems most agreeable and consistent, that it should come from some intermediate body between the governed and the governors, that is between the Congress and the people, let a CONTINENTAL CONFERENCE be held, in the following manner, and for the following purpose . . . to frame a Continental Charter, or Charter of the United Colonies; (answering to what is called the Magna Charta of England) fixing the number and manner of choosing members of Congress, members of Assembly, with their date of sitting, and drawing the line of business and jurisdiction between them: always remembering, that our strength is continental, not provincial: Securing freedom and property to all men, and above all things the free exercise of religion, according to the dictates of conscience; with such other matter as is necessary for a charter to contain. Immediately after which, the said conference to dissolve, and the bodies which shall be chosen conformable to the said charter, to be the legislators and governors of this continent for the time being: Whose peace and happiness, may God preserve, Amen. . . .

But where says some is the king of America? I'll tell you Friend, he reigns above, and does not make havoc of mankind like the Royal of Britain. Yet that we may not appear to be defective even in earthly honors, let a day be solemnly set apart for proclaiming the charter; let it be brought forth placed on the divine law, the word of God; let a crown be placed thereon, by which the world may know, that so far as we approve of monarchy, that in America the LAW IS KING. For as in absolute governments the king is law, so in free countries the law OUGHT TO be king; and there ought to be no other. But lest any ill use should afterwards arise, let the crown at the conclusion of the ceremony be demolished, and scattered among the people whose right it is.

A government of our own is our natural right: And when a man seriously reflects on the precariousness of human affairs, he will become convinced, that it is infinitely wiser and safer, to form a constitution of our own in a cool deliberate manner, while we have it in our power, than to trust such an interesting event to time and chance.

There are thousands and tens of thousands; who would think it glorious to expel from the continent, that barbarous and hellish power, which has stirred up the Indians and Negroes to destroy us; the cruelty has a double guilt, it is dealing brutally by us, and treacherously by them. To talk of friendship with those in whom our reason forbids us to have faith, and our affections, (wounded through a thousand pores) instruct us to detest, is madness and folly. Every day wears out the little remains of kindred between us and them, and can there be any reason to hope, that as the relationship expires, the affection will increase, or that we shall agree better, when we have ten times more and greater concerns to quarrel over than ever?

Ye that tell us of harmony and reconciliation, can ye restore to us the time that is past? Can ye give to prostitution its former innocence? Neither can ye reconcile Britain and America. The last cord now is broken, the people of England are presenting addresses against us. There are injuries which nature cannot forgive; she would cease to be nature if she did. As well can the lover forgive the ravisher of his mistress, as the continent forgive the murders of Britain. The Almighty has implanted in us these inextinguishable feelings for good and wise purposes. They are the guardians of his image in our hearts. They distinguish us from the herd of common animals. The social compact would dissolve, and justice be extirpated the earth, or have only a casual existence were we callous to the touches of affection. The robber and the murderer, would often escape unpunished, did not the injuries which our tempers sustain, provoke us into justice.[13]

O ye that love mankind! Ye that dare oppose, not only the tyranny, but the tyrant, stand forth! Every spot of the old world is overrun with oppression. Freedom has been hunted round the globe. Asia, and Africa, have long expelled her. Europe regards her like a stranger, and England has given her warning to depart. O! receive the fugitive, and prepare in time an asylum for mankind.

OF THE PRESENT ABILITY OF AMERICA, WITH SOME MISCELLANEOUS REFLECTIONS

Section 6: American resources for winning the war

I have never met with a man, either in England or America, who has not confessed his opinion, that a separation between the countries, would take place one time or other. And there is no instance in which we have shown less judgment, than in endeavoring to describe, what we call, the ripeness or fitness of the Continent for independence.

As all men allow the measure, and vary only in their opinion of the time, let us, in order to remove mistakes, take a general survey of things and endeavor if possible, to find out the very time. But we need not go far, the inquiry ceases at once, for the TIME HAS FOUND US. The general concurrence, the glorious union of all things prove the fact.

Paine addresses the fact that the British can call upon a much larger population for war, turning shortfalls into advantages regarding Americans' ability to stand up to British might.

It is not in numbers but in unity, that our great strength lies; yet our present numbers are sufficient to repel the force of all the world. The Continent hath, at this time, the largest body of armed and disciplined men of any power under Heaven; and is just arrived at that pitch of strength, in which no single colony is able to support itself, and the whole, who united can accomplish the matter, and either more, or, less than this, might be fatal in its effects. Our land force is already sufficient, and as to naval affairs, we cannot be insensible, that Britain would never suffer an American man of war to be built while the continent remained in her hands. Wherefore we should be no forwarder an hundred years hence in that branch, than we are now; but the truth is, we should be less so, because the timber of the country is every day diminishing, and that which will remain at last, will be far off and difficult to procure.

---

13. Note the criminal and often sexual imagery invoked in this paragraph: "prostitution," "ravisher," "robber," "murderer."

Were the continent crowded with inhabitants, her sufferings under the present circumstances would be intolerable. The more sea port towns we had, the more should we have both to defend and to lose. Our present numbers are so happily proportioned to our wants, that no man need be idle. The diminution of trade affords an army, and the necessities of an army create a new trade.

Debts we have none; and whatever we may contract on this account will serve as a glorious memento of our virtue. Can we but leave posterity with a settled form of government, an independent constitution of its own, the purchase at any price will be cheap. But to expend millions for the sake of getting a few acts repealed, and routing the present ministry only, is unworthy the charge, and is using posterity with the utmost cruelty; because it is leaving them the great work to do, and a debt upon their backs, from which they derive no advantage. Such a thought is unworthy a man of honor, and is the true characteristic of a narrow heart and a peddling politician.

The debt we may contract does not deserve our regard if the work be but accomplished. No nation ought to be without a debt. A national debt is a national bond; and when it bears no interest, is in no case a grievance. Britain is oppressed with a debt of upwards of one hundred and forty millions sterling, for which she pays upwards of four millions interest. And as a compensation for her debt, she has a large navy; America is without a debt, and without a navy; yet for the twentieth part of the English national debt, could have a navy as large again. The navy of England is not worth, at this time, more than three millions and a half sterling. . . .

No country on the globe is so happily situated, so internally capable of raising a fleet as America. Tar, timber, iron, and cordage are her natural produce. We need go abroad for nothing. Whereas the Dutch, who make large profits by hiring out their ships of war to the Spaniards and Portuguese, are obliged to import most of the materials they use. We ought to view the building a fleet as an article of commerce, it being the natural manufactory of this country. It is the best money we can lay out. A navy when finished is worth more than it cost. And is that nice point in national policy, in which commerce and protection are united. Let us build; if we want them not, we can sell; and by that means replace our paper currency with ready gold and silver . . .

Despite the advantages of the British navy, the greatest in the world, America can quickly build a comparable one.

The English list of ships of war is long and formidable, but not a tenth part of them are at any one time fit for service, numbers of them not in being; yet their names are pompously continued in the list, if only a plank be left of the ship: and not a fifth part, of such as are fit for service, can be spared on any one station at one time. The East, and West Indies, Mediterranean, Africa, and other parts over which Britain extends her claim, make large demands upon her navy. From a mixture of prejudice and inattention, we have contracted a false notion respecting the navy of England, and have talked as if we should have the whole of it to encounter at once, and for that reason, supposed that we must have one as large; which not being instantly practicable, have been made use of by a set of disguised tories[14] to discourage our beginning thereon. Nothing can be farther from truth than this; for if America had only a twentieth part of the naval force of Britain, she would be by far an over match for her; because, as we neither have, nor claim any foreign dominion, our whole force would be employed on our own coast, where we should, in the long run, have two to one the advantage of those who had three or four thousand miles to sail over, before they could attack us, and the same distance to return in order to refit and recruit. And although Britain by her fleet, has a check over our trade to Europe, we have as large a one over her trade to the West Indies, which, by laying in the neighborhood of the Continent, is entirely at its mercy. . . .

In almost every article of defense we abound. Hemp flourishes even to rankness, so that we need not want cordage. Our iron is superior to that of other countries. Our small arms equal to any in the world. Cannon we can cast at pleasure. Saltpeter and gunpowder we are every day producing. Our knowledge is hourly improving. Resolution is our inherent character, and courage has never yet forsaken us. Wherefore, what is it that we want? Why is it that we hesitate? From Britain we can expect nothing but ruin. If she is once admitted to the government of America again, this Continent will not be worth living in. Jealousies will be always arising; insurrections will be constantly happening; and who will go forth to quell them? Who will venture his life to reduce his own countrymen to a foreign obedience? The difference between Pennsylvania and Connecticut, respecting some unlocated lands, shows the insignificance of a British government, and fully proves that nothing but Continental authority can regulate Continental matters.

Paine suggests using "unoccupied" land to pay for war and fund the newly independent government, and hints that it could be used to pay soldiers later who volunteer now.

Another reason why the present time is preferable to all others, is, that the fewer our numbers are, the more land there is yet unoccupied, which instead of being lavished by the king on his worthless dependents, may be hereafter applied, not only to the discharge of the present debt, but to the constant support of government. No nation under heaven has such an advantage as this.

The infant state of the Colonies, as it is called, so far from being against, is an argument in favor of independence. We are sufficiently numerous, and were we more so, we might be less united. It is a matter worthy of observation, that the more a country is peopled, the smaller their armies are. In military numbers, the ancients far exceeded the moderns: and the reason is evident, for trade being the consequence of population, men become too much absorbed thereby to attend to anything else. Commerce diminishes the spirit, both of patriotism and military

---

14. Loyalists were often known as "Tories," which was the name of a leading English political faction.

defense. And history sufficiently informs us, that the bravest achievements were always accomplished in the non-age of a nation. With the increase of commerce England has lost its spirit. The city of London, notwithstanding its numbers, submits to continued insults with the patience of a coward. The more men have to lose, the less willing are they to venture. The rich are in general slaves to fear, and submit to courtly power with the trembling duplicity of a spaniel.

Youth is the seed-time of good habits, as well in nations as in individuals. It might be difficult, if not impossible, to form the Continent into one government half a century hence. The vast variety of interests, occasioned by an increase of trade and population, would create confusion. Colony would be against colony. Each being able might scorn each other's assistance: and while the proud and foolish gloried in their little distinctions, the wise would lament that the union had not been formed before. Wherefore, the PRESENT TIME is the TRUE TIME for establishing it. The intimacy which is contracted in infancy, and the friendship which is formed in misfortune, are, of all others, the most lasting and unalterable. Our present union is marked with both these characters: we are young, and we have been distressed; but our concord has withstood our troubles, and fixes a memorable area for posterity to glory in.

The present time, likewise, is that peculiar time, which never happens to a nation but once, viz., the time of forming itself into a government. Most nations have let slip the opportunity, and by that means have been compelled to receive laws from their conquerors, instead of making laws for themselves. First, they had a king, and then a form of government; whereas, the articles or charter of government should be formed first, and men delegated to execute them afterwards: but from the errors of other nations, let us learn wisdom, and lay hold of the present opportunity—TO BEGIN GOVERNMENT AT THE RIGHT END. . . .

Section 7: Independence, now

TO CONCLUDE: However strange it may appear to some, or however unwilling they may be to think so, matters not, but many strong and striking reasons may be given, to show, that nothing can settle our affairs so expeditiously as an open and determined declaration for independence. Some of which are:

FIRST. It is the custom of nations, when any two are at war, for some other powers, not engaged in the quarrel, to step in as mediators, and bring about the preliminaries of a peace: but while America calls herself the subject of Great Britain, no power, however well disposed she may be, can offer her mediation. Wherefore, in our present state we may quarrel on forever.

SECONDLY. It is unreasonable to suppose, that France or Spain will give us any kind of assistance, if we mean only to make use of that assistance for the purpose of repairing the breach, and strengthening the connection between Britain and America; because, those powers would be sufferers by the consequences.

THIRDLY. While we profess ourselves the subjects of Britain, we must, in the eye of foreign nations, be considered as rebels. The precedent is somewhat dangerous TO THEIR PEACE, for men to be in arms under the name of subjects; we on the spot, can solve the paradox: but to unite resistance and subjection, requires an idea much too refined for common understanding.

FOURTHLY. Were a manifesto to be published and dispatched to foreign courts,[15] setting forth the miseries we have endured, and the peaceable methods we have ineffectually used for redress; declaring, at the same time, that not being able, any longer to live happily or safely under the cruel disposition of the British court, we had been driven to the necessity of breaking off all connection with her; at the same time assuring all such courts of our peaceable disposition towards them, and of our desire of entering into trade with them. Such a memorial would produce more good effects to this Continent, than if a ship were freighted with petitions to Britain.

Under our present denomination of British subjects we can neither be received nor heard abroad: The custom of all courts is against us, and will be so, until, by an independence, we take rank with other nations.

These proceedings may at first appear strange and difficult; but, like all other steps which we have already passed over, will in a little time become familiar and agreeable; and, until an independence is declared, the continent will feel itself like a man who continues putting off some unpleasant business from day to day, yet knows it must be done, hates to set about it, wishes it over, and is continually haunted with the thoughts of its necessity.

---

15. Paine foreshadows a Declaration of Independence, which would persuade foreign governments to be allies to the colonists in the fight.

JAMES CHALMERS

From *Plain Truth,* 1776

James Chalmers was born in Scotland in 1727. He emigrated first to the West Indies and then to the Eastern Shore of Maryland in 1760, where he became a wealthy landowner and slaveowner. He wrote this Loyalist rejoinder to Common Sense *in March 1776 under the name Candidus in order to attack Paine at every point while avoiding being sued for libel. Chalmers' pamphlet was suppressed by some Patriot-leaning areas. He personally led a regiment of Loyalists during the Revolutionary*

War, and afterwards he fled to England. Editor's note: This document has been broken into sections and headings have been added to facilitate both reading and referencing.

SOURCE: *Merrill Jensen, ed.,* Tracts of the American Revolution: 1773–1776 *(Indianapolis: Bobbs-Merrill, 1967), 447–498.*

INTRODUCTION

*J*F indignant at the Doctrine contained in the Pamphlet, entitled COMMON SENSE: I have expressed myself, in the following Observations, with some ardor; I entreat the Reader to impute my indignation, to honest zeal against the Author's Insidious Tenets. Animated and impelled by every inducement of the Human Heart; I love, and (if I dare so express myself,) I adore my Country. Passionately devoted to true Liberty; I glow with the purest flame of Patriotism. Silver'd with age as I am, if I know myself, my humble Sword shall not be wanting to my Country; (if the most Honorable Terms are not tendered by the British Nation) to whose Sacred Cause, I am most fervently devoted. The judicious Reader, will not impute my honest, tho' bold Remarks, to unfriendly designs against my Children—against my Country; but to abhorrence of Independency; which if effected, would inevitably plunge our once pre-eminently envied Country into Ruin, Horror, and Desolation.

PLAIN TRUTH; CONTAINING REMARKS ON A LATE PAMPHLET, ENTITLED COMMON SENSE.

I HAVE now before me the Pamphlet, entitled COMMON SENSE; on which I shall remark with freedom and candor.

Section 1: A Defense of the British government, versus the defects of democracy

His [Paine's] first indecent attack is against the English constitution; which with all its imperfections, is, and ever will be the pride and envy of mankind. To this panegyric involuntarily our author subscribes, by granting individuals to be safer in England, than in any other part of Europe. He indeed insidiously attributes this pre-eminent excellence to the constitution of the people, rather than to our excellent constitution. To such contemptible subterfuge is our Author reduced. I would ask him, why did not the constitution of the people afford them superior safety, in the reign of Richard the Third, Henry the Eighth, and other tyrannic princes? Many pages might indeed be filled with encomiums bestowed on our excellent constitution, by illustrious authors of different nations.

This beautiful system (according to MONTESQUIEU) our constitution is a compound of Monarchy, Aristocracy, and Democracy. But it is often said, that the Sovereign, by honors and appointments, influences the Commons. The profound and elegant HUME[1] agitating this question, thinks, to this circumstance, we are in part indebted for our supreme felicity; since without such control in the Crown, our Constitution would immediately degenerate into Democracy; a Government, which in the sequel, I hope to prove ineligible. Were I asked marks of the best government, and the purpose of political society, I would reply, the increase, preservation, and prosperity of its members, in no quarter of the Globe, are those marks so certainly to be found, as in Great Britain, and her dependencies. After our Author has employed several pages, to break the mounds of society by debasing Monarchs: he says, "The plain truth is, that the antiquity of English Monarchy will not bear looking into." HUME treating of the original contract, has the following melancholy, but sensible observation, "Yet reason tells us, that there is no property in durable objects, such as lands, and houses, when carefully examined, in passing from hand to hand, but must in some period, have been founded in fraud and injustice. The necessities of human society, neither in private or public life, will allow of such an accurate enquiry; and there is no virtue or moral duty, but what may, with facility, be refined away, if we indulge a false philosophy, in sifting and scrutinizing, by every captious rule of logic, in every light or position in which it may be placed."

I will humbly attempt to describe good Kings by the following unerring rule. The best Princes are constantly calumniated by the envenomed tongues and pens of the most worthless of their subjects. For this melancholy truth, do I appeal to the testimony of impartial historians, and long experience. The many unmerited insults offered to our gracious Sovereign; by the unprincipled [John] Wilkes,[2] and others down to this late Author; will forever disgrace humanity. For he says, "that monarchy was the most prosperous invention the Devil ever set on foot for the promotion of idolatry. It is the pride of Kings which throws mankind into confusion: In short, continues this Author, monarchy and succession, have laid not this or that kingdom only, but the world in blood and ashes." How deplorably wretched the condition of mankind, could they believe such execrable flagitious jargon. Unhappily indeed, mankind in every age are susceptible of delusion; but surely our Author's poison carries its antidote with it. Attentive to the spirit of his publication, we fancy ourselves in the barbarous fifteenth century: in which period our Author would have figured with his "Common Sense—and blood will attend it."

---

1. David Hume (1708–1776), philosopher of the Scottish Enlightenment.
2. John Wilkes (1725–1797), member of Parliament who was expelled for being an outlaw and then re-elected by his constituency, feted in the colonies as a defender of the people and supporter of colonial rights as well.

After his terrible anathema against our venerable constitution, and monarchy; let us briefly examine a democratical state; and see whether or not it is a government less sanguinary. This government is extremely plausible, and indeed flattering to the pride of mankind. The demagogues therefore, to seduce the people into their criminal designs ever hold up democracy to them: although conscious it never did, nor ever will answer in practice. If we believe a great Author, "There never existed, nor ever will exist a real democracy in the World." If we examine the republics of Greece and Rome, we ever find them in a state of war domestic or foreign. Our Author therefore makes no mention of these ancient States.

The excellent Montesquieu declares, "that a democracy supposes the concurrence of a number of circumstances rarely united. In the first place, it is requisite that the state itself should be of small extent; so that the people might be easily assembled and personally known to each other. Secondly, the simplicity of their manners, should be such as to prevent a multiplicity of affairs, and perplexity in discussing them: And thirdly, there should subsist a great degree of equality between them, in point of right and authority: Lastly, there should be little or no luxury, for luxury must either be the effect of wealth, or it must make it necessary. It corrupts at once, both rich and poor: The one, by the possession, and the other, by the want of it." To this may be added continues the same Author, "that no government is so subject to CIVIL WARS, and INTESTINE COMMOTIONS, as that of the democratical or popular form; because, no other tends so strongly and so constantly to alter, nor requires so much vigilance, and fortitude to preserve it from alteration." It is indeed, in such a constitution, particularly, that a Citizen should always be armed with fortitude, constancy; and should every day, in the sincerity of his heart, guard against corruption, arising either from selfishness in himself, or in his compatriots; for if it once enters into public transactions, to root it out afterwards would be miraculous. . . .

Section 2: America's horrendous military odds versus the British empire, with no likely foreign aid

I shall humbly endeavor to show that our author shamefully misrepresents facts, is ignorant of the true state of Great Britain and her Colonies, utterly unqualified for the arduous task, he has presumptuously assumed; and ardently intent on seducing us to that precipice on which himself stands trembling. To elucidate my strictures, I must with fidelity expose the circumstances of Great Britain and her colonies. If therefore, in the energy of description, I unfold certain bold and honest truths with simplicity, the judicious reader will remember, that true knowledge of our situation, is as essential to our safety, as ignorance thereof may endanger it. In the English provinces, exclusive of negro and other slaves, we have one hundred and sixty thousand; or one hundred and seventy thousand men capable of bearing arms. If we deduct the people called Quakers, Anabaptists, and other religionists averse to arms; a considerable part of the emigrants, and those having a grateful predilection for the ancient constitution and parent state, we shall certainly reduce the first number to sixty or seventy thousand men. Now admitting those equal to the Roman legions, can we suppose them capable of defending against the power of Britain, a country nearly twelve hundred miles extending on the ocean. Suppose our troops assembled in New England, if the Britons see not fit to assail them, they haste to and desolate our other provinces, which eventually would reduce New England. If by dividing our forces, we pretend to defend our provinces, we also are infallibly undone. Our most fertile provinces, filled with unnumbered domestic enemies, slaves, intersected by navigable rivers, everywhere accessible to the fleets and armies of Britain, can make no defense. If without the medium of passion and prejudice, we view our other provinces, half armed, destitute of money and a navy: We must confess that no power ever engaged such POTENT ANTAGONISTS, under such peculiar circumstances of infelicity. In the better days of Rome, she permitted no regular troops to defend her. Men destitute of property she admitted not into her militia, (her only army). I have been extremely concerned at the separation of the Connecticut men from our army. It augur'd not an ardent enthusiasm for liberty and glory. We still have an army before Boston, and I should be extremely happy to hear substantial proofs of their glory. I am still hopeful of great things from our army before Boston, when joined by the regiments now forming, which WANT OF BREAD will probably soon fill. Notwithstanding the predilection I have for my countrymen, I remark with grief, that hitherto our troops have displayed but few marks of Spartan or Roman enthusiasm. In the sincerity of my heart, I adjure the reader to believe, that no person is more sensibly afflicted by hearing the enemies of America remark, that no General ever fell singly and so ingloriously unrevenged before the inauspicious affair of Quebec.[3] I am under no doubt, however, that we shall become as famed for martial courage, as any nation ever the sun beheld.

With the utmost deference to the honorable Congress, I do not view the most distant gleam of aid from foreign powers. The princes alone, capable of [aiding] us, are the Sovereigns of France and Spain. If according to our Author, we possess an eighth part of the habitable globe, and actually have a check on the West India commerce of England; the French indigo and other valuable West India commodities, and the Spanish galleons, are in great jeopardy from our power. The French and Spaniards are therefore wretched politicians, if they do not assist England, in reducing her colonies to obedience.—Pleasantry apart! Can we be so deluded, to expect aid from those princes, which inspiring their subjects with a relish for liberty, might eventually shake their arbitrary thrones.—Natural avowed enemies

---

3. This refers to the failed American invasion of Canada in the winter of 1775–76, led by General Richard Montgomery (who died in the abortive attempt) and Benedict Arnold.

to our sacred cause: Will they cherish, will they support the flame of liberty in America? Ardently intent on extinguishing its latent dying sparks in their respective dominions. Can we believe that those princes will offer an example so dangerous to their subjects and colonies, by aiding those provinces to independence? If independent, aggrandized by infinite numbers from every part of Europe, this Continent would rapidly attain power astonishing to imagination. Soon, very soon would we be conditioned to conquer Mexico, and all their West India settlements, which to annoy, or possess, we indeed are most happily situated. Simple and obvious as these truths are, can they be unknown to the people and princes of Europe? Say, ye friends of liberty and mankind, would no danger accrue from an army of French and Spaniards in the bosom of America?

Let us now briefly view the pre-eminently envied state of Great Britain. If we regard the power of Britain, unembarrassed with Continental connections, and the political balance, we may justly pronounce her what our author does, AMERICA;—"A match for all Europe." Amazing were the efforts of England, in the war of Queen Anne, when little benefitted by colony commerce, and e'er she had availed herself of the courage, good sense, and numbers of the people of Scotland and Ireland.

That England then prescribed laws to Europe, will be long remembered. Last war, her glory was, if possible, more eminently exalted; in every quarter of the globe did victory hover round her armies and navies, and her fame re-echoed from pole to pole. At present Great Britain is the umpire of Europe.

Section 3: Britain's interests in holding onto the colonies

Can a reasonable being for a moment believe that Great Britain, whose political existence depends on our constitutional obedience, who but yesterday made such prodigious efforts to save us from France, will not exert herself as powerfully to preserve us from our frantic schemes of independency. Can we a moment doubt, that the Sovereign of Great Britain and his ministers, whose glory as well as personal safety depends on our obedience, will not exert every nerve of the British power, to save themselves and us from ruin.

I am perfectly satisfied, that we are in no condition to set the world at defiance, that commerce and the protection of Great Britain will secure us peace, and the friendship of all Europe; but I deny it is the interest of all Europe to have America a free-port, unless they are desirous of depopulating their dominions. His assertions, that barrenness of gold and silver will secure us from invaders, is indeed highly pleasant. Have we not a much better security from invasions, viz. the most numerous and best disciplined army under heaven; or has our author already disbanded it. Pray how much gold and silver do the mines of Flanders produce? And what country so often has seen its unhappy fields drenched with blood, and fertilized with human gore. The princes of Europe have long dreaded the migration of their subjects to America; and we are sensible, that the king of Prussia is said more than once to have hanged Newlanders, or those who seduced his subjects to emigrate. I also humbly apprehend, that Britain is a part of Europe. Now, *old gentleman*, as you have clearly shown, that we have a check upon her West India trade, is it her interest to give us a greater check upon it, by permitting America (as you express it,) to become a free port. Can we suppose it to be her interest to lose her valuable commerce to the Colonies, which effectually she would do, by giving up America to become your free port. If therefore it is the interest of all Europe, to have America a free port: The people of Britain are extremely simple to expend so many millions sterling to prevent it. "It is repugnant to the nature of things, to all examples from former ages, to suppose that this Continent can long remain subject to any external power."

Antiquity affords us no eclaricisement[4] respecting the future government of America. I see no reason to doubt, that Great Britain, may not long retain us in constitutional obedience. Time, the destroyer of human affairs, may indeed, end her political life by a gentle decay. Like Rome, she may be constrained to defend herself from the Huns, and Alaricks of the North. Ungratefully should we endeavor to precipitate her political demise, she will devise every expedient to retain our obedience; and rather than fail, will participate those provinces amongst the potent states of Europe.

Section 4: The delusions of Paine and the colonial leadership

"Every quiet method of peace has been ineffectual; our prayers have been rejected with disdain." I do not indeed agree with the people of England in saying, that those, who so successfully labored to widen the breach—desired nothing less than peace. That they who shortly were to command the most numerous and best disciplined army under Heaven, and a navy fit to contend with the fleets of England, imagining the *time had found us*, disdained to be just. I highly venerate a majority of the Delegates. I have not indeed the honor of knowing all the worthy members; however, I wish the Gentlemen of the Congress, e'er they entered on their important charge, had been better acquainted with the strength of our friends in parliament. I sincerely lament, that the King did not receive the last excellent petition from the Congress; and I as sincerely wish, the Gentlemen of the Congress had not addressed themselves at that juncture, to the people of Ireland. "As to government matters," (continues our Author,) "it is not in the power of Britain to do this Continent justice: The business of it will soon be too weighty and intricate to be managed with any tolerable degree of convenience, by a power so very distant from

---

4. An explanation of something that has not been explicable before.

us, and so very ignorant of us; for if they cannot conquer us, they cannot govern us. The difference between Pennsylvania and Connecticut, respecting some unlocated lands, shows the insignificance of a British government, and fully proves, that nothing but Continental authority can regulate Continental matters."

Until the present unhappy period, Great Britain has afforded to all mankind, the most perfect proof of her wise, lenient, and magnanimous government of the Colonies—The proofs to which we already have alluded, viz. Our supreme felicity, and amazing increase . . .

Innumerable are the advantages of our connection with Britain; and a just dependence on her, is a sure way to avoid the horrors and calamities of war. Wars in Europe, will probably than heretofore become less frequent; religious rancor, which formerly animated princes to arms, is succeeded by a spirit of philosophy extremely friendly to peace. The princes of Europe are or ought to be convinced by sad experience, that the objects of conquest, are vastly inadequate to the immense charge of their armaments. Prudential motives, therefore, in future, will often dictate negotiation, instead of war. Be it however admitted, that our speculations are nugatory, and that as usual, we are involved in war. In this case we really do not participate a twentieth part of the misery and hardships of war, experienced by the other subjects of the empire. As future wars will probably be carried on by Britain in her proper element, her success will hardly be doubtful, nor can this be thought audacity, if we remember the great things effected by Britain in her naval wars, then secondary objects to her Germanic connections, to which she now politically seems indifferent. Our sailors navigating our vessels to the West Indies during war, are exempted from impressment, and if our trade to any part of Europe is then stagnated, it flows with uncommon rapidity in the West Indies, nor is the object of captures inconsiderable.

Our author surely forgets, that when independent, we cannot trade with Europe, without political connections, and that all treaties made by England or other commercial states are, or ought to be, ultimately subservient to their commerce. "But (says our author,) admitting that matters were made up, what would be the event? I answer the ruin of the Continent, and that for several reasons." Reconciliation would conduct us to our former happy state. The happiness of the governed is without doubt the true interest of the governors, and if we aim not at independence, there cannot be a doubt, of receiving every advantage relative to laws and commerce that we can desire.

This Continent fifty years hence, infallibly will be richer, and much better peopled than at present; consequently abler to affect a revolution. But alas! e'er that period, our author will forever be forgotten; impelled therefore by his villainous ambition, he would rashly precipitate his country into every species of horror, misery, and desolation, rather than forego his fancied protectorship. "But if you have, (says our author) and still can shake hands with the murderers, then are ye unworthy the name of husband, father, friend, or lover, and whatever may be your rank or title in life, you have the heart of a coward, and the spirit of a sycophant, &c. To talk of friendship with those in whom our reason forbids us to have faith, and our affections wounded through a thousand pores, instructs us to detest is madness and folly."

Ye that are not drunk with fanaticism answer me? Are these words dictated by peace, or base foul revenge, the constant attendant on cowards and sycophants? Does our author so perfectly versed in scripture, mean to conduct us to peace or desolation? or is he fit to legislate for men or devils? Nations after desolating each other (happily for mankind,) forgive, forget, and reconcile; like individuals who quarrel, reconcile, and become friends. Following the laudable example of the CONGRESS; we lately have most readily shaken hands with our inveterate enemies the Canadians, who have scalped nearly as many of our people as the British troops have done: Why therefore may we not forgive and reconcile—By no means, it blasts our author's ambitious purposes. The English and Scotch, since the first Edward's time, have alternately slaughtered each other, (in the field of Bannockburn, more men fell than are now in the New-England provinces) to the amount of several hundred thousand: And now view each other as subjects, despising the efforts of certain turbulent spirits, tending to rekindle the ancient animosity.

Nations, like individuals, in the hour of passion attend to no mediation. But when heartily drubbed, and tired of war, are very readily reconciled, without the intervention of mediators; by whom, belligerents were never reconciled, until their interests or passions dictated the pacification. If we may use our author's elegant language, mediation is "farcical." I grant however, that the idea of our forcing England by arms to treat with us is brilliant. "It is unreasonable continues (our author) to suppose that France and Spain will give us any kind of assistance, if we mean only to make use of that assistance for the purpose of repairing the breach, and strengthening the connection between Britain and America; because those powers would be sufferers by the consequences."

Considering "we have the most numerous, and best disciplined army under Heaven; and a fleet fit to contend with the navy of Britain;" we must suppose our Author's brain affected by dwelling constantly on his beloved independency, else he would not have the imbecility to require the assistance of France and Spain. The manner of his prevailing on France and Spain to assist us, is also a strong proof of his insanity. Did those powers, hesitate to succor the Scotch rebels in 1745, because they did not declare themselves independent. It then was their interest to create a diversion, alas! too serious in the sequel for the deluded rebels in that kingdom; and were they now interested in aiding us, they undoubtedly would do it in spite of quibbles. In such case, e'er this time, their armies

Chalmers questions Paine's readings of history and even his sanity regarding American chances of obtaining foreign aid in a war against Britain.

and navies had joined us without interruption: For we must confess, that the efforts of Britain hitherto, would not have precluded the republic of Genoa from aiding us.

Suppose our author, had a son or an apprentice eloped to his intimate acquaintance, and desired to enter into his service: If this person replied to the youth; I know your apprenticeship is unexpired, notwithstanding declare yourself a freeman, and I will hire and protect you. I demand, would such odious, ridiculous duplicity, render our supposed person, less criminal in the eyes of our Author, or render the example less dangerous to his own apprentice. "Were a manifesto (says our author) dispatched to foreign courts, &c." This also is a conclusive proof of our author's *maniacum delirium.* Our author "challenges the warmest advocate for reconciliation to show a single advantage this Continent can reap, by being connected with Great Britain. I repeat the challenge, not a single advantage is derived: Our corn will fetch its price in any market in Europe:" Were the author's assertions respecting our power, as real as delusive, a reconciliation on liberal principles with Great Britain, would be most excellent policy. I wave similarity of manners, laws, and customs, most friendly indeed to perpetual alliance. The greatest part of our plank, staves, shingles, hoops, corn, beef, pork herrings, and many other articles, could find no vent, but in the English Islands. The demand for our flour would also be considerably lessened. The Spaniards have no demand for these articles; and the French little or none. Britain would be a principal mart for our lumber, part of our grain, naval stores, tobacco, and many other articles, which perhaps are not generally wanted in any kingdom in Europe.

Notwithstanding our Author's fine words about toleration: Ye sons of peace and true Christianity; believe me, it were folly supreme, madness, to expect angelic toleration from New-England, where she has constantly been detested, persecuted and execrated. Even in vain would our Author: or our CROMWELL cherish toleration; for the people of New-England, not yet arrived in the seventeenth or eighteenth century, would reprobate her.—It is more than probable to suppose, that the New-England governments would have no objection to an Agrarian law; nor is it unreasonable to suppose, that such division of property would be very agreeable to the soldiers. Indeed their General could not perhaps with safety to his existence as a General, refute them so reasonable a gratification, particularly, as he will have more than one occasion for their services. Let us however admit that our General and troops, contradicting the experience of ages; do not assume the sovereignty. Released from foreign war; we would probably be plunged into all the misery of anarchy and intestine war. Can we suppose that the people of the South, would submit to have the seat of Empire at Philadelphia, or in New England; or that the people oppressed by a change of government, contrasting their misery with their former happy state, would not invite Britain to reassume the sovereignty.

Volumes were insufficient to describe the horror, misery and desolation, awaiting the people at large in the Siren form of American independence. In short, I affirm that it would be most excellent policy in those who wish for TRUE LIBERTY to submit by an advantageous reconciliation to the authority of Great Britain; "to accomplish in the long run, what they cannot do by hypocrisy, fraud and force in the short one."

INDEPENDENCE AND SLAVERY ARE SYNONYMOUS TERMS.

FINIS

SELECTED BIBLIOGRAPHY

Appleby, Joyce. *Liberalism and Republicanism in the Historical Imagination.* Cambridge, MA: Harvard University Press, 1992.

Bailyn, Bernard. *Faces of Revolution: Personalities and Themes in the Struggle for American Independence.* New York: Alfred A. Knopf, 1990.

Bailyn, Bernard. *The Ideological Origins of the American Revolution.* Cambridge, MA: Harvard University Press, 1967.

Berkin, Carol. *Revolutionary Mothers: Women in the Struggle for America's Independence.* New York: Vintage Books, 2005.

Berlin, Ira. *Many Thousands Gone: The First Two Centuries of Slavery in North America.* Cambridge, MA: Harvard University Press, 1998.

Breen, T. H. *The Marketplace of Revolution: How Consumer Politics Shaped American Independence.* New York: Oxford University Press, 2004.

Burrows, Edwin G., and Mike Wallace. *Gotham: A History of New York City to 1898.* New York: Oxford University Press, 1999.

Countryman, Edward. *A People in Revolution: The American Revolution and Political Society in New York, 1760–1790.* Baltimore: Johns Hopkins University Press, 1981.

Egnal, Marc, and Joseph A. Ernst. "An Economic Interpretation of the American Revolution." *William and Mary Quarterly,* 3rd Series, XXIX (1972): 3–32.

Ellis, Edward Robb. *The Epic of New York City: A Narrative History.* New York: Kodansha, 1997.

Foner, Eric. *Tom Paine and Revolutionary America.* New York: Oxford University Press, 1976.

Greene, Jack P. *Negotiated Authorities: Essays in Colonial Political and Constitutional History.* Charlottesville: University Press of Virginia, 1994.

———. *Peripheries and Center: Constitutional Development in the Extended Polities of the British Empire and the United States, 1607–1788.* Athens, GA: University of Georgia Press, 1986.

———. *Pursuits of Happiness: The Social Development of Early Modern British Colonies and the Formation of American Culture.* Chapel Hill: University of North Carolina Press, 1988.

Greene, Jack P., "Society, Ideology, and Politics," Richard Bushman, "Massachusetts Farmers and the Revolution," and Michael Kammen, "American Revolution as a Crise de Conscience" in *Society, Freedom and Conscience: The Coming of the Revolution in Virginia, Massachusetts, and New York,* edited by Richard Jellison. New York: W. W. Norton, 1976.

Greene, Jack P., and J. R. Pole, eds. *A Companion to the American Revolution.* United Kingdom: Blackwell Publishing, 2000.

Hodges, Graham Russell. *Root and Branch: African Americans in New York and East Jersey, 1613–1863.* Chapel Hill: University of North Carolina Press, 1999.

Jackson, Kenneth T., ed. *The Encyclopedia of New York City.* New Haven: Yale University Press, 1995.

Kerber, Linda. *No Constitutional Right to be Ladies: Women and the Obligations of Citizenship.* New York: Hill and Wang, 1998.

Ketchum, Richard M. *Divided Loyalties: How the American Revolution Came to New York.* New York: Henry Holt and Company, 2002.

Lepore, Jill. *New York Burning: Liberty, Slavery, and Conspiracy in Eighteenth-Century Manhattan.* New York: Alfred A. Knopf, 2005.

Maier, Pauline. *From Resistance to Revolution: Colonial Radicals and the Development of American Opposition* to Britain, 1765–1776. New York: Alfred A. Knopf, 1972.

———. The Old Revolutionaries: Political Lives in the Age of Samuel Adams. New York: W. W. Norton, 1990.

Martin, James Kirby and Mark Edward Lender. A Respectable Army: The Military Origins of the Republic, 1763–1789. Wheeling, IL: Harlan Davidson, 1982.

Marshall, P. J., ed. The Oxford History of the British Empire: Volume II: The Eighteenth Century. Oxford: Oxford University Press, 1998.

McCusker, John J., and Russell R. Menard. The Economy of British America, 1607–1789. Chapel Hill: University of North Carolina Press, 1985.

Nash, Gary. The Unknown American Revolution: The Unruly Birth of Democracy and the Struggle to Create America. New York: Viking, 2005.

———. The Urban Crucible: Social Change, Political Consciousness, and the Origins of the American Revolution. Cambridge, MA: Harvard University Press, 1979.

Norton, Mary Beth, and Ruth Alexander. Major Problems in American Women's History, 4th ed. Boston: Houghton Mifflin, 2007.

Perkins, Edwin J. The Economy of Colonial America. New York: Columbia University Press, 1980.

Raphael, Ray. A People's History of the American Revolution: How Common People Shaped the Fight for Independence. New York: New Press, 2001.

Reid, John Phillip. In Defiance of the Law: The Standing Army Controversy, the Two Constitutions, and the Coming of the American Revolution. Chapel Hill: University of North Carolina Press, 1981.

Rhoden, Nancy L., and Ian K. Steele, eds. The Human Tradition in the American Revolution. Wilmington: Scholarly Resources, 2000.

Salmon, Marylynn. Women and the Law of Property in Early America. Chapel Hill: University of North Carolina Press, 1986.

Schecter, Barnet. The Battle for New York: The City at the Heart of the American Revolution. New York: Walker and Company, 2002.

Schama, Simon. Rough Crossings: Britain, the Slaves, and the American Revolution. New York: Harper Collins, 2006.

Shy, John. A People Numerous and Armed: Reflections on the Military Struggle for American Independence. New York: Oxford University Press, 1976.

Wood, Gordon S. The American Revolution: A History. New York: The Modern Library, 2002.

———. The Creation of the American Republic, 1776–1787. Chapel Hill: University of North Carolina Press, 1969.

———. The Radicalism of the American Revolution. New York: Alfred A. Knopf, 1992.

Young, Alfred F., ed. The American Revolution: Explorations in the History of American Radicalism. DeKalb, IL: Northern Illinois University Press, 1976.

Young, Alfred F. "George Robert Twelves Hewes (1742–1840): A Boston Shoemaker and the Memory of the American Revolution." William and Mary Quarterly, 3rd Series, XXXVIII (1981): 561–623.

———. Liberty Tree: Ordinary People and the American Revolution. New York: New York University Press, 2006.

ENDNOTES

Part One: Introduction

1. This prologue, as well as parts of the prologue to the John Locke excerpts on pages 99–102, was contributed by Mark C. Carnes, professor of history, Barnard College, Columbia University. The author is extremely grateful for these contributions.

2. Carol Berkin, *Revolutionary Mothers: Women in the Struggle for America's Independence* (New York: Random House, 2005), 62.

Part Two: Historical Context

1. "Examination of Benjamin Franklin in the House of Commons," February 13, 1766, in Jack P. Greene, ed., *Colonies to Nation, 1763–1789* (New York: McGraw-Hill, 1967), 73.

2. Robert V. Wells, "Population and Family in Early America," in Jack P. Greene and J. R. Pole, eds., *A Companion to the American Revolution* (Oxford: Blackwell Publishing, 2000), 39–50; Edwin J. Perkins, "Socio-economic Development of the Colonies," in Greene and Pole, 51–59; Jack P. Greene, "The Origins of the New Colonial Policy, 1748–1763," in Greene and Pole, 101–111. The population estimates for England can be found in E. A. Wrigley and R. S. Schofield, *The Population History of England 1541–1871: A Reconstruction* (Cambridge: Cambridge University Press, 1989), 207–15.

3. Jack P. Greene, ed., *Settlements to Society, 1607–1763: A Documentary History of Colonial America* (New York: W. W. Norton, 1975), 238–39.

4. Gordon Wood, *The Radicalism of the American Revolution* (New York: Alfred A. Knopf, 1992), 11–92.

5. See Gary Nash, *The Urban Crucible: Social Change, Political Consciousness, and the Origins of the American Revolution* (Cambridge, MA: Harvard University Press, 1979).

6. Gary Nash, *The Urban Crucible: The Northern Seaports and the Origins of the American Revolution* (Cambridge, MA: Harvard University Press, 1986), 220.

7. Peter Force, ed., *American Archives*, 4th series (Washington, D.C.: 1837), 342–43.

8. Graham Russell Hodges, *Root & Branch: African Americans in New York and East Jersey, 1613–1863* (Chapel Hill: University of North Carolina Press, 1989), 137.

9. Jill Lepore, *New York Burning: Liberty, Slavery, and Conspiracy in Eighteenth-Century Manhattan* (New York: Alfred A. Knopf, 2005).

10. William Blackstone, *Commentaries on the Laws of England*, vol. 1 (1765), 442.

11. Carol Berkin, *Revolutionary Mothers: Women in the Struggle for America's Independence* (New York: Random House, 2005), 14–15.

12. Sara M. Evans, *Born for Liberty: A History of Women in America* (New York: The Free Press, 1999), 49.

13. Edwin G. Burrows and Mike Wallace, *Gotham: A History of New York City to 1898* (New York: Oxford University Press, 1999), 212.

14. Abigail Adams, "Letter from Abigail Adams to John Adams," March 31, 1776, *Adams Family Papers: An Electronic Archive*, www.masshist.org/digitaladams/aea (accessed June 9, 2009).

15. This economic analysis is primarily drawn from Marc Egnal and Joseph Ernst, "An Economic Interpretation of the American Revolution," *William and Mary Quarterly*, 3rd series, XXIX (1972), 3–32. A similar process occurred in Virginia and Maryland, with Scottish tobacco traders starting in the 1740s to subvert the large planters' economic authority through a system of small shops, easy credit, faster shipping, and access to the French tobacco market that enabled a better tobacco price. The result was to turn the small planters' dealings from their large planter neighbors to

the Scots, who similarly encouraged overconsumption and indebtedness among consumers. The credit crisis of the mid-1760s took effect and average tobacco planters found themselves facing economic ruin.

16. Edmund S. Morgan, *Prologue to Revolution: Sources and Documents on the Stamp Act Crisis, 1764–66* (Chapel Hill: University of North Carolina Press, 2004), 32.

17. Bernard Bailyn, *The Ideological Origins of the American Revolution* (Cambridge, MA: Harvard University Press, 1967), 56–57.

Part Five: Core Texts

1. This section and the accompanying questions for discussion in the Instructor's Manual were written by me and Mark C. Carnes, professor of history at Barnard College.

2. John Locke, *Second Treatise of Government*, edited by C. B. MacPherson (Indianapolis: Hackett Publishing Company, 1980), vii–xxi.

3. Bernard Bailyn, *The Ideological Origins of the American Revolution* (Cambridge MA: Harvard University Press, 1967), 27–28.

ACKNOWLEDGMENTS

Many thanks to all of the undergraduate players in courses at Pace University, and at dozens of other colleges and universities throughout the United States, plus Canada, Australia, and Egypt. Pace University itself, through Dean Nira Herrmann of the Dyson College of Arts and Sciences as well as then–associate provost Beverly Kahn, provided support both moral and logistical for bringing Reacting to Pace.

Many thanks to the Reacting to the Past headquarters at Barnard College, without which this work would not have been possible. Mark Carnes not only encouraged this effort beginning in 2002, he provided money for it (through a Reacting development grant) and then authored both a vignette (fiction writing being my weakness) and an introduction for the John Locke section. Dana Johnson was invaluable throughout for her logistical skill, for arranging my play-tests of the game book at various Reacting to the Past conferences, and for guiding the first edition of this work through hazardous shoals to ultimate publication. The Reacting Board has also given this effort its unwavering support.

Among the many instructors who have played the game with me at a conference, used my game in their classroom, or both, I wish to personally thank (in no particular order): Paula Lazrus (St. John's University), Ann Davison (Queens College), Deb DiSimone (College of Staten Island), Donna Scimeca (College of Staten Island), Richard Powers (College of Staten Island), Nick Proctor (Simpson College), Jeff Hyson (St. Joseph's University), John Burney (Doane College), Pat Coby (Smith College), Jace Weaver (University of Georgia), Laura Weaver (University of Georgia), Andy Schocket (Bowling Green State University), Michael Winship (University of Georgia), Tracy Lightcap (LaGrange College), Mark Higbee (Eastern Michigan University), John Moser (Ashland University), and Jason Locke (Piedmont Community College). Their thoughtful questions about game mechanics greatly improved the clarity of the game book and the accompanying instructor's manual. They all deserve special thanks, as does every instructor who ever played the game at a conference, or sent me an e-mail about the game materials or mechanisms.

Finally, thanks to my wife Nancy Reagin, and my children Mary Offutt-Reagin and Seth Offutt-Reagin. Their contributions have been intangible yet nonetheless real and indispensable.